# BATTLE HONOURS
# of the
# BRITISH AND INDIAN ARMIES
# 1695–1914

# BATTLE HONOURS
# of the
# BRITISH AND INDIAN ARMIES
# 1695–1914

by

**N. B. Leslie**

Leo Cooper
London

First published 1970 by
LEO COOPER LIMITED
196 Shaftesbury Avenue, London WC1

ISBN 0 85052 004 5

Typeset by Gavin Martin Ltd, London and
printed in Great Britain by
Lewis Reprints Limited, Port Talbot, Glamorgan

THIS BOOK
IS FOR
MY WIFE

# Contents

## PREFACE

The histories of the British and Indian Armies are particularly associated with the founding of Britain's Eastern Empire. When the British Army was raised in the 17th Century, its early campaigns were for the maintenance of the Balance of Power in Europe. With the acquisition of Empire — casual and reluctant though it was — the British Army was aided by Auxiliaries, particularly those raised in India, and this is reflected in the number of honours the two Armies share.

In military histories, when writing of campaigns, it is usual to refer to regiments by the name of the Colonel, or by the number by which it was known. It is often difficult and tedious for the layman to identify regiments by their modern County titles, although after 1783 most regiments had subsidiary County titles, or were 'Royal' regiments.

When the Army was reorganised in 1881 units were localised, each to its own regimental district, and linked to form regiments, given County titles, and the use of numbers was discontinued. When the Regiments were linked the battle honours were combined. Some regiments, with many honours were linked with others, who through no fault of theirs, had few. There were some uneasy partnerships, but these difficulties were overcome, and the new regiments were as proud of their new titles as their forbears had been of their numbers. This work brings together for easy reference the honours awarded to both Armies. As the British Army was engaged in many parts of the world simultaneously, there is an overlapping of dates. To avoid confusion it has been found convenient to arrange the work by Continents; Europe, Asia, Africa, America and the West Indies, and the Antipodes. Before each section, the battles are listed in chronological order, the campaign in which each was fought is shown, and the date of the battle or campaign given. In the list of battles following, the first column gives in abbreviated form the title by which the regiment was known in 1914 — a complete list of numbers with full title and date of formation will be found at the beginning of this book. The second column gives the title by which the regiment was known at the time of the battle and the third column shows the date on which the honour was awarded. Some of the dates given here may appear to conflict with those claimed by regiments, but those given here are from contemporary official records. The honours awarded up to 1914 represent the achievement of the regular British Army — "a perfect thing apart" — which all but disappeared in the Great War. The honours granted after the two World Wars were earned not only by the Regular Army but by Service and Territorial battalions, who shared in all campaigns and added lustre to already famous names. The honours awarded for the two World Wars can be referred to in any Army List.

This work could not have been undertaken without the facilities for research in military history available at the Ministry of Defence (Central & Army) Library (the old War Office Library), where some unique records are housed.

I must express my thanks to Mr. D.W. King, OBE, FLA, for his interest and encouragement. I would also like to thank so many members of the Library staff for their interest. They have listened to me with unfailing patience on a subject I find of absorbing interest — the British Army.

My wife, my sons and my brothers have taken the keenest interest in this work and but for their insistence it would never have been offered for publication. My particular thanks to my son Hugh for his advice on technical matters, and my brother John and David Male for his assistance in checking. To Mr. Leo Cooper, who shares my interest in the British Army and whose enthusiasm had encouraged me enormously, my grateful thanks.

## INTRODUCTION

*"I would have you fix your eyes upon the greatness of your country until you have become filled with the love of her, and when her glory stirs your heart reflect that this Empire has been won by men who knew their duty, and dared to do it, who in the hour of battle had ever the fear of disgrace before their eyes, and who did they fall lose everything before honour, and freely gave their lives to their country, as the best offerings they could present."*

Honours on Colours, what an inspired idea, but whose? Probably of Continental origin the first indication of their adoption in the British Army was the honour EMSDORF on the guidons of the 15th Light Dragoons. This appeared in a Royal Warrant of the December 19 1768 which related to a "General View of the Differences and Distinctions of the several Corps of Cavalry in the Clothing, Horse-Furniture, and Standards."

Sixteen years later on the April 14 1784 the Commanding Officers of the 12th, 39th, 56th & 58th Regiments were informed that

> "I am commanded to acquaint you that, in commemoration of the Glorious Defence made by those Regiments of Infantry which composed the Garrison of Gibraltar during the late memorable siege of that Fortress, of which the Regiment under your command was one, His Majesty has been graciously pleased to permit you to have the word GIBRALTAR put upon your Grenadier & Light Infantry Caps, as also upon your Accoutrements, Drums and like wise upon the second Colour of the Regiment underneath the number of it."

From this it would appear that the custom was now established of commemorating campaigns and victories in this fashion, but curiously as the custom was likely to be continued as other regiments wished to have their deeds recorded, it was not thought necessary to lay down rules for the grant of future awards.

Fifty years later, on the December 9 1836 the regiments who were awarded GIBRALTAR were advised that

> "His Majesty has approved of the 12th, 39th, 56th & 58th Regiments which have been permitted to bear the word GIBRALTAR in their Colours and Appointments, in commemoration of their distinguished Gallantry in the Defence of Gibraltar in the year 1782, also THE CASTLE & KEY, being part of the Armorial Bearings of that Fortress together with the motto 'MONTIS INSIGNIA CALPE'."

The dates 1779-1783 were added in 1909. The distinction GIBRALTAR 1780-1783 with THE CASTLE & KEY and motto were granted to The Highland Light Infantry in 1908.

Whilst awards were for actions, they were not the first Colour distinction to be awarded to a Regiment. William III granted the 18th Regiment of Foot the privilege of bearing his arms THE LION OF NASSAU with the motto VIRTUTIS NAMURCENSIS PRAEMIUM on their Colours, as a record of their services at the Siege of Namur in 1695. It has never been clear why this regiment was selected for this signal honour, but it is thought that the reasons were political. Fourteen regiments, including the 18th Foot who were present at the Siege were granted NAMUR 1695 in 1910.

The 19th Century opened with two awards. On the January 1 1801, the authorities at the Horse Guards wrote to the Commanding Officers of the 12th 2nd Bn. 20th, 23rd, 25th, 37th and 51st Regiments that

> "I am directed by His Royal Highness the Commander-in-Chief to inform you that His Majesty has signified his Gracious Permission for the Regiment under your Command to bear the word MINDEN in its Colours in Remembrance of the Battle of the 1st August 1759 in which the Regiment so honourably distinguished itself."

The honour was granted to the 2nd Battalion of the 20th Foot which was subsequently disbanded. A regrant of the award was made in 1820.

Why was this particular battle selected for commemoration at this time? It is impossible to give an answer. Eighty years were to elapse before Marlborough's campaigns were commemorated.

On the July 6 1802 a number of Cavalry and Infantry regiments were informed of the grant of EGYPT with the Sphinx in a laurel wreath. The grant to some regiments would indicate that it was not considered necessary for a complete regiment to have been present at an action. This is shown by the grant to the 11th Light Dragoons and the 40th Foot. The former was represented by a detachment and the latter by Flank Companies.

MAIDA was granted to six regiments on the February 24 1807 "..... for Gallantry displayed on the Plains of Maida ..... on the 4th July 1806." As a medal was granted for the campaign (the first to be awarded to the Army for a land battle), it may be thought that future grants of honours would be dependent on the grant of a medal. This however was not established, Peninsula honours were generally associated with the grant of a medal or clasp, but not in every case. There is an honour PENINSULA but no medal or clasp and BENEVENTE an honour was granted but no clasp issued.

That honours were to be granted not only for actions but for distinguished services is evident from Horse Guards letters of April 16 and July 6 1807. In the first letter the ELEPHANT with ASSAYE was granted to three regiments, the 19th Light Dragoons, the 74th and 78th Regiments, for the action, but the ELEPHANT only to one, the 94th Regiment for "distinguished service in India". In the second letter the 75th Regiment was granted the ROYAL TIGER with the word INDIA for "distinguished service of the Corps in India during the period of 19 years."

For over thirty years from 1811, the bulk of honours for the Peninsular War were granted. In some cases the award was granted to a single regiment, in others to several regiments at the same time. Some were granted to Flank Companies, these were later extended to the Regiment as a whole. Many Peninsular honours were earned by 2nd and 3rd Battalions, most of which were disbanded in 1816 on the reduction of the Army, but in many cases the surviving battalion adopted the honour, for which no authority can be found. That the Duke of Wellington considered that an award should be covered by the grant of a medal for an action is clear from his letter of November 16 1816 in this he said,

> "One of the rules is that an officer shall receive a medal only for a particular action to which the Corps to which he belongs has been engaged with musketry. This was not the case of the Cavalry at Busaco nor with much of the Infantry, the action not having been a general one, only those of the Infantry are in the list of whose Corps were engaged with musketry."

From Waterloo to the Crimea awards were mainly for services in India and the East Indies. Those for the British Army by the Queen, and the troops of the East India Company, by the Governor General, or in some cases by the Governor of a Presidency. It had been the custom for some time for the East India Company to grant what they called 'honorary standards' to a regiment for distinguished service. In 1781 the 2nd Carnatic Battalion (subsequently the 80th Carnatic Infantry) were granted a Colour with the inscription in the Vernacular HYDER ALI, SHOLINGHUR, to commemorate the victory of the September 26 1781. During the next twenty years standards were granted to various regiments bearing such words as 'LAKE' and 'VICTORY'. The honours for the Mahratta War of 1803 were granted in 1829. The first award for the Madras Army was AMBOOR granted to the 10th Madras Infantry.

As in the British Army what appears to be the first honour in which a battle was named appeared on the guidons of a Cavalry regiment. This grant appeared in Governor General's Order of the February 27 1819 which stated

> "The Governor General in Council is pleased to permit the 6th Regiment of Bengal Light Cavalry to bear embroidered in the corner of the Regimental Standard in English and Persian characters as an honourable tribute of applause from the Supreme Government the word SEETABULDEE 27th NOVEMBER 1817, in Commemoration of the brilliant and decisive charge made that day by some troops of the regiment headed by Captain Fitzgerald, when the British troops were treacherously attacked by the forces of the Rajah of Nagpore."

Two curious grants were made in the middle of the 19th Century. In the first instance, a cavalry regiment disbanded for mutiny disappeared from the Army List. On the augmentation of the Army in 1854, a new regiment was raised, given the old number and later granted the honours of the disbanded regiment. The second case is odder still. In 1817 the 97th Regiment, which had a particularly distinguished record was renumbered 96th, and on the reduction of the Army in 1818, disbanded. In 1824, a new 96th was raised, and in 1874 the honours awarded to the original 97th were granted to the new regiment. If it was considered necessary that these honours should be revived, surely they should have been given to the 97th and not the 96th Regiment, a regiment that had not the remotest connection with the original recipient.

A Committee was appointed in 1882, under the presidency of Major General Sir Archibald Alison and it has been suggested that the report laid down certain principles for the future granting of honours, but the terms of reference were "to . . . . . consider the claims of Regiments which took part in

(a) the campaigns of the Duke of Marlborough

(b) the wars between the British and French in North America."

In paragraph 2 of the report it states ". . . . . that it appeared to us that some general principle with regard to the particular victories to be commemorated should be decided upon. This principle is in our opinion was as follows viz, that in dealing with events so long past that the names of such victories only should be retained, as, either in themselves or by their results, had left a mark in history which renders the name familiar not only to the British Army, but to every educated gentleman."

If it was considered that 'victories only' should be commemorated this was surely not novel, all previous honours were granted for that reason, not for defeats. But an exception to this principle existed. Two honours borne by regiments, one granted in the 19th Century and the other in the 18th were not strictly for victories. In the first case the garrison after a gallant defence capitulated and the latter the garrison were starved into surrender. In paragraph 5 of the report the principle of what proportion of a regiment should be present is referred to with particular reference to a Guards regiment at Oudenarde and Malplaquet. In these battles the regiment was represented by four companies. The Committee questioned whether in the circumstances the honour should be granted. As the award was subsequently made, the Committee did not consider it necessary for the whole regiment to have been engaged. For this there was the precedent EGYPT.

In paragraph 7 in discussing the Siege of Lille the report says "further in the British Service the principle exists that when a distinction is conferred for a siege they should be granted not only to the corps absolutely conducting but for those covering it." When BADAJOS was awarded two regiments who were present, but took no active part in the actual storming were not granted the honour; the rule laid down by the Duke of Wellington in his previously quoted letter was strictly applied. He added "In the same manner the Badajos medal is for those engaged in the siege and storm of that place."

The suggestion therefore that the Alison Committee laid down new rules for the future granting of honours is odd, as nothing in the report was said that had not already been established by precedent.

When the awards for the Sudan Expedition of 1898 were being considered the then Adjutant General stated firmly "It has been ruled again and again that no distinction on Colours or in Army Lists shall be granted for any action which was not represented by a special clasp for that act." This certainly confirmed that an honour should follow the award of a medal or clasp, but the Adjutant General did not amplify the ruling by stating what portion of a regiment should have been present in order to qualify for the grant of an honour. That honours, for the South African War, should follow the grant of a clasp were confirmed and approved by the Commander-in-Chief who ruled that "the best and simplest course will be to accept the medal clasps as they stand, provided always that the Headquarters and 50 per cent of the Regiment had been present."

In future therefore the grant of a battle honour would be governed by two conditions (a) the grant of a medal or clasp providing always that (b) the Headquarters and 50 per cent of the regiment had been present at the action. Under the 50 per cent rule the Auxiliary Forces i.e. Imperial Yeomanry, and Volunteers would not qualify, because of circumstances peculiar to themselves. It was not possible for a complete Yeomanry or Volunteer unit to be present at the seat of war, but in order that those units which were represented in South Africa should not be overlooked, for their not inconsiderable services, the Army Council recommended that "Corps which furnished parties of 20 or over for service in South Africa should be granted the honour with the year or years during which they served during the war". It was further laid down that, in the case of a Naval action, the Headquarters rule should be dispensed with, and no grant would be considered for an operation connected with civil strife.

If the ruling for South African honours had been strictly observed, it would have resulted in twenty-six new honours being added to the colours; this was considered to be excessive, and it was finally decided that seven actions only would be commemorated. Two honours peculiar to the Militia were granted MEDITERRANEAN and ST. HELENA. These however lapsed in 1910 when as the result of Army Order 251 the distinctions borne by regular battalions were also borne by Special Reserve Battalion belonging to those regiments.

After the South African War, there was a revival of interest in battle honours and a Permanent Committee was appointed to advise the Adjutant General on all questions connected with honours and distinctions. Many applications were made by regiments for the recognition of battles long forgotten but nevertheless worthy of being remembered and many grants were made but the many anomalies, about which so much could be written, were not rectified, and to have attempted to do so was considered an all but impossible task.

The Committee was considering applications down to the outbreak of war in 1914. In the holocaust that followed the old British Army disappeared. The new armies would fight far bloodier battles than Ferozeshah or Badajos, and prove worthy descendants of their predecessors, and would add laurels to the imperishable glory of an Army that has lasted for over three hundred years.

## A LIST OF REGIMENTS OF THE BRITISH & INDIAN ARMIES WITH TITLES BORNE IN 1914, TOGETHER WITH DATES OF FORMATION

|  |  | |
|---|---|---|
| 1st Life Guards | 1660 | |
| 2nd Life Guards | 1660 | |
| Royal Horse Guards (The Blues) | 1661 | |
| 1st (King's) Dragoon Guards | 1685 | |
| 2nd Dragoon Guards (Queen's Bays) | 1685 | |
| 3rd (Prince of Wales's) Dragoon Guards | 1685 | |
| 4th (Royal Irish) Dragoon Guards | 1685 | |
| 5th (Princess Charlotte of Wales's) Dragoon Guards | 1685 | |
| 6th Dragoon Guards (Carabiniers) | 1685 | |
| 7th (Princess Royal's) Dragoon Guards | 1688 | |
| 1st (Royal) Dragoons | 1683 | |
| 2nd Dragoons (Royal Scots Greys) | 1681 | |
| 3rd (King's Own) Hussars | 1685 | |
| 4th (Queen's Own) Hussars | 1685 | |
| 5th (Royal Irish) Lancers | 1858 | |
| 6th (Inniskilling) Dragoons | 1689 | |
| 7th (Queen's Own) Hussars | 1690 | |
| 8th (King's Royal Irish) Hussars | 1693 | |
| 9th (Queen's Royal) Lancers | 1715 | |
| 10th (Prince of Wales's Own Royal) Hussars | 1715 | |
| 11th (Prince Albert's Own) Hussars | 1715 | |
| 12th (Prince of Wales's Royal) Lancers | 1715 | |
| 13th Hussars | 1715 | |
| 14th (King's) Hussars | 1715 | |
| 15th (The King's) Hussars | 1759 | |
| 16th (The Queen's) Lancers | 1759 | |
| 17th (Duke of Cambridge's Own) Lancers | 1759 | |
| 18th (Queen Mary's Own) Hussars | 1858 | |
| 19th (Queen Alexandra's Own Royal) Hussars | 1858 | |
| 20th Hussars | 1860 | |
| 21st (Empress of India's) Lancers | 1861 | |
| Grenadier Guards | 1660 | |
| Coldstream Guards | 1650 | |
| Scots Guards | 1660 | |
| Irish Guards | 1900 | |
| The Royal Scots (Lothian Regiment) | 1633 | 1st Foot |
| The Queen's (Royal West Surrey Regiment) | 1661 | 2nd Foot |
| The Buffs (East Kent Regiment) | 1665 | 3rd Foot |
| The King's Own (Royal Lancaster Regiment) | 1680 | 4th Foot |
| The Northumberland Fusiliers | 1674 | 5th Foot |
| The Royal Warwickshire Regiment | 1673 | 6th Foot |
| The Royal Fusiliers (City of London Regiment) | 1685 | 7th Foot |
| The King's (Liverpool Regiment) | 1685 | 8th Foot |
| The Norfolk Regiment | 1685 | 9th Foot |
| The Lincolnshire Regiment | 1685 | 10th Foot |
| The Devonshire Regiment | 1685 | 11th Foot |
| The Suffolk Regiment | 1685 | 12th Foot |
| Prince Albert's (Somerset Light Infantry) | 1685 | 13th Foot |
| The Prince of Wales's Own (West Yorkshire Regiment) | 1685 | 14th Foot |
| The East Yorkshire Regiment | 1685 | 15th Foot |
| The Bedfordshire Regiment | 1688 | 16th Foot |
| The Leicestershire Regiment | 1688 | 17th Foot |
| The Royal Irish Regiment | 1684 | 18th Foot |
| Alexandra, Princess of Wales's Own (Yorkshire Regiment) | 1688 | 19th Foot |
| The Lancashire Fusiliers | 1688 | 20th Foot |
| The Royal Scots Fusiliers | 1678 | 21st Foot |
| The Cheshire Regiment | 1689 | 22nd Foot |
| The Royal Welsh Fusiliers | 1689 | 23rd Foot |
| The South Wales Borderers | 1689 | 24th Foot |
| The King's Own Scottish Borderers | 1689 | 25th Foot |
| 1st Bn. The Cameronians (Scottish Rifles) | 1689 | 26th Foot |
| 1st Bn. The Royal Inniskilling Fusiliers | 1689 | 27th Foot |
| 1st Bn. The Gloucestershire Regiment | 1694 | 28th Foot |
| 1st Bn. The Worcestershire Regiment | 1702 | 29th Foot |
| 1st Bn. The East Lancashire Regiment | 1702 | 30th Foot |

N.B. Welsh Guards formed in 1915.

## BRITISH REGIMENTS (Cont.)

| | | |
|---|---|---|
| 1st Bn. The East Surrey Regiment | 1702 | 31st Foot |
| 1st Bn. The Duke of Cornwall's Light Infantry | 1702 | 32nd Foot |
| 1st Bn. The Duke of Wellington's (West Riding Regiment) | 1702 | 33rd Foot |
| 1st Bn. The Border Regiment | 1702 | 34th Foot |
| 1st Bn. The Royal Sussex Regiment | 1701 | 35th Foot |
| 2nd Bn. The Worcestershire Regiment | 1701 | 36th Foot |
| 1st Bn. The Hampshire Regiment | 1702 | 37th Foot |
| 1st Bn. The South Staffordshire Regiment | 1705 | 38th Foot |
| 1st Bn. The Dorsetshire Regiment | 1702 | 39th Foot |
| 1st Bn. The Prince of Wales's Volunteers (South Lancashire Regiment) | 1717 | 40th Foot |
| 1st Bn. The Welsh Regiment | 1719 | 41st Foot |
| 1st Bn. The Black Watch (Royal Highlanders) | 1739 | 42nd Foot |
| 1st Bn. The Oxfordshire & Buckinghamshire Light Infantry | 1741 | 43rd Foot |
| 1st Bn. The Essex Regiment | 1741 | 44th Foot |
| 1st Bn. The Sherwood Foresters (Nottinghamshire & Derbyshire Regiment) | 1741 | 45th Foot |
| 2nd Bn. The Duke of Cornwall's Light Infantry | 1741 | 46th Foot |
| 1st Bn. The Loyal North Lancashire Regiment | 1741 | 47th Foot |
| 1st Bn. The Northamptonshire Regiment | 1741 | 48th Foot |
| 1st Bn. Princess Charlotte of Wales's (Royal Berkshire Regiment) | 1743 | 49th Foot |
| 1st Bn. The Queen's Own (Royal West Kent Regiment) | 1755 | 50th Foot |
| 1st Bn. The King's Own (Yorkshire Light Infantry) | 1755 | 51st Foot |
| 2nd Bn. The Oxfordshire & Buckinghamshire Light Infantry | 1755 | 52nd Foot |
| 1st Bn. The King's (Shropshire Light Infantry) | 1755 | 53rd Foot |
| 2nd Bn. The Dorsetshire Regiment | 1755 | 54th Foot |
| 2nd Bn. The Border Regiment | 1755 | 55th Foot |
| 2nd Bn. The Essex Regiment | 1755 | 56th Foot |
| 1st Bn. The Duke of Cambridge's (Middlesex Regiment) | 1755 | 57th Foot |
| 2nd Bn. The Northamptonshire Regiment | 1755 | 58th Foot |
| 2nd Bn. The East Lancashire Regiment | 1755 | 59th Foot |
| The King's Royal Rifle Corps | 1755 | 60th Foot |
| 2nd Bn. The Gloucestershire Regiment | 1758 | 61st Foot |
| 1st Bn. The Duke of Edinburgh's (Wiltshire Regiment) | 1756 | 62nd Foot |
| 1st Bn. The Manchester Regiment | 1758 | 63rd Foot |
| 1st Bn. The Prince of Wales's (North Staffordshire Regiment) | 1758 | 64th Foot |
| 1st Bn. The York & Lancaster Regiment | 1758 | 65th Foot |
| 2nd Bn. Princess Charlotte of Wales's (Royal Berkshire Regiment) | 1758 | 66th Foot |
| 2nd Bn. The Hampshire Regiment | 1758 | 67th Foot |
| 1st Bn. The Durham Light Infantry | 1758 | 68th Foot |
| 2nd Bn. The Welsh Regiment | 1758 | 69th Foot |
| 2nd Bn. The East Surrey Regiment | 1758 | 70th Foot |
| 1st Bn. The Highland Light Infantry | 1777 | 71st Foot |
| 1st Bn. Seaforth Highlanders (Ross-shire Buffs, The Duke of Albany's) | 1778 | 72nd Foot |
| 2nd Bn. The Black Watch (Royal Highlanders) | 1786 | 73rd Foot |
| 2nd Bn. The Highland Light Infantry | 1787 | 74th Foot |
| 1st Bn. The Gordon Highlanders | 1787 | 75th Foot |
| 2nd Bn. The Duke of Wellington's (West Riding Regiment) | 1787 | 76th Foot |
| 2nd Bn. The Duke of Cambridge's Own (Middlesex Regiment) | 1787 | 77th Foot |
| 2nd Bn. Seaforth Highlanders (Ross-shire Buffs, The Duke of Albany's) | 1793 | 78th Foot |
| The Queen's Own Cameron Highlanders | 1793 | 79th Foot |
| 2nd Bn. The South Staffordshire Regiment | 1793 | 80th Foot |
| 2nd Bn. The Loyal North Lancashire Regiment | 1793 | 81st Foot |
| 2nd Bn. The Prince of Wales's Volunteers (South Lancashire Regiment) | 1793 | 82nd Foot |
| 1st Bn. The Royal Irish Rifles | 1793 | 83rd Foot |
| 2nd Bn. The York & Lancaster Regiment | 1794 | 84th Foot |
| 2nd Bn. The King's (Shropshire Light Infantry) | 1794 | 85th Foot |
| 2nd Bn. The Royal Irish Rifles | 1793 | 86th Foot |
| 1st Bn. Princess Victoria's (Royal Irish Fusiliers) | 1793 | 87th Foot |
| 1st Bn. The Connaught Rangers | 1793 | 88th Foot |
| 2nd Bn. Princess Victoria's (Royal Irish Fusiliers) | 1793 | 89th Foot |
| 2nd Bn. The Cameronians (Scottish Rifles) | 1794 | 90th Foot |
| 1st Bn. Princess Louise's (Argyll & Sutherland Highlanders) | 1794 | 91st Foot |
| 2nd Bn. The Gordon Highlanders | 1797 | 92nd Foot |
| 2nd Bn. Princess Louise's (Argyll & Sutherland Highlanders) | 1800 | 93rd Foot |
| 2nd Bn. The Connaught Rangers | 1823 | 94th Foot |
| 2nd Bn. The Sherwood Foresters (Nottinghamshire & Derbyshire Regiment) | 1823 | 95th Foot |
| 2nd Bn. The Manchester Regiment | 1824 | 96th Foot |

## BRITISH REGIMENTS (Cont.)

| | | |
|---|---|---|
| 2nd Bn. The Queen's Own (Royal West Kent Regiment) | 1824 | 97th Foot |
| 2nd Bn. The Prince of Wales's (North Staffordshire Regiment) | 1824 | 98th Foot |
| 2nd Bn. The Duke of Edinburgh's (Wiltshire Regiment) | 1824 | 99th Foot |
| 1st Bn. The Prince of Wales's Leinster Regiment (Royal Canadians) | 1858 | 100th Foot |
| 1st Bn. The Royal Munster Fusiliers (From 1756 with H.E.I.C.) | 1861 | 101st Foot |
| 1st Bn. The Royal Dublin Fusiliers (From 1746 with H.E.I.C.) | 1861 | 102nd Foot |
| 2nd Bn. The Royal Dublin Fusiliers (From 1661 with H.E.I.C.) | 1861 | 103rd Foot |
| 2nd Bn. The Royal Munster Fusiliers (From 1839 with H.E.I.C.) | 1861 | 104th Foot |
| 2nd Bn. The King's Own (Yorkshire Light Infantry) (From 1839 with H.E.I.C.) | 1861 | 105th Foot |
| 2nd Bn. The Durham Light Infantry (From 1826 with H.E.I.C.) | 1861 | 106th Foot |
| 2nd Bn. The Royal Sussex Regiment (From 1854 with H.E.I.C.) | 1861 | 107th Foot |
| 2nd Bn. The Royal Inniskilling Fusiliers (From 1854 with H.E.I.C.) | 1861 | 108th Foot |
| 2nd Bn. The Prince of Wales's Leinster Regiment (Royal Canadians) (From 1853 with H.E.I.C.) | 1861 | 109th Foot |
| The Rifle Brigade (The Prince Consort's Own) | 1800 | |

## INDIAN ARMY

| | |
|---|---|
| Governor General's Body Guard | 1773 |
| Governor's Body Guard, Madras | 1778 |
| Governor's Body Guard, Bombay | 1865 |
| Governor's Body Guard, Bengal | 1912 |
| 1st Duke of York's Own Lancers (Skinner's Horse) | 1803 |
| 2nd Lancers (Gardner's Horse) | 1809 |
| 3rd Skinner's Horse | 1814 |
| 4th Cavalry | 1838 |
| 5th Cavalry | 1841 |
| 6th King Edward's Own Cavalry | 1842 |
| 7th Hariana Lancers | 1846 |
| 8th Cavalry | 1846 |
| 9th Hodson's Horse | 1857 |
| 10th Duke of Cambridge's Own Lancers (Hodson's Horse) | 1857 |
| 11th King Edward's Own Lancers (Probyn's Horse) | 1857 |
| 12th Cavalry | 1857 |
| 13th Duke of Connaught's Lancers (Watson's Horse) | 1858 |
| 14th Murray's Jat Lancers | 1857 |
| 15th Lancers (Cureton's Multanis) | 1858 |
| 16th Cavalry | 1857 |
| 17th Cavalry | 1857 |
| 18th King George's Own Lancers | 1858 |
| 19th Lancers (Fane's Horse) | 1860 |
| 20th Deccan Horse | 1826 |
| 21st Prince Albert Victor's Own Cavalry (Frontier Force) (Daly's Horse) | 1849 |
| 22nd Sam Browne's Cavalry (Frontier Force) | 1849 |
| 23rd Cavalry (Frontier Force) | 1849 |
| 25th Cavalry (Frontier Force) | 1849 |
| 26th King George's Own Light Cavalry | 1787 |
| 27th Light Cavalry | 1784 |
| 28th Light Cavalry | 1784 |
| 29th Lancers (Deccan Horse) | 1826 |
| 30th Lancers (Gordon's Horse) | 1826 |
| 31st Duke of Connaught's Own Lancers | 1817 |
| 32nd Lancers | 1817 |
| 33rd Queen Victoria's Own Light Cavalry | 1820 |
| 34th Prince Albert Victor's Own Poona Horse | 1817 |
| 35th Scinde Horse | 1839 |
| 36th Jacob's Horse | 1846 |
| 37th Lancers (Baluch Horse) | 1885 |
| 38th King George's Own Central India Horse | 1858 |
| 39th King George's Own Central India Horse | 1858 |

B

| | |
|---|---|
| Queen Victoria's Own Corps of Guides (Frontier Force) (Lumsden's) | 1846-47 |
| 21st Kohat Mountain Battery (Frontier Force) | 1851 |
| 22nd Derajat Mountain Battery (Frontier Force) | 1849 |
| 23rd Peshawar Mountain Battery (Frontier Force) | 1853 |
| 24th Hazara Mountain Battery (Frontier Force) | 1851 |
| 25th Mountain Battery | 1836 |
| 26th Jacob's Mountain Battery | 1843 |
| 27th Mountain Battery | 1886 |
| 28th Mountain Battery | 1886 |
| 29th Mountain Battery | 1898-99 |
| 30th Mountain Battery | 1900-01 |
| 31st Mountain Battery | 1907 |
| 32nd Mountain Battery | 1907 |
| The Frontier Garrison Artillery | 1851 |
| 1st King George's Own Sappers & Miners | 1803 |
| 2nd Queen Victoria's Own Sappers & Miners | 1780 |
| 3rd Sappers & Miners | 1820 |
| 1st Brahmans | 1776 |
| 2nd Queen Victoria's Own Rajput Light Infantry | 1798 |
| 3rd Brahmans | 1798 |
| 4th Prince Albert Victor's Rajputs | 1798 |
| 5th Light Infantry | 1803 |
| 6th Jat Light Infantry | 1803 |
| 7th Duke of Connaught's Own Rajputs | 1824 |
| 8th Rajputs | 1814 |
| 9th Bhopal Infantry | 1859 |
| 10th Jats | 1823 |
| 11th Rajputs | 1825 |
| 12th Pioneers (The Kelat-i-Ghilzie Regiment) | 1838 |
| 13th Rajputs (The Shekhawati Regiment) | 1835 |
| 14th King George's Own Ferozepore Sikhs | 1846 |
| 15th Ludhiana Sikhs | 1846 |
| 16th Rajputs (The Lucknow Regiment) | 1857 |
| 17th Infantry (The Loyal Regiment) | 1858 |
| 18th Infantry | 1795 |
| 19th Punjabis | 1857 |

| | |
|---|---|
| 20th Duke of Cambridge's Own Infantry (Brownlow's Punjabis) | 1857 |
| 21st Punjabis | 1857 |
| 22nd Punjabis | 1857 |
| 23rd Sikh Pioneers | 1857 |
| 24th Punjabis | 1857 |
| 25th Punjabis | 1857 |
| 26th Punjabis | 1857 |
| 27th Punjabis | 1857 |
| 28th Punjabis | 1857 |
| 29th Punjabis | 1857 |
| 30th Punjabis | 1857 |
| 31st Punjabis | 1857 |
| 32nd Sikh Pioneers | 1857 |
| 33rd Punjabis | 1857 |
| 34th Sikh Pioneers | 1887 |
| 35th Sikhs | 1887 |
| 36th Sikhs | 1887 |
| 37th Dogras | 1887 |
| 38th Dogras | 1858 |
| 39th Garhwal Rifles | 1887 |
| 40th Pathans | 1858 |
| 41st Dogras | 1900 |
| 42nd Deoli Regiment | 1857 |
| 43rd Erinpura Regiment | 1860 |
| 44th Merwera Infantry | 1822 |
| 45th Rattray's Sikhs | 1856 |
| 46th Punjabis | 1900 |
| 47th Sikhs | 1901 |
| 48th Pioneers | 1901 |
| 51st Sikhs (Frontier Force) | 1846-47 |
| 52nd Sikhs (Frontier Force) | 1846-47 |
| 53rd Sikhs (Frontier Force) | 1846-47 |
| 54th Sikhs (Frontier Force) | 1846-47 |
| 55th Coke's Rifles (Frontier Force) | 1849 |
| 56th Punjabi Rifles (Frontier Force) | 1849 |
| 57th Wilde's Rifles (Frontier Force) | 1849 |

| | |
|---|---|
| 58th Vaughan's Rifles (Frontier Force) | 1849 |
| 59th Scinde Rifles (Frontier Force) | 1843 |
| 61st King George's Own Pioneers | 1758 |
| 62nd Punjabis | 1759 |
| 63rd Palamcottah Light Infantry | 1759 |
| 64th Pioneers | 1759 |
| 66th Punjabis | 1761 |
| 67th Punjabis | 1761 |
| 69th Punjabis | 1762-65 |
| 72nd Punjabis | 1767 |
| 73rd Carnatic Infantry | 1776 |
| 74th Punjabis | 1776 |
| 75th Carnatic Infantry | 1776 |
| 76th Punjabis | 1776 |
| 79th Carnatic Infantry | 1777 |
| 80th Carnatic Infantry | 1777 |
| 81st Pioneers | 1786 |
| 82nd Punjabis | 1788 |
| 83rd Wallajahbad Light Infantry | 1794 |
| 84th Punjabis | 1794 |
| 86th Carnatic Infantry | 1794 |
| 87th Punjabis | 1798 |
| 88th Carnatic Infantry | 1798 |
| 89th Punjabis | 1798 |
| 90th Punjabis | 1799 |
| 91st Punjabis (Light Infantry) | 1800 |
| 92nd Punjabis | 1800 |
| 93rd Burma Infantry | 1800 |
| 94th Russell's Infantry | 1813 |
| 95th Russell's Infantry | 1813 |
| 96th Berar Infantry | 1797 |
| 97th Deccan Infantry | 1794 |
| 98th Infantry | 1788 |
| 99th Deccan Infantry | 1788 |
| The 101st Grenadiers | 1779 |
| 102nd King Edward's Own Grenadiers | 1796 |
| 103rd Mahratta Light Infantry | 1768 |
| 104th Wellesley's Rifles | 1775 |
| 105th Mahratta Light Infantry | 1788 |
| 106th Hazara Pioneers | 1904 |
| 107th Pioneers | 1788 |
| 108th Infantry | 1768 |
| 109th Infantry | 1788 |
| 110th Mahratta Light Infantry | 1797 |
| 112th Infantry | 1798 |
| 113th Infantry | 1800 |
| 114th Mahrattas | 1800 |
| 116th Mahrattas | 1800 |
| 117th Mahrattas | 1800 |
| 119th Infantry (The Mooltan Regiment) | 1817 |
| 120th Rajputana Infantry | 1817 |
| 121st Pioneers | 1777 |
| 122nd Rajputana Infantry | 1818 |
| 123rd Outram's Rifles | 1820 |
| 124th Duchess of Connaught's Own Baluchistan Infantry | 1820 |
| 125th Napier's Rifles | 1820 |
| 126th Baluchistan Infantry | 1825 |
| 127th Queen Mary's Own Baluch Light Infantry | 1844 |
| 128th Pioneers | 1846 |
| 129th Duke of Connaught's Own Baluchis | 1846 |
| 130th King George's Own Baluchis (Jacob's Rifles) | 1858 |
| 1st King George's Own Gurkha Rifles (The Malaun Regiment) | 1815 |
| 2nd King Edward's Own Gurkha Rifles (The Sirmoor Rifles) | 1815 |
| 3rd Queen Alexandra's Own Gurkha Rifles | 1815 |
| 4th Gurkha Rifles | 1857 |
| 5th Gurkha Rifles (Frontier Force) | 1858 |
| 6th Gurkha Rifles | 1817 |
| 7th Gurkha Rifles | 1902 |
| 8th Gurkha Rifles | 1824 |
| 9th Gurkha Rifles | 1817 |
| 10th Gurkha Rifles | 1890 |

# EUROPE

| | | | |
|---|---|---|---|
| **NAMUR 1695** | War of the League of Augsburg | | 3rd to 6th July 1695 |
| **GIBRALTAR 1704-1705** | Capture & Defence | | 1704-1705 |
| **BLENHEIM** | War of the Spanish Succession | | 13th August 1704 |
| **RAMILLIES** | " " | | 23rd May 1706 |
| **OUDENARDE** | " " | | 11th July 1708 |
| **MALPLAQUET** | " " | | 11th September 1709 |
| **DETTINGEN** | War of the Austrian Succession | | 27th June 1743 |
| **MINDEN** | Seven Years War | | 1st August 1759 |
| **EMSDORFF** | " " | | 16th July 1760 |
| **WARBURG** | " " | | 31st July 1760 |
| **BELLEISLE** | " " | | 7th June 1761 |
| **WILHELMSTAHL** | " " | | 24th June 1762 |
| **GIBRALTAR 1779-1783** | War of American Independence 1775-1783 | | 1779-1783 |
| **JERSEY** | | Defence | 6th January 1781 |
| **LINCELLES** | French Revolutionary Wars 1793-1802 | | 18th August 1793 |
| **NIEUPORT** | " " | | 20th to 30th October 1793 |
| **VILLERS-EN-CAUCHIES** | " " | | 24th April 1794 |
| **BEAUMONT** | " " | | 26th April 1794 |
| **WILLEMS** | " " | | 10th May 1794 |
| **TOURNAY** | " " | | 23rd May 1794 |
| **NAVAL CROWN** | " " | | 1st June 1794 |
| **ST. VINCENT** | " " | | 14th February 1797 |
| **FISHGUARD** | " " | | 24th February 1797 |
| **EGMONT-OP-ZEE** | " " | | 2nd October 1799 |
| **1800** | " " | Defence of Malta | 1800 |
| **COPENHAGEN** | " " | | 2nd April 1801 |
| **NAVAL CROWN** | " " | | 2nd April 1801 |
| **MAIDA** | Napoleonic Wars 1803-1815 | | 4th July 1806 |
| **ROLICA** | Peninsular War | | 17th August 1808 |

| | | |
|---|---|---|
| VIMIERA | Peninsular War | 21st August 1808 |
| SAHAGUN | ” ” | 20th December 1808 |
| CORUNNA | ” ” | 16th January 1809 |
| DUORO | ” ” | 10th to 12th May 1809 |
| TALAVERA | ” ” | 27th to 28th July 1809 |
| BUSACO | ” ” | 27th September 1810 |
| BARROSA | ” ” | 5th March 1811 |
| FUENTES D'ONOR | ” ” | 5th May 1811 |
| ALBUHERA | ” ” | 16th May 1811 |
| ARROYO DOS MOLINOS | ” ” | 28th October 1811 |
| TARIFA | ” ” | 31st December 1811 |
| CIUDAD RODRIGO | ” ” | 8th to 19th January 1812 |
| BADAJOS | ” ” | 17th March to 7th April 1812 |
| ALMARAZ | ” ” | 20th May 1812 |
| SALAMANCA | ” ” | 22nd July 1812 |
| VITTORIA | ” ” | 21st June 1813 |
| PYRENEES | ” ” | 25th July to 2nd August 1813 |
| SAN SEBASTIAN | ” ” | 9th June to 9th September 1813 |
| NIVELLE | ” ” | 10th to 12th November 1813 |
| NIVE | ” ” | 9th December 1813 |
| ORTHES | ” ” | 27th February 1814 |
| TOULOUSE | ” ” | 10th April 1814 |
| PENINSULA | ” ” | 1808-1814 |
| WATERLOO | The Hundred Days | 18th June 1815 |
| ALMA | Crimean War | 20th September 1854 |
| BALACLAVA | ” ” | 25th October 1854 |
| INKERMAN | ” ” | 5th November 1854 |
| SEVASTOPOL | ” ” | 1854-1855 |
| MEDITERRANEAN | ” ” | |

| | ABBREVIATED TITLE | FORMER TITLE | DATE OF AWARD |
|---|---|---|---|
| **NAMUR 1695** | Grenadier Guards | 1st Regt. of Foot Guards (Col: The Earl of Romney) | Army Order 45/1910 |
| | Coldstream Guards | Coldstream Regt. of Foot Guards (Col: Lord Cutts) | Army Order 45/1910 |
| | Scots Guards | Scots Regt. of Foot Guards (Col: Maj-Gen. George Ramsay) | Army Order 45/1910 |
| | The Royal Scots | Royal Regt. of Foot (Col: The Earl of Orkney) | Army Order 45/1910 |
| | The Queen's (Royal West Surrey Regt.) | The Queen Dowager's Regt. (Col: Brig. William Selwyn) | Army Order 45/1910 |
| | The King's (Royal Lancaster Regt.) | The Queen's Regt. of Foot (Col: Col. Henry Trelawny) | Army Order 45/1910 |
| | The Royal Warwickshire Regt. | Col. Columbine's Regt. of Foot (Col: Ventris Columbine) | Army Order 45/1910 |
| | The Royal Fusiliers | The Royal Regt. of Fusiliers (Col: Edward Fitzpatrick) | Army Order 45/1910 |
| | The West Yorkshire Regt. | Col. Tidcomb's Regt. of Foot (Col: John Tidcomb) | Army Order 45/1910 |
| | The Bedfordshire Regt. | Col. Hon. James Stanley's Regt. of Foot (Col: Hon. James Stanley) | Army Order 45/1910 |
| | The Leicestershire Regt. | Col. Courthorpe's Regt. of Foot (Col: James Courthorpe) | Army Order 45/1910 |
| | The Royal Irish Regt. | Col. Hamilton's Regt. of Foot (Col: Frederick Hamilton) | Army Order 45/1910 |
| | The Royal Welsh Fusiliers | Col. Ingoldsby's Regt. of Foot (Col: Richard Ingoldsby) | Army Order 45/1910 |
| | The King's Own Scottish Borderers | Col. Maitland's Regt. of Foot (Col: James Maitland) | Army Order 45/1910 |

| | | | |
|---|---|---|---|
| **GIBRALTAR 1704-1705 (Capture – Defence)** | Grenadier Guards | 1st Regt. of Foot Guards (Col: The Duke of Marlborough) | Army Order 180/1909 |
| | Coldstream Guards | Coldstream Regt. of Foot Guards (Col: Lord Cutts) | Army Order 180/1909 |
| | The King's Own (Royal Lancaster Regt.) | *The Queen's Own Regt. of Marines (Col: Lt-Gen. William Seymour) | Army Order 180/1909 |
| | The Somerset L.I. | The Earl of Barrymore's Regt. of Foot (Col: The Earl of Barrymore) | Army Order 180/1909 |
| | 1st Bn. The East Lancashire Regt. | Col. Thomas Saunderson's Regt. of Marines (Col: Thomas Saunderson) | Army Order 180/1909 |
| | 1st Bn. The East Surrey Regt. | Col. George Villier's Regt. of Marines (Col: George Villiers) | Army Order 180/1909 |
| | 1st Bn. The Duke of Cornwall's L.I. | Col. Edward Fox's Regt. of Marines (Col: Edward Fox) | Army Order 180/1909 |
| | 1st Bn. The Royal Sussex Regt. | The Earl of Donegall's Regt. of Foot (Col: The Earl of Donegall) | Army Order 180/1909 |
| **BLENHEIM** | 1st (King's) Dragoon Guards | The Queen's (or 2nd) Regt. of Horse (Col: Henry Lumley) | 13th March 1882 |
| | 3rd Dragoon Guards | Maj-Gen. Wood's Regt. of Horse (Col: Cornelius Wood) | 13th March 1882 |
| | 5th Dragoon Guards | Brig-Gen. Cadogan's Regt. of Horse (Col: William Cadogan) | 13th March 1882 |
| | 6th Dragoon Guards | The King's Carabiniers (Col: Hugh Wyndham) | 13th March 1882 |
| | 7th Dragoon Guards | The Duke of Schomberg's Regt. of Horse (Col: Gen. the Duke of Schomberg) | 13th March 1882 |
| | 2nd Dragoons (Royal Scots Greys) | Her Majesty's Regt. of (North) British Dragoons (Col: Maj-Gen. The Earl of Stair) | 13th March 1882 |
| | 5th Royal Irish Lancers | Royal Regt. of Irish Dragoons (Col: Maj-Gen. Charles Ross) | 13th March 1882 |

* Temporarily constituted a Regiment of Marines in 1702.
Reverted to the Line in 1711.

| | | | |
|---|---|---|---|
| **BLENHEIM (Cont.)** | Grenadier Guards | 1st Regt. of Foot Guards (Col: The Duke of Marlborough) | 13th March 1882 |
| | The Royal Scots | The Royal Regt. of Foot (Col: The Earl of Orkney) | 13th March 1882 |
| | The Buffs (East Kent Regt.) | General Churchill's Regt. of Foot (Col: Charles Churchill) | 13th March 1882 |
| | The King's (Liverpool Regt.) | Brig-Gen. Webb's Regt. of Foot (Col: John Richmond Webb) | 13th March 1882 |
| | The Lincolnshire Regt. | Lord North & Grey's Regt. of Foot (Col: Lord North & Grey) | 13th March 1882 |
| | The East Yorkshire Regt. | Brig-Gen. Howe's Regt. of Foot (Col: Emmanuel Howe) | 13th March 1882 |
| | The Bedfordshire Regt. | The Earl of Derby's Regt. of Foot (Col: Maj-Gen. The Earl of Derby) | 13th March 1882 |
| | The Royal Irish Regt. | The Royal Regt. of Ireland (Col: Brig-Gen. Frederick Hamilton) | 13th March 1882 |
| | The Royal Scots Fusiliers | Brig-Gen. Row's Regt. of Fuziliers (Col: Archibald Row) | 13th March 1882 |
| | The Royal Welsh Fusiliers | Lt-Gen. Ingoldsby's Regt. of Fusiliers (Col: Richard Ingoldsby) | 13th March 1882 |
| | The South Wales Borderers | The Duke of Marlborough's (Late) Regt. of Foot (Col: William Tatton) | 13th March 1882 |
| | 1st Bn. The Cameronians | Brig-Gen. Ferguson's Regt. of Foot (Col: James Ferguson) | 13th March 1882 |
| | 1st Bn. The Hampshire Regt. | Brig-Gen. Meredyth's Regt. of Foot (Col: Thomas Meredyth) | 13th March 1882 |
| **RAMILLIES** | 1st (King's) Dragoon Guards | The Queen's (or 2nd) Regt. of Horse (Col: Henry Lumley) | 13th March 1882 |
| | 3rd Dragoon Guards | Maj-Gen. Wood's Regt. of Horse (Col: Cornelius Wood) | 13th March 1882 |
| | 5th Dragoon Guards | Brig-Gen. Cadogan's Regt. of Horse (Col: William Cadogan) | 13th March 1882 |

| | | | |
|---|---|---|---|
| **RAMILLIES (Cont.)** | 6th Dragoon Guards | The King's Carabiniers<br>(Col: Hugh Wyndham) | 13th March 1882 |
| | 7th Dragoon Guards | The Duke of Schomberg's Regt. of Horse<br>(Col: Gen. The Duke of Schomberg) | 13th March 1882 |
| | 2nd Dragoons (Royal Scots Greys) | Royal Regt. of Scots Dragoons<br>(Col: Lt-Gen. Lord John Hay) | 13th March 1882 |
| | 5th Royal Irish Lancers | Royal Regt. of Irish Dragoons<br>(Col: Maj-Gen. Charles Ross) | 13th March 1882 |
| | Grenadier Guards | 1st Regt. of Foot Guards<br>(Col: The Duke of Marlborough) | 13th March 1882 |
| | The Royal Scots | The Royal Regt. of Foot<br>(Col: The Earl of Orkney) | 13th March 1882 |
| | The Buffs (East Kent Regt.) | Gen. Churchill's Regt. of Foot<br>(afterwards Argyll's)<br>(Col: Charles Churchill) | 13th March 1882 |
| | The King's (Liverpool Regt.) | Brig-Gen. Webb's Regt. of Foot<br>(Col: John Richmond Webb) | 13th March 1882 |
| | The Lincolnshire Regt. | Lord North & Grey's Regt. of Foot<br>(Col: Maj-Gen. Lord North & Grey) | 13th March 1882 |
| | The East Yorkshire Regt. | Brig-Gen. Howe's Regt. of Foot<br>(Col: Emmanuel Howe) | 13th March 1882 |
| | The Bedfordshire Regt. | Col. Godfrey's Regt. of Foot (late Derby's)<br>(Col: Francis Godfrey) | 13th March 1882 |
| | The Royal Irish Regt. | The Royal Regt. of Ireland<br>(Col: Lt-Gen. Richard Ingoldsby) (late F. Hamilton) | 13th March 1882 |
| | The Royal Scots Fusiliers | Royal Regt. of Scots Fusiliers<br>(Col: Lord Mordaunt) (afterwards de Lalo's) | 13th March 1882 |
| | The Royal Welsh Fusiliers | Her Majesty's Regt. of Welch Fuziliers<br>(Col: Brig-Gen. Joseph Sabine) (late Ingoldsby's) | 13th March 1882 |
| | The South Wales Borderers | Col. Tatton's Regt. of Foot<br>(Col: William Tatton) (late Marlborough's) | 13th March 1882 |
| | 1st Bn. The Cameronians | Brig-Gen. Lord Dalrymple's Regt. of Foot<br>(Col: Lord Dalrymple) | 13th March 1882 |

| Battle | Regiment | Predecessor | Date |
|---|---|---|---|
| **RAMILLIES (Cont.)** | 1st Bn. The Gloucestershire Regt. | Col. de Lalo's Regt. of Foot (Col: Sampson de Lalo) | 13th March 1882 |
| | 1st Bn. The Worcestershire Regt. | Brig-Gen. Farrington's Regt. of Foot (Col: Thomas Farrington) | 13th March 1882 |
| | 1st Bn. The Hampshire Regt. | Brig-Gen. Meredyth's Regt. of Foot (Col: Thomas Meredyth) | 13th March 1882 |
| **OUDENARDE** | 1st (King's) Dragoon Guards | The Queen's Regt. of Horse (Col: Henry Lumley) | 13th March 1882 |
| | 3rd Dragoon Guards | Lt-Gen. Wood's Regt. of Horse (Col: Cornelius Wood) | 13th March 1882 |
| | 5th Dragoon Guards | Lt-Gen. Cadogan's Regt. of Horse (Col: William Cadogan) | 13th March 1882 |
| | 6th Dragoon Guards | Her Majesty's Regt. of Carabiniers (Col: Hugh Wyndham) | 13th March 1882 |
| | 7th Dragoon Guards | The Duke of Schomberg's Regt. of Horse (Col: Gen. The Duke of Schomberg) | 13th March 1882 |
| | 2nd Dragoons (Royal Scots Greys) | Her Majesty's Regt. of (North) British Dragoons (Col: Maj-Gen. The Earl of Stair) | 13th March 1882 |
| | 5th Royal Irish Lancers | Her Majesty's Royal Regt. of Dragoons of Ireland (Col: Lt-Gen. Charles Ross) | 13th March 1882 |
| | Grenadier Guards | 1st Regt. of Foot Guards (Col: The Duke of Marlborough) | 13th March 1882 |
| | Coldstream Guards | Coldstream Regt. of Foot Guards (Col: Gen. Charles Churchill) | 13th March 1882 |
| | The Royal Scots | The Royal Regt. of Foot (Col: Lt-Gen. The Earl of Orkney) | 13th March 1882 |
| | The Buffs (East Kent Regt.) | HRH Prince George of Denmark's Regt. of Foot (Col: Lt-Gen. The Duke of Argyll) | 13th March 1882 |
| | The King's (Liverpool Regt.) | Lt-Gen. Webb's Regt. of Foot (Col: John Richmond Webb) | 13th March 1882 |
| | The Lincolnshire Regt. | Lord North & Grey's Regt. of Foot (Col: Maj-Gen. Lord North & Grey) | 13th March 1882 |

| | | | |
|---|---|---|---|
| **OUDENARDE (Cont.)** | The East Yorkshire Regt. | Maj-Gen. Howe's Regt. of Foot (Col: Emmanuel Howe) | 13th March 1882 |
| | The Bedfordshire Regt. | Col. Godfrey's Regt. of Foot (Col: Francis Godfrey) | 13th March 1882 |
| | The Royal Irish Regt. | Her Majesty's Royal Regt. of Foot of Ireland (Col: Richard Ingoldsby) | 13th March 1882 |
| | The Royal Scots Fusiliers | Her Majesty's Regt. of Royal (North) British Fuziliers (Col: Sampson de Lalo) | 13th March 1882 |
| | The Royal Welsh Fusiliers | Her Majesty's Regt. of (Royal) Welch Fuziliers (Col: Brig-Gen. Joseph Sabine) | 13th March 1882 |
| | The South Wales Borderers | Brig-Gen. Primrose's Regt. of Foot (Col: Gilbert Primrose) | 13th March 1882 |
| | 1st Bn. The Cameronians | Col. Preston's Regt. of Foot (Col: George Preston) | 13th March 1882 |
| | 1st Bn. The Hampshire Regt. | Lt-Gen. Meredyth's Regt. of Foot (Col: Thomas Meredyth) | 13th March 1882 |
| **MALPLAQUET** | 1st King's Dragoon Guards | The Queen's Regt. of Horse (Col: Henry Lumley) | 13th March 1882 |
| | 3rd Dragoon Guards | Lt-Gen. Wood's Regt. of Horse (Col: Cornelius Wood) | 13th March 1882 |
| | 5th Dragoon Guards | Lt-Gen. Cadogan's Regt. of Horse (Col: William Cadogan) | 13th March 1882 |
| | 6th Dragoon Guards | Her Majesty's First Regt. of Carabiniers (Col: Lt-Gen. Francis Palmes) | 13th March 1882 |
| | 7th Dragoon Guards | The Duke of Schomberg's Regt. of Horse (Col: Gen. The Duke of Schomberg) | 13th March 1882 |
| | 2nd Dragoons (Royal Scots Greys) | Her Majesty's Royal Regt. of (North) British Dragoons (Col: Maj-Gen. The Earl of Stair) | 13th March 1882 |
| | 5th Royal Irish Lancers | Her Majesty's Royal Regt. of Dragoons of Ireland (Col: Lt-Gen. Charles Ross) | 13th March 1882 |

| | | | |
|---|---|---|---|
| **MALPLAQUET (Cont.)** | Grenadier Guards | 1st Regt. of Foot Guards<br>(Col: The Duke of Marlborough) | 13th March 1882 |
| | Coldstream Guards | Coldstream Regt. of Foot Guards<br>(Col: Gen. Charles Churchill) | 13th March 1882 |
| | The Royal Scots | The Royal Regt. of Foot<br>(Col: Lt-Gen. The Earl of Orkney) | 13th March 1882 |
| | The Buffs (East Kent Regt.) | HRH Prince George of Denmark's Regt. of Foot<br>(Col: Lt-Gen. The Duke of Argyll) | 13th March 1882 |
| | The King's (Liverpool Regt.) | Lt-Gen. Webb's Regt. of Foot<br>(Col: John Richmond Webb) | 13th March 1882 |
| | The Lincolnshire Regt. | Lord North & Grey's Regt. of Foot<br>(Col: Maj-Gen. Lord North & Grey) | 13th March 1882 |
| | The East Yorkshire Regt. | Lt-Gen. Howe's Regt. of Foot<br>(Col: Emmanuel Howe) | 13th March 1882 |
| | The Bedfordshire Regt. | Col. Godfrey's Regt. of Foot<br>(Col: Francis Godfrey) | 13th March 1882 |
| | The Royal Irish Regt. | Her Majesty's Royal Regt. of Foot of Ireland<br>(Col: Richard Ingoldsby) | 13th March 1882 |
| | The Green Howards (Yorkshire Regt.) | Lt-Gen. Erle's Regt. of Foot<br>(Col: Thomas Erle) | 13th March 1882 |
| | The Royal Scots Fusiliers | Her Majesty's Regt. of Royal (North) British Fuziliers<br>(Col: Brig-Gen. Samson de Lalo) | 13th March 1882 |
| | The Royal Welsh Fusiliers | Her Majesty's Regt. of (Royal) Welch Fuziliers<br>(Col: Brig-Gen. Joseph Sabine) | 13th March 1882 |
| | The South Wales Borderers | Brig-Gen. Primrose's Regt. of Foot<br>(Col: Gilbert Primrose) | 13th March 1882 |
| | 1st Bn. The Cameronians | Col. Preston's Regt. of Foot<br>(Col: George Preston) | 13th March 1882 |
| | 1st Bn. The Hampshire Regt. | Lt-Gen. Meredyth's Regt. of Foot<br>(Col: Thomas Meredyth) | 13th March 1882 |

| DETTINGEN | 1st Life Guards | *3rd Troop of Life Guards<br>(Col: The Earl of Albemarle) | 11th September 1882 |
|---|---|---|---|
| | 2nd Life Guards | *4th Troop of Life Guards<br>(Col: The Earl of Craufurd) | 11th September 1882 |
| | Royal Horse Guards | Royal Regt. of Horse Guards<br>(Col: The Earl of Hertford) | 11th September 1882 |
| | 1st King's Dragoon Guards | The King's Own Regt. of Horse<br>(Col: Lt-Gen. Sir Philip Honywood) | 11th September 1882 |
| | 7th Dragoon Guards | Lt-Gen. Ligonier's Regt. of Horse<br>(Col: Lt-Gen. John Ligonier) | 11th September 1882 |
| | 1st Royal Dragoons | Royal Regt. of Dragoons<br>(Col: Maj-Gen. Henry Hawley) | 11th September 1882 |
| | 2nd Dragoons (Royal Scots Greys) | Royal Regt. of North British Dragoons<br>(Col: Lt-Gen. James Campbell) | 11th September 1882 |
| | 3rd Hussars | King's Own Regt. of Dragoons<br>(Col: Brig-Gen. Humphrey Bland) (late Honywood's) | 11th September 1882 |
| | 4th Hussars | Lt-Gen. Rich's Regt. of Dragoons<br>(Col: Lt-Gen. Sir Robert Rich) | 11th September 1882 |
| | 6th (Inniskilling) Dragoons | The Earl of Stair's Regt. of Dragoons<br>(Col: Maj-Gen. The Earl of Stair) | 11th September 1882 |
| | 7th Hussars | The Queen's Own Regt. of Dragoons<br>(Col: Maj-Gen. Sir John Cope) | 11th September 1882 |
| | Grenadier Guards | 1st Regt. of Foot Guards<br>(Col: Maj-Gen. The Duke of Cumberland) | 11th September 1882 |
| | Coldstream Guards | Coldstream Regt. of Foot Guards<br>(Col: Charles, Duke of Marlborough) | 11th September 1882 |
| | Scots Guards | 3rd Regt. of Foot Guards<br>(Col: The Earl of Dunmore) | 11th September 1882 |
| | The Buffs (East Kent Regt.) | Maj-Gen. Howard's Regt. of Foot<br>(Col: Thomas Howard) | 11th September 1882 |
| | The King's (Liverpool Regt.) | The King's Regt. of Foot<br>(Col: Brig-Gen. Richard Onslow) | 11th September 1882 |

* 3rd and 4th Troops disbanded 1746

| | | | |
|---|---|---|---|
| **DETTINGEN (Cont.)** | The Devonshire Regt. | Col. Sowle's Regt. of Foot<br>(Col: Robinson Sowle) | 11th September 1882 |
| | The Suffolk Regt. | Col. Durore's Regt. of Foot<br>(Col: Scipio Durore) | 11th September 1882 |
| | The Somerset L.I. | Brig-Gen. Pulteney's Regt. of Foot<br>(Col: Henry Pulteney) | 11th September 1882 |
| | The Lancashire Fusiliers | Col. Bligh's Regt. of Foot<br>(Col: Thomas Bligh) | 11th September 1882 |
| | The Royal Scots Fusiliers | Royal North British Regt. of Fuziliers<br>(Col: Maj-Gen. John Campbell) | 11th September 1882 |
| | The Royal Welsh Fusiliers | Royal Regt. of Welch Fuziliers<br>(Col: Newsham Peers) | 11th September 1882 |
| | 1st Bn. The East Surrey Regt. | Brig-Gen. Handasyd's Regt. of Foot<br>(Col: William Handasyd) | 11th September 1882 |
| | 1st Bn. The Duke of Cornwall's L.I. | Brig-Gen. Huske's Regt. of Foot<br>(Col: John Huske) | 11th September 1882 |
| | 1st Bn. Duke of Wellington's Regt. | Col. Johnson's Regt. of Foot<br>(Col: John Johnson) | 11th September 1882 |
| | 1st Bn. The Hampshire Regt. | Col. Ponsonby's Regt. of Foot<br>(Col: Henry Ponsonby) | 11th September 1882 |
| **MINDEN** | The Suffolk Regt. | 12th Regt. of Foot<br>(Col: Lt-Gen. Robert Napier) | 1st January 1801 |
| | The Lancashire Fusiliers | 2nd Bn. 20th Regt. of Foot<br>(Col: Maj-Gen. William Kingsley) | 1st January 1801 |
| | | To Regiment | 22nd December 1820 |
| | The Royal Welsh Fusiliers | 23rd Regt. of Foot (Royal Welch Fuziliers)<br>(Col: Lt-Gen. John Huske) | 1st January 1801 |
| | The King's Own Scottish Borderers | 25th Regt. of Foot<br>(Col: Lt-Gen. The Earl of Home) | 1st January 1801 |
| | 1st Bn. The Hampshire Regt. | 37th Regt. of Foot<br>(Col: Lt-Gen. Hon. James Stuart) | 1st January 1801 |
| | 1st Bn. The King's Own Yorkshire L.I. | 51st Regt. of Foot<br>(Col: Maj-Gen. Thomas Brudenell) | 1st January 1801 |

| | | | |
|---|---|---|---|
| **EMSDORFF** | 15th King's Hussars | 15th Regt. of (Light) Dragoons<br>(Col: Maj-Gen. George Augustus Elliott) | Royal Warrant 1768 |
| **WARBURG** | Royal Horse Guards | Royal Regt. of Horse Guards<br>(Col: Lt-Gen. The Marquis of Granby) | Army Order 180/1909 |
| | 1st King's Dragoon Guards | 1st (or the King's) Regt. of Dragoon Guards<br>(Col: Lt-Gen. Humphrey Bland) | Army Order 180/1909 |
| | 2nd Dragoon Guards | 2nd (or the Queen's) Regt. of Dragoon Guards<br>(Col: Lt-Gen. Hon. J. Waldegrave) | Army Order 180/1909 |
| | 3rd Dragoon Guards | 3rd Regt. of Dragoon Guards<br>(Col: Lt-Gen. Hon. Sir Charles Howard) | Army Order 180/1909 |
| | 6th Dragoon Guards | 3rd Irish Horse or Carabiniers<br>(Col: Lt-Gen. Louis Dejean) | Army Order 180/1909 |
| | 7th Dragoon Guards | 4th (or Black) Irish Horse<br>(Col: Lt-Gen. Philip Honywood) | Army Order 180/1909 |
| | 1st Royal Dragoons | 1st (or Royal) Regt. of Dragoons<br>(Col: Lt-Gen. Henry Seymour Conway) | Army Order 180/1909 |
| | 2nd Dragoons (Royal Scots Greys) | 2nd (or Royal North British) Regt. of Dragoons<br>(Col: Lt-Gen. John Campbell) (Duke of Argyll) | Army Order 180/1909 |
| | 6th Inniskilling Dragoons | 6th (or Inneskilling) Regt. of Dragoons<br>(Col: Lt-Gen. Hon. James Cholmondeley) | Army Order 180/1909 |
| | 7th Hussars | 7th (or the Queen's) Regt. of Dragoons<br>(Col: Lt-Gen. John Mostyn) (late Cope's) | Army Order 180/1909 |
| | 10th Hussars | 10th Regt. of Dragoons<br>(Col: Lt-Gen. Sir John Mordaunt) | Army Order 180/1909 |
| | 11th Hussars | 11th Regt. of Dragoons<br>(Col: Lt-Gen. The Earl of Ancram) | Army Order 180/1909 |

| | | | |
|---|---|---|---|
| **BELLEISLE** | The Buffs (East Kent Regt.) | 3rd Regt. of Foot or the Buffs (Col: Maj-Gen. George Howard) | Army Order 136/1951 |
| | The Norfolk Regt. | 9th Regt. of Foot (Col: Maj-Gen. William Whitmore) | Army Order 136/1951 |
| | The Yorkshire Regt. (The Green Howards) | 19th Regt. of Foot (Col: Lt-Gen. Lord George Beauclerk) | Army Order 136/1951 |
| | The Royal Scots Fusiliers | 21st Regt. of Foot (or Royal North British Fuzileers) (Col: Lt-Gen. The Earl of Panmure) | Army Order 136/1951 |
| | 1st Bn. The East Lancashire Regt. | 30th Regt. of Foot (Col: Lt-Gen. The Earl of Loudon) | Army Order 136/1951 |
| | 2nd Bn. The Worcestershire Regt. | 36th Regt. of Foot (Col: Lt-Gen. Lord Robert Manners) | Army Order 136/1951 |
| | 2nd Bn. The Hampshire Regt. | 67th Regt. of Foot (Col: Lt-Gen. Hamilton Lambert) | Army Order 136/1951 |
| | 2nd Bn. The Welsh Regt. | 69th Regt. of Foot (Col: Maj-Gen. Charles Colville) | Army Order 136/1951 |
| **WILHELMSTAHL** | The Northumberland Fusiliers | 5th Regt. of Foot (Col: Maj-Gen. Studholme Hodgson) | 7th May 1836 |
| **GIBRALTAR 1779-1783** Date added Army Order 180/1909 Castle & Key with Motto 'Montis Insignia Calpe' | The Suffolk Regt. | 12th Regt. of Foot (Col: Maj-Gen. William Picton) | 14th April 1784 |
| | 1st Bn. The Dorsetshire Regt. | 39th Regt. of Foot (Col: Lt-Gen. Robert Boyd) | 14th April 1784 |
| | 2nd Bn. The Essex Regt. | 56th Regt. of Foot (Col: Lt-Gen. Hunt Walsh) | 14th April 1784 |
| | 2nd Bn. The Northamptonshire Regt. | 58th Regt. of Foot (Col: Lt-Gen. Lancelot Baugh) | 14th April 1784 |
| **GIBRALTAR 1780-1783** | 1st Bn. The Highland L.I. | *73rd (Highland) Regt. of Foot (Col: Maj-Gen. Lord MacLeod) | Army Order 73/1908 |

* Renumbered 71st in 1786

| | | | |
|---|---|---|---|
| **JERSEY** | 1st or West Bn. Royal Jersey (L.I.) | North-West Regt. of Jersey Militia | 3rd June 1881 |
| | 2nd or East Bn. Royal Jersey (L.I.) | East Regt. of Jersey Militia | |
| | 3rd or South Bn. Royal Jersey (L.I.) | South-West Regt. of Jersey Militia | |
| **LINCELLES** | Grenadier Guards | 1st Regt. of Foot Guards (Col: Gen. HRH The Duke of Gloucester) | 20th June 1811 |
| | Coldstream Guards | Coldstream Regt. of Foot Guards (Col: Lt-Gen. HRH The Duke of York) | 20th June 1811 |
| | Scots Guards | 3rd Regt. of Foot Guards (Col: Gen. The Duke of Argyll) | 20th June 1811 |
| **NIEUPORT** | 1st Bn. The King's Shropshire L.I. | 53rd (Shropshire) Regt. of Foot (Col: Lt-Gen. Robert Dalrymple-Horn-Elphinstone) | 10th March 1825 |
| **VILLERS EN CAUCHIES Name to read as above Army Order 216/1911** | 15th King's Hussars | 15th (or the King's) Regt. of (Light) Dragoons (Col: Gen. Lord Dorchester) | c. 1817 or 1818 |
| **BEAUMONT** | Royal Horse Guards | Royal Regt. of Horse Guards (Col: F.M. Henry Seymour Conway) | Army Order 211/1909 |
| | 1st King's Dragoon Guards | 1st (or King's) Regt. of Dragoon Guards (Col: F.M. Sir George Howard) | Army Order 211/1909 |
| | 3rd Dragoon Guards | 3rd (Prince of Wales's) Regt. of Dragoon Guards (Col: Lt-Gen. William Fawcett) | Army Order 211/1909 |
| | 5th Dragoon Guards | 5th Regt. of Dragoon Guards (Col: Maj-Gen. Thomas Bland) | Army Order 211/1909 |
| | 1st Royal Dragoons | 1st (Royal) Regt. of Dragoons (Col: Gen. The Earl of Pembroke) | Army Order 211/1909 |
| | 7th Hussars | 7th (or Queen's Own) Regt. of (Light) Dragoons (Col: Gen. Sir Henry Clinton) | Army Order 211/1909 |
| | 11th Hussars | 11th Regt. of (Light) Dragoons (Col: Gen. Studholme Hodgson) | Army Order 211/1909 |
| | 16th Lancers | 16th (or the Queen's) Regt. of (Light) Dragoons (Col: Lt-Gen. Hon. William Harcourt) | Army Order 211/1909 |

| | | | |
|---|---|---|---|
| **WILLEMS** | Royal Horse Guards | Royal Regt. of Horse Guards (Col: F.M. Henry Seymour Conway) | Army Order 211/1909 |
| | 2nd Dragoon Guards | 2nd (or the Queen's) Regt. of Dragoon Guards (Col: Gen. Marquis Townshend) | Army Order 211/1909 |
| | 3rd Dragoon Guards | 3rd (Prince of Wales's) Regt. of Dragoon Guards (Col: Lt-Gen. William Fawcett) | Army Order 211/1909 |
| | 6th Dragoon Guards | 6th Regt. of Dragoon Guards (Carabiniers) (Col: Lt-Gen. The Earl of Carhampton) | Army Order 211/1909 |
| | 1st Royal Dragoons | 1st (Royal) Regt. of Dragoons (Col: Gen. The Earl of Pembroke) | Army Order 211/1909 |
| | 2nd Dragoons (Royal Scots Greys) | 2nd (or Royal North British) Regt. of Dragoons (Col: Gen. James Johnston) | Army Order 211/1909 |
| | 6th Inniskilling Dragoons | 6th (Inniskilling) Regt. of Dragoons (Col: Gen. James Johnston) | Army Order 211/1909 |
| | 7th Hussars | 7th (or Queen's Own) Regt. of (Light) Dragoons (Col: Gen. Sir Henry Clinton) | Army Order 211/1909 |
| | 11th Hussars | 11th Regt. of (Light) Dragoons (Col: Gen. Studholme Hodgson) | Army Order 211/1909 |
| | 15th Hussars | 15th (or the King's) Regt. of (Light) Dragoons (Col: Gen. Lord Dorchester) | Army Order 211/1909 |
| | 16th Lancers | 16th (or the Queen's) Regt. of (Light) Dragoons (Col: Lt-Gen. Hon. William Harcourt) | Army Order 211/1909 |
| **TOURNAY** | The West Yorkshire Regt. | 14th (Bedfordshire) Regt. of Foot (Col: Maj-Gen. George Hotham) | 24th February 1836 |
| | 1st Bn. The Hampshire Regt. | 37th (North Hampshire) Regt. of Foot (Col: Lt-Gen. Sir John Dalling) | 13th June 1826 |
| | 1st Bn. The King's Shropshire L.I. | 53rd (Shropshire) Regt. of Foot (Col: Gen. Robert Dalrymple-Horn-Elphinstone) | 10th March 1825 |
| **NAVAL CROWN Superscribed 1st June 1794** | The Queen's (Royal West Surrey Regt.) | 2nd (The Queen's Royal) Regt. of Foot (Col: Maj-Gen. Alexander Stewart) | Army Order 312/1909 |
| | 1st Bn. The Worcestershire Regt. | 29th (Worcestershire) Regt. of Foot (Col: Col. William, Lord Cathcart) | Army Order 312/1909 |

C*

| | | | |
|---|---|---|---|
| **ST VINCENT** | 2nd Bn. The Welsh Regt. | 69th (South Lincolnshire) Regt. of Foot (Col: Gen. Sir Cornelius Cuyler) | Army Order 121/1891 |
| **FISHGUARD** | Pembrokeshire Yeomanry | Gentlemen & Yeomanry of Pembroke | 28th May 1853 |
| **EGMONT OP ZEE** | 15th Hussars | 15th (the King's) Regt. of (Light) Dragoons (Col: Gen. Lord Dorchester) | 8th April 1820 |
| | Grenadier Guards | 1st Regt. of Foot Guards (Col: HRH William Duke of Gloucester) | Army Order 295/1913 |
| | The Royal Scots | 1st (or the Royal) Regt. of Foot (Col: Gen. Lord Adam Gordon) | 25th July 1821 |
| | The Lancashire Fusiliers | 20th (East Devonshire) Regt. of Foot (Col: Lt-Gen. Charles Leigh) | 27th March 1820 |
| | The King's Own Scottish Borderers | 25th (Sussex) Regt. of Foot (Col: Gen. Lord George Gordon-Lennox) | 10th February 1820 |
| | 1st Bn. The Royal Berkshire Regt. | 49th (Hertfordshire) Regt. of Foot (Col: Gen. Sir Alexander Maitland) | 19th February 1819 |
| | 1st Bn. The Manchester Regt. | 63rd (West Suffolk) Regt. of Foot (Col: Lt-Gen. The Earl of Balcarres) | 18th June 1830 |
| | The Queen's Own Cameron Highlanders | 79th Regt. of Foot (or Cameronian Volunteers) (Col: Sir Alan Cameron) | 2nd October 1818 |
| | 2nd Bn. The Gordon Highlanders | *92nd Regt. of Foot (Col: Maj-Gen. The Marquis of Huntley) | 31st August 1814 |
| | * Originally granted on 15th February 1813 as BERGEN-OP-ZOOM | | |
| **'1800'** | The King's Own Malta Regt. of Militia | | 23rd September 1897 |
| **COPENHAGEN** | 1st Bn. The Royal Berkshire Regt. | 49th (Hertfordshire) Regt. of Foot (Col: Gen. Sir Alexander Maitland) | 19th February 1819 |
| | The Rifle Brigade | A Corps of Riflemen (Col: Col. Coote Manningham) | 22nd March 1821 |

| | | | |
|---|---|---|---|
| **NAVAL CROWN** | 1st Bn. The Royal Berkshire Regt. | 49th (Hertfordshire) Regt. of Foot | Army Order 136/1951 |
| **Superscribed 2nd April 1801** | The Rifle Brigade | A Corps of Riflemen | Army Order 136/1951 |
| **MAIDA** | The Lancashire Fusiliers | 20th (East Devonshire) Regt. of Foot | 24th February 1807 |
| | 1st Bn. The Royal Inniskilling Fusiliers | 27th (Inniskilling) Regt. of Foot | 24th February 1807 |
| | 2nd Bn. The Gloucestershire Regt. | 61st (South Gloucestershire) Regt. of Foot | 10th February 1808 |
| | 1st Bn. The Royal Sussex Regt. | 35th (Sussex) Regt. of Foot | |
| | | To Flank Companies | 10th February 1808 |
| | | To Regiment | 27th June 1818 |
| | 2nd Bn. The Loyal North Lancashire Regt. | 81st Regt. of Foot | 24th February 1807 |
| | 2nd Bn. The Northamptonshire Regt. | 58th (Rutlandshire) Regt. of Foot | 24th February 1807 |
| | 2nd Bn. Seaforth Highlanders | 78th (Highland) Regt. of Foot (Ross-shire Buffs) | 24th February 1807 |
| **ROLICA** | The Northumberland Fusiliers | 1st Bn. 5th (Northumberland) Regt. of Foot | 25th September 1817 |
| **Originally awarded as ROLEIA.** | The Royal Warwickshire Regt. | 1st Bn. 6th (1st Warwickshire) Regt. of Foot | 26th April 1827 |
| **.O. 216/1911 directed that award** | The Norfolk Regt. | 1st Bn. 9th (East Norfolk) Regt. of Foot | 23rd September 1820 |
| **should read ROLICA.** | 1st Bn. The Worcestershire Regt. | 1st Bn. 29th (Worcestershire) Regt. of Foot | 2nd March 1812 |
| | 2nd Bn. The Worcestershire Regt. | 1st Bn. 36th (Herefordshire) Regt. of Foot | 26th May 1833 |
| | 1st Bn. The Duke of Cornwall's L.I. | 1st Bn. 32nd (Cornwall) Regt. of Foot | 23rd January 1826 |
| | 1st Bn. The South Staffordshire Regt. | 1st Bn. 38th (1st Staffordshire) Regt. of Foot | 14th November 1831 |
| | 1st Bn. P.W.V. (South Lancashire) Regt. | 1st Bn. 40th (2nd Somersetshire) Regt. of Foot | 6th April 1824 |
| | 2nd Bn. P.W.V. (South Lancashire) Regt. | 1st Bn. 82nd Regt. of Foot (Prince of Wales's Volunteers) | 7th September 1825 |
| | 1st Bn. The Sherwood Foresters | 1st Bn. 45th (Nottinghamshire) Regt. of Foot | 4th December 1817 |
| | The King's Royal Rifle Corps | *5th Bn. 60th (Royal American) Regt. of Foot | 21st September 1821 |
| | 1st Bn. The Highland L.I. | 1st Bn. 71st (Highland) Regt. of Foot | 16th April 1818 |
| | 1st Bn. Argyll & Sutherland Highlanders | 1st Bn. 91st (Argyllshire Highlanders) Regt. of Foot | 16th January 1833 |
| | The Rifle Brigade | 2nd Bn. 95th Regt. of Foot (Rifle Corps) | 4th January 1821 |
| **VIMIERA** | 20th Hussars | 20th Regt. of (Light) Dragoons | Army Order 392/1890 |
| | The Queen's (Royal West Surrey Regt.) | 2nd (the Queen's Royal) Regt. of Foot | 15th June 1833 |
| | The Northumberland Fusiliers | 1st Bn. 5th (Northumberland) Regt. of Foot | 10th December 1825 |

* Granted to old 2nd & 3rd Bns. for services of 5th Bn.

| | | | |
|---|---|---|---|
| VIMIERA (Cont.) | The Royal Warwickshire Regt. | 1st Bn. 6th (1st Warwickshire) Regt. of Foot | 26th April 1827 |
| | The Norfolk Regt. | 1st & 2nd Bns. 9th (East Norfolk) Regt. of Foot | 23rd September 1820 |
| | The Lancashire Fusiliers | 1st Bn. 20th (East Devonshire) Regt. of Foot | 26th April 1838 |
| | 1st Bn. The Worcestershire Regt. | 1st Bn. 29th (Worcestershire) Regt. of Foot | 8th August 1818 |
| | 2nd Bn. The Worcestershire Regt. | 1st Bn. 36th (Herefordshire) Regt. of Foot | 26th July 1816 |
| | 1st Bn. The Duke of Cornwall's L.I. | 1st Bn. 32nd (Cornwall) Regt. of Foot | 23rd January 1826 |
| | 1st Bn. The South Staffordshire Regt. | 1st Bn. 38th (1st Staffordshire) Regt. of Foot | 14th November 1831 |
| | 1st Bn. P.W.V. (South Lancashire) Regt. | 1st Bn. 40th (2nd Somersetshire) Regt. of Foot | 6th April 1824 |
| | 2nd Bn. P.W.V. (South Lancashire) Regt. | 1st Bn. 82nd Regt. of Foot (Prince of Wales's Volunteers) | 20th September 1824 |
| | 1st Bn. Oxf & Bucks Lt. Infty. | 2nd Bn. 43rd (Monmouthshire Light Infantry) Regt. | 13th February 1821 |
| | 2nd Bn. Oxf & Bucks Lt. Infty. | 2nd Bn. 52nd (Oxfordshire Light Infantry) Regt. | 13th February 1821 |
| | 1st Bn. The Sherwood Foresters | 1st Bn. 45th (Nottinghamshire) Regt. of Foot | 4th December 1817 |
| | 1st Bn. The Queen's Own (Royal West Kent Regt.) | 1st Bn. 50th (West Kent) Regt. of Foot | 14th November 1812 |
| | The King's Royal Rifle Corps | 5th Bn. 60th (Royal American) Regt. of Foot | 21st September 1821 |
| | 1st Bn. Highland L.I. | 1st Bn. 71st (Glasgow Highland) Regt. of Foot | 16th April 1818 |
| | 1st Bn. Argyll & Sutherland Highlanders | 91st (Argyllshire Highlander) Regt. of Foot | 16th January 1833 |
| | The Rifle Brigade | 1st & 2nd Bns. 95th Regt. of Foot (Rifle Corps) | 4th January 1821 |
| SAHAGUN | 15th Hussars | 15th (the King's) Regt. of Light Dragoons (Hussars) | 23rd February 1832 |
| CORUNNA | Grenadier Guards | 1st & 3rd Bns. 1st Regt. of Foot Guards | 13th December 1811 |
| | The Royal Scots | 3rd Bn. 1st (Royal) Regt. of Foot | |
| | | To 1st and 2nd Bns. | 28th May 1832 |
| | The Queen's (Royal West Surrey) Regt. | 2nd (Queen's Royal) Regt. of Foot | 15th June 1833 |
| | The King's Own (Royal Lancaster Regt.) | 1st Bn. 4th (King's Own) Regt. of Foot | 20th February 1812 |
| | The Northumberland Fusiliers | 1st Bn. 5th (Northumberland) Regt. of Foot | 20th December 1825 |
| | The Royal Warwickshire Regt. | 1st Bn. 6th (1st Warwickshire) Regt. of Foot | 23rd May 1827 |
| | The Norfolk Regt. | 1st Bn. 9th (East Norfolk) Regt. of Foot | 4th June 1835 |
| | The West Yorkshire Regt. | 2nd Bn. 14th (Buckinghamshire) Regt. of Foot | 30th November 1811 |
| | The Lancashire Fusiliers | 20th (East Devonshire) Regt. of Foot | 26th April 1838 |

| | | | |
|---|---|---|---|
| **CORUNNA (Cont.)** | The Royal Welsh Fusiliers | 2nd Bn. 23rd Regt. of Foot (Royal Welsh Fuzileers) | February 1835 |
| | 1st Bn. The Cameronians | 1st Bn. 26th (Cameronian) Regt. of Foot | 17th April 1823 |
| | 1st Bn. The Gloucestershire Regt. | 1st Bn. 28th (North Gloucestershire) Regt. of Foot | 11th June 1832 |
| | 2nd Bn. The Worcestershire Regt. | 1st Bn. 36th (Herefordshire) Regt. of Foot | 26th May 1833 |
| | 2nd Bn. The East Lancashire Regt. | 2nd Bn. 59th (2nd Nottinghamshire) Regt. of Foot | 29th April 1812 |
| | 1st Bn. The Duke of Cornwall's L.I. | 1st Bn. 32nd (Cornwall) Regt. of Foot | 8th April 1842 |
| | 2nd Bn. The Duke of Wellington's Regt. | 2nd Bn. 76th (Hindoostan) Regt. of Foot | Army Order 51/1908 |
| | 1st Bn. The South Staffordshire Regt. | 1st Bn. 38th (1st Staffordshire) Regt. of Foot | 14th November 1831 |
| | 2nd Bn. P.W.V. (South Lancashire) Regt. | 1st Bn. 82nd Regt. of Foot (Prince of Wales's Volunteers) | Army Order 51/1908 |
| | 1st Bn. The Black Watch | 1st Bn. 42nd (Royal Highland) Regt. of Foot | 20th February 1812 |
| | 1st Bn. The Queen's Own (Royal West Kent Regt.) | 1st Bn. 50th (West Kent) Regt. of Foot | 20th February 1812 |
| | 1st Bn. The King's Own Yorkshire L.I. | 51st (2nd Yorkshire West Riding) Regt. of Foot | 9th August 1834 |
| | 1st Bn. Oxf & Bucks Lt. Infty. | 2nd Bn. 43rd (Monmouthshire Light Infantry) Regt. | 13th February 1821 |
| | 2nd Bn. Oxf & Bucks Lt. Infty. | 1st Bn. 52nd (Oxfordshire Light Infantry) Regt. | 13th February 1821 |
| | 2nd Bn. The Loyal North Lancashire Regt. | 2nd Bn. 81st Regt. of Foot | 20th February 1812 |
| | | Distinction to Regiment | 18th July 1816 |
| | 1st Bn. The Highland L.I. | 1st Bn. 71st (Highland) Regt. of Foot | 11th May 1835 |
| | 2nd Bn. The Gordon Highlanders | 1st Bn. 92nd (Highland) Regt. of Foot | 16th February 1830 |
| | The Queen's Own Cameron Highlanders | 1st Bn. 79th Regt. of Foot (Cameron Highlanders) | Army Order 51/1908 |
| | 1st Bn. Argyll & Sutherland Highlanders | 1st Bn. 91st Regt. of Foot | 9th January 1833 |
| | The Rifle Brigade | 95th Regt. of Foot (or Rifle Corps) | 1st March 1821 |
| **DOURO** | 14th Hussars | 14th (Duchess of York's Own) Regt. of (Light) Dragoons | 22nd July 1837 |
| | The Buffs (East Kent Regt.) | 1st Bn. 3rd (East Kent) Regt. of Foot (or the Buffs) | 10th September 1813 |
| | 1st Bn. The Northamptonshire Regt. | 1st Bn. 48th (Northamptonshire) Regt. of Foot | 22nd January 1818 |
| | 2nd Bn. The Royal Berkshire Regt. | 2nd Bn. 66th (Berkshire) Regt. of Foot | 14th August 1815 |
| | | To Regiment | 30th July 1823 |

| | | | |
|---|---|---|---|
| TALAVERA | 3rd Dragoon Guards | 3rd (Prince of Wales's) Regt. of Dragoon Guards | 9th May 1826 |
| | 4th Hussars | 4th (Queen's Own) Regt. of Dragoons | 6th April 1819 |
| | 14th Hussars | 14th (Duchess of York's Own) Regt. of (Light) Dragoons | 17th February 1820 |
| | 16th Lancers | 16th (the Queen's) Regt. of (Light) Dragoons | 16th April 1818 |
| | Coldstream Guards | 1st Bn. Coldstream Regt. of Foot Guards | 11th February 1812 |
| | Scots Guards | 1st Bn. 3rd Regt. of Foot Guards | 11th February 1812 |
| | The Buffs (East Kent Regt.) | 1st Bn. 3rd (East Kent) Regt. of Foot (or the Buffs) | 4th January 1823 |
| | The Royal Fusiliers | 2nd Bn. 7th Regt. of Foot (Royal Fusiliers) | 12th November 1819 |
| | The South Wales Borderers | 2nd Bn. 24th (2nd Warwickshire) Regt. of Foot | 29th July 1817 |
| | 2nd Bn. The Gloucestershire Regt. | 1st Bn. 61st (South Gloucestershire) Regt. of Foot | 8th October 1821 |
| | 1st Bn. The Worcestershire Regt. | 29th (Worcestershire) Regt. of Foot | 8th August 1818 |
| | 1st Bn. The East Surrey Regt. | 2nd Bn. 31st (Huntingdonshire) Regt. of Foot | 4th January 1823 |
| | 1st Bn. P.W.V. (South Lancashire Regt.) | 1st Bn. 40th (2nd Somersetshire) Regt. of Foot | 6th April 1824 |
| | 1st Bn. The Sherwood Foresters | 1st Bn. 45th (Nottinghamshire) Regt. of Foot | 30th January 1817 |
| | 1st Bn. The Northamptonshire Regt. | 1st Bn. 48th (Northamptonshire) Regt. of Foot | 6th November 1816 |
| | 1st Bn. The King's Shropshire L.I. | 2nd Bn. 53rd (Shropshire) Regt. of Foot | 8th August 1818 |
| | The King's Royal Rifle Corps | 5th Bn. 60th (Royal American) Regt. of Foot | 21st September 1821 |
| | 2nd Bn. The Royal Berkshire Regt. | 2nd Bn. 66th (Berkshire) Regt. of Foot | 11th January 1823 |
| | 1st Bn. The Royal Irish Rifles | 2nd Bn. 83rd Regt. of Foot | 4th August 1819 |
| | 1st Bn. The Royal Irish Fusiliers | 2nd Bn. 87th (Prince of Wales's Irish) Regt. of Foot | 27th January 1824 |
| | 1st Bn. The Connaught Rangers | 1st Bn. 88th Regt. of Foot (or Connaught Rangers) | 28th August 1817 |
| BUSACO | The Royal Scots | 3rd Bn. 1st (or Royal) Regt. of Foot | 21st June 1817 |
| | The Northumberland Fusiliers | 2nd Bn. 5th (Northumberland) Regt. of Foot | 10th December 1825 |
| | The Royal Fusiliers | 1st Bn. 7th Regt. of Foot (or Royal Fuzileers) | Army Order 218/1910 |
| | The Norfolk Regt. | 1st Bn. 9th (East Norfolk) Regt. of Foot | 18th February 1819 |
| | The South Wales Borderers | 2nd Bn. 24th (2nd Warwickshire) Regt. of Foot | Army Order 218/1910 |
| | 2nd Bn. The Gloucestershire Regt. | 1st Bn. 61st (South Gloucestershire) Regt. of Foot | Army Order 218/1910 |
| | 1st Bn. The South Staffordshire Regt. | 2nd Bn. 38th (1st Staffordshire) Regt. of Foot | 29th August 1831 |
| | 1st Bn. The Black Watch | 42nd (or Royal Highland) Regt. of Foot | Army Order 218/1910 |
| | 1st Bn. Oxf & Bucks Lt. Infty. | 1st Bn. 43rd (Monmouthshire Light Infantry)Regt. | 13th February 1821 |
| | 2nd Bn. Oxf & Bucks Lt. Infty. | 1st Bn. 52nd (Oxfordshire Light Infantry) Regt. | 13th February 1821 |

| | | | |
|---|---|---|---|
| **BUSACO (Cont.)** | 1st Bn. The Sherwood Foresters | 1st Bn. 45th (Nottinghamshire) Regt. of Foot | 30th January 1817 |
| | The King's Royal Rifle Corps | 5th Bn. 60th (Royal American) Regt. of Foot | 25th April 1879 |
| | 2nd Bn. The Highland L.I. | 1st Bn. 74th (Highland) Regt. of Foot | 16th June 1817 |
| | The Queen's Own Cameron Highlanders | 1st Bn. 79th Regt. of Foot (or Cameron Highlanders) | Army Order 218/1910 |
| | 1st Bn. The Royal Irish Rifles | 2nd Bn. 83rd Regt. of Foot | 10th May 1827 |
| | 1st Bn. The Connaught Rangers | 1st Bn. 88th Regt. of Foot (or Connaught Rangers) | 28th August 1817 |
| | The Rifle Brigade | 1st Bn. 95th Regt. of Foot (or Rifle Corps) | 4th January 1821 |
| **BARROSA** | Grenadier Guards | 2nd Bn. 1st Regt. of Foot Guards | 13th December 1811 |
| | Coldstream Guards | 2nd Bn. Coldstream Regt. of Foot Guards | 11th February 1812 |
| | Scots Guards | 2nd Bn. 3rd Regt. of Foot Guards | 11th February 1812 |
| | 1st Bn. The Gloucestershire Regt. | 1st Bn. 28th (North Gloucestershire) Regt. of Foot | 30th November 1814 |
| | 2nd Bn. The Hampshire Regt. | 2nd Bn. 67th (South Hampshire) Regt. of Foot | 26th May 1817 |
| | 1st Bn. The Royal Irish Fusiliers | 2nd Bn. 87th (Prince of Wales's Own Irish) Regt. of Foot | 11th April 1811 |
| | The Rifle Brigade | 95th Regt. of Foot (or Rifle Corps) | 4th January 1821 |
| **FUENTES D'ONOR** | 1st Royal Dragoons | 1st (Royal) Regt. of Dragoons | Army Order 218/1910 |
| | 14th Hussars | 14th (Duchess of York's Own) Regt. of (Light) Dragoons | 17th February 1820 |
| | 16th Lancers | 16th (the Queen's) Regt. of (Light) Dragoons | 16th April 1818 |
| | Coldstream Guards | 1st Bn. Coldstream Regt. of Foot Guards | Army Order 218/1910 |
| | Scots Guards | 1st Bn. 3rd Regt. of Foot Guards | Army Order 218/1910 |
| | The South Wales Borderers | 2nd Bn. 24th (2nd Warwickshire) Regt. of Foot | 28th July 1817 |
| | 1st Bn. The Black Watch | 2nd Bn. 42nd (Royal Highland) Regt. of Foot | 4th December 1817 |
| | 1st Bn. Oxf & Bucks Lt. Infty. | 1st Bn. 43rd (Monmouthshire Light Infantry) Regt. | 13th February 1821 |
| | 2nd Bn. Oxf & Bucks Lt. Infty. | 1st & 2nd Bns. 52nd (Oxfordshire Light Infantry) Regt. | 13th February 1821 |
| | 1st Bn. The Sherwood Foresters | 1st Bn. 45th (Nottinghamshire) Regt. of Foot | 22nd December 1820 |
| | 1st Bn. The King's Own Yorkshire L.I. | 2nd Bn. 51st (2nd Yorkshire, West Riding) Regt. of Foot | 27th November 1871 |
| | 2nd Bn. The King's Shropshire L.I. | 85th (Bucks Volunteers) (Light Infantry) Regt. | 8th July 1826 |
| | The King's Royal Rifle Corps | 5th Bn. (Royal American) Regt. of Foot | 21st September 1821 |
| | 1st Bn. The Highland L.I. | 1st Bn. 71st (Highland) Light Infantry Regt. | 16th April 1818 |

| | | | |
|---|---|---|---|
| **FUENTES D'ONOR (Cont.)** | 2nd Bn. The Highland L.I. | 74th (Highland) Regt. of Foot | 16th June 1817 |
| | 2nd Bn. The Gordon Highlanders | 92nd (Highland) Regt. of Foot | 16th February 1830 |
| | The Queen's Own Cameron Highlanders | 1st Bn. 79th Regt. of Foot (or Cameron Highlanders) | 16th April 1818 |
| | 1st Bn. The Royal Irish Rifles | 2nd Bn. 83rd Regt. of Foot | 4th August 1819 |
| | 1st Bn. The Connaught Rangers | 2nd Bn. 88th Regt. of Foot (or Connaught Rangers) | 28th August 1817 |
| | The Rifle Brigade | 1st, 2nd & 4th Bns. 95th Regt. of Foot (or Rifle Corps) | 4th January 1821 |
| **ALBUHERA** | 3rd Dragoon Guards | 3rd (Prince of Wales's) Regt. of Dragoon Guards | 5th April 1837 |
| | 4th Hussars | 4th (the Queen's Own) Regt. of Dragoons | 6th April 1819 |
| | 13th Hussars | 13th Regt. of (Light) Dragoons | Army Order 38/1890 |
| | The Buffs (East Kent Regt.) | 1st Bn. 3rd (East Kent) Regt. of Foot or The Buffs | 4th January 1823 |
| | The Royal Fusiliers | 1st & 2nd Bns. 7th Regt. of Foot (or Royal Fuzileers) | 5th September 1816 |
| | The Royal Welsh Fusiliers | 1st Bn. 23rd Regt. of Foot (or Royal Welsh Fuzileers) | 18th November 1816 |
| | 1st Bn. The Gloucestershire Regt. | 2nd Bn. 28th (North Gloucestershire) Regt. of Foot | 28th May 1816 |
| | 1st Bn. The Worcestershire Regt. | 29th (Worcestershire) Regt. of Foot | 8th August 1818 |
| | 1st Bn. The East Surrey Regt. | 2nd Bn. 31st (Huntingdonshire) Regt. of Foot | 5th June 1816 |
| | 1st Bn. The Border Regt. | 2nd Bn. 34th (Cumberland) Regt. of Foot | 13th June 1817 |
| | | Distinction to Regiment | 18th September 1817 |
| | 1st Bn. The Dorsetshire Regt. | 2nd Bn. 39th (Dorsetshire) Regt. of Foot | 22nd October 1816 |
| | 1st Bn. The Northamptonshire Regt. | 1st & 2nd Bns. 48th (Northamptonshire) Regt. of Foot | 22nd January 1818 |
| | 2nd Bn. The Royal Berkshire Regt. | 2nd Bn. 66th (Berkshire) Regt. of Foot | 11th January 1823 |
| | 1st Bn. The Middlesex Regt. | 1st Bn. 57th (West Middlesex) Regt. of Foot | 1st February 1816 |
| | The King's Royal Rifle Corps | 5th Bn. 60th (Royal American) Regt. of Foot | 12th January 1825 |
| **ARROYO DOS MOLINOS** | 1st Bn. The Border Regt. | 2nd Bn. 34th (Cumberland) Regt. of Foot | 30th May 1845 |
| **TARIFA** | 1st Bn. The Loyal North Lancashire Regt. | 2nd Bn. 47th (Lancashire) Regt. of Foot | 13th June 1816 |
| | 1st Bn. The Royal Irish Fusiliers | 2nd Bn. 87th (Prince of Wales's Own Irish) Regt. of Foot | 7th October 1812 |
| **CIUDAD RODRIGO** | The Northumberland Fusiliers | 2nd Bn. 5th (Northumberland) Regt. of Foot | 25th September 1817 |
| | 1st Bn. Oxf & Bucks Lt. Infty. | 1st Bn. 43rd (Monmouthshire Light Infantry) Regt. | 13th February 1821 |

| | | | |
|---|---|---|---|
| CIUDAD RODRIGO (Cont.) | 2nd Bn. Oxf & Bucks Lt. Infty. | 1st & 2nd Bns. 52nd (Oxfordshire Light Infantry) Regt. | 13th February 1821 |
| | 1st Bn. The Sherwood Foresters | 1st Bn. 45th (Nottinghamshire) Regt. of Foot | 4th December 1817 |
| | 2nd Bn. The Middlesex Regt. | 77th (East Middlesex) Regt. of Foot | 4th December 1817 |
| | The King's Royal Rifle Corps | 5th Bn. 60th (Royal American) Regt. of Foot | 21st September 1821 |
| | 2nd Bn. The Highland L.I. | 74th (Highland) Regt. of Foot | 16th June 1817 |
| | 1st Bn. The Royal Irish Rifles | 2nd Bn. 83rd Regt. of Foot | 4th August 1819 |
| | 1st Bn. The Connaught Rangers | 1st Bn. 88th Regt. of Foot (Connaught Rangers) | 28th August 1817 |
| | 2nd Bn. The Connaught Rangers | 94th Regt. of Foot | 22nd January 1818 |
| | The Rifle Brigade | 1st, 2nd & 3rd Bns. 95th Regt. of Foot (Rifle Corps) | 4th January 1821 |
| BADAJOS | The King's Own (Royal Lancaster Regt.) | 1st Bn. 4th (King's Own) Regt. of Foot | 4th January 1823 |
| | The Northumberland Fusiliers | 2nd Bn. 5th (Northumberland) Regt. of Foot | 28th May 1818 |
| | The Royal Fusiliers | 1st Bn. 7th Regt. of Foot (Royal Fuzileers) | 12th November 1819 |
| | The Royal Welsh Fusiliers | 1st Bn. 23rd Regt. of Foot (Royal Welsh Fuzileers) | 15th May 1821 |
| | 1st Bn. The Royal Inniskilling Fusiliers | 3rd Bn. 27th (Inniskilling) Regt. of Foot | 22nd October 1821 |
| | 1st Bn. The East Lancashire Regt. | 2nd Bn. 30th (Cambridgeshire) Regt. of Foot | 26th March 1825 |
| | 1st Bn. The South Staffordshire Regt. | 2nd Bn. 38th (1st Staffordshire) Regt. of Foot | 29th August 1831 |
| | 1st Bn. P.W.V. (South Lancashire Regt.) | 1st Bn. 40th (2nd Somersetshire) Regt. of Foot | 6th April 1824 |
| | 1st Bn. Oxf & Bucks Lt. Infty. | 1st Bn. 43rd (Monmouthshire Light Infantry) Regt. | 13th February 1821 |
| | 2nd Bn. Oxf & Bucks Lt. Infty. | 1st Bn. 52nd (Oxfordshire Light Infantry) Regt. | 13th February 1821 |
| | 1st Bn. The Essex Regt. | 2nd Bn. 44th (East Essex) Regt. of Foot | 4th January 1820 |
| | 1st Bn. The Sherwood Foresters | 1st Bn. 45th (Nottinghamshire) Regt. of Foot | 4th December 1817 |
| | 1st Bn. The Northamptonshire Regt. | 1st Bn. 48th (Northamptonshire) Regt. of Foot | 22nd January 1818 |
| | 2nd Bn. The Middlesex Regt. | 77th (East Middlesex) Regt. of Foot | 4th December 1817 |
| | The King's Royal Rifle Corps | 5th Bn. 60th (Royal American) Regt. of Foot | 21st September 1821 |
| | 2nd Bn. The Highland L.I. | 74th (Highland) Regt. of Foot | 16th June 1817 |
| | 1st Bn. The Royal Irish Rifles | 2nd Bn. 83rd Regt. of Foot | 4th August 1819 |
| | 1st Bn. The Connaught Rangers | 1st Bn. 88th Regt. of Foot (Connaught Rangers) | 2nd October 1818 |
| | 2nd Bn. The Connaught Rangers | 94th Regt. of Foot | 22nd January 1818 |
| | The Rifle Brigade | 95th Regt. of Foot (Rifle Corps) | 4th January 1821 |

| | | | |
|---|---|---|---|
| **ALMARAZ** | 1st Bn. The Queen's Own (Royal West Kent) Regt. | 1st Bn. 50th (West Kent) Regt. of Foot | 11th December 1815 |
| | 1st Bn. The Highland L.I. | 1st Bn. 71st (Highland) Regt. of Foot (Light Infantry) | 24th November 1815 |
| | 2nd Bn. The Gordon Highlanders | 1st Bn. 92nd (Highland) Regt. of Foot | 18th February 1830 |
| **SALAMANCA** | 5th Dragoon Guards | 5th (Princess Charlotte of Wales's) Regt. of Dragoon Guards | 26th October 1814 |
| | 3rd Hussars | 3rd (King's Own) Regt. of Dragoons | 26th October 1814 |
| | 4th Hussars | 4th (Queen's Own) Regt. of Dragoons | 26th October 1814 |
| | 11th Hussars | 11th Regt. of (Light) Dragoons | 26th July 1838 |
| | 12th Lancers | 12th (Prince of Wales's) Regt. of (Light) Dragoons | Army Order 136/1951 |
| | 14th Hussars | 14th (Duchess of York's Own) Regt. of (Light) Dragoons | 17th February 1820 |
| | 16th Lancers | 16th (the Queen's) Regt. of (Light) Dragoons | 16th April 1818 |
| | Coldstream Guards | Coldstream Regt. of Foot Guards | Army Order 136/1951 |
| | Scots Guards | 3rd Regt. of Foot Guards | Army Order 136/1951 |
| | The Royal Scots | 3rd Bn. 1st (Royal Scots) Regt. of Foot | 21st June 1817 |
| | The Queen's (Royal West Surrey Regt.) | 2nd (Queen's Royal) Regt. of Foot | 9th July 1816 |
| | The King's Own (Royal Lancaster Regt.) | 1st & 2nd Bns. 4th (King's Own) Regt. of Foot | 4th January 1823 |
| | The Northumberland Fusiliers | 1st & 2nd Bns. 5th (Northumberland) Regt. of Foot | 25th September 1817 |
| | The Royal Fusiliers | 1st Bn. 7th Regt. of Foot (or Royal Fuzileers) | 12th November 1819 |
| | The Norfolk Regt. | 1st Bn. 9th (East Norfolk) Regt. of Foot | 18th February 1819 |
| | The Devonshire Regt. | 1st Bn. 11th (Devonshire) Regt. of Foot | 9th July 1816 |
| | The Royal Welsh Fusiliers | 1st Bn. 23rd Regt. of Foot (or Royal Welsh Fuzileers) | 15th May 1821 |
| | The South Wales Borderers | 2nd Bn. 24th (2nd Warwickshire) Regt. of Foot | 20th September 1824 |
| | 1st Bn. The Royal Inniskilling Fusiliers | 3rd Bn. 27th (Inniskilling) Regt. of Foot | 22nd October 1821 |
| | 2nd Bn. The Gloucestershire Regt. | 1st Bn. 61st (South Gloucestershire) Regt. of Foot | 9th July 1816 |
| | 2nd Bn. The Worcestershire Regt. | 1st Bn. 36th (Herefordshire) Regt. of Foot | 26th July 1816 |
| | 1st Bn. The East Lancashire Regt. | 2nd Bn. 30th (Cambridgeshire) Regt. of Foot | 26th March 1825 |
| | 1st Bn. The Duke of Cornwall's L.I. | 1st Bn. 32nd (Cornwall) Regt. of Foot | 9th July 1816 |
| | 1st Bn. The South Staffordshire Regt. | 1st Bn. 38th (1st Staffordshire) Regt. of Foot | 19th March 1817 |
| | 1st Bn. P.W.V. (South Lancashire Regt.) | 1st Bn. 40th (2nd Somersetshire) Regt. of Foot | 6th April 1824 |
| | 1st Bn. The Black Watch | 1st Bn. 42nd (Royal Highland) Regt. of Foot | Army Order 136/1951 |
| | 1st Bn. Oxf & Bucks Lt. Infty. | 1st Bn. 43rd (Monmouthshire Light Infantry) Regt. | 13th February 1821 |

| | | | |
|---|---|---|---|
| **SALAMANCA (Cont.)** | 2nd Bn. Oxf & Bucks Lt. Infty. | 1st Bn. 52nd (Oxfordshire Light Infantry) Regt. | 13th February 1821 |
| | 1st Bn. The Essex Regt. | 2nd Bn. 44th (East Essex) Regt. of Foot | 4th January 1820 |
| | 1st Bn. The Sherwood Foresters | 1st Bn. 45th (Nottinghamshire) Regt. of Foot | 4th December 1817 |
| | 1st Bn. The Northamptonshire Regt. | 1st Bn. 48th (Northamptonshire) Regt. of Foot | 22nd January 1818 |
| | 2nd Bn. The Northamptonshire Regt. | 2nd Bn. 58th (Rutlandshire) Regt. of Foot | 14th February 1821 |
| | 1st Bn. The King's Own Yorkshire L.I. | 51st (2nd Yorkshire, West Riding) Regt. of Foot | 9th August 1834 |
| | 1st Bn. The King's Shropshire L.I. | 2nd Bn. 53rd (Shropshire) Regt. of Foot | 9th July 1816 |
| | The King's Royal Rifle Corps | 5th Bn. 60th (Royal American) Regt. of Foot | 21st September 1821 |
| | 1st Bn. The Durham L.I. | 68th (Durham) Regt. of Foot (Light Infantry) | 20th June 1823 |
| | 2nd Bn. The Highland L.I. | 74th (Highland) Regt. of Foot | 16th June 1817 |
| | The Queen's Own Cameron Highlanders | 1st Bn. 79th Regt. of Foot (or Cameron Highlanders) | 16th April 1818 |
| | 1st Bn. The Royal Irish Rifles | 2nd Bn. 83rd Regt. of Foot | 4th August 1819 |
| | 1st Bn. The Connaught Rangers | 1st Bn. 88th Regt. of Foot (or Connaught Rangers) | 28th August 1817 |
| | 2nd Bn. The Connaught Rangers | *94th Regt. of Foot | 22nd January 1818 |
| | The Rifle Brigade | 95th Regt. of Foot (or Rifle Corps) | 4th January 1821 |

* Regranted 18th March 1874

| | | | |
|---|---|---|---|
| **VITTORIA** | 3rd Dragoon Guards | 3rd (Prince of Wales's) Regt. of Dragoon Guards | 9th May 1826 |
| | 5th Dragoon Guards | 5th (Princess Charlotte of Wales's) Regt. of Dragoon Guards | 14th February 1820 |
| | 3rd Hussars | 3rd (King's Own) Regt. of Dragoons | 7th September 1821 |
| | 4th Hussars | 4th (Queen's Own) Regt. of Dragoons | 6th April 1819 |
| | 13th Hussars | 13th Regt. of (Light) Dragoons | Army Order 38/1890 |
| | 14th Hussars | 14th (Duchess of York's Own) Regt. of (Light) Dragoons | 17th February 1820 |
| | 15th Hussars | 15th (the King's) Regt. of (Light) Dragoons (Hussars) | 23rd February 1832 |
| | 16th Lancers | 16th (the Queen's) Regt. of (Light) Dragoons | 16th April 1818 |
| | The Royal Scots | 3rd Bn. 1st (Royal Scots) Regt. of Foot | 21st June 1817 |
| | The Queen's (Royal West Surrey Regt.) | 2nd (Queen's Royal) Regt. of Foot | 4th August 1819 |
| | The Buffs (East Kent Regt.) | 1st Bn. 3rd (East Kent) Regt. of Foot or the Buffs | 19th August 1890 |
| | The King's Own (Royal Lancaster Regt.) | 1st Bn. 4th (the King's Own) Regt. of Foot | 4th January 1823 |
| | The Northumberland Fusiliers | 1st Bn. 5th (Northumberland) Regt. of Foot | 25th September 1817 |

| | | | |
|---|---|---|---|
| **VITTORIA (Cont.)** | The Royal Warwickshire Regt. | 1st Bn. 6th (1st Warwickshire) Regt. of Foot | 26th April 1827 |
| | The Royal Fusiliers | 1st Bn. 7th Regt. of Foot (or Royal Fuzileers) | 12th November 1819 |
| | The Norfolk Regt. | 1st Bn. 9th (East Norfolk) Regt. of Foot | 18th February 1819 |
| | The Lancashire Fusiliers | 20th (East Devonshire) Regt. of Foot | 12th May 1826 |
| | The Royal Welsh Fusiliers | 1st Bn. 23rd Regt. of Foot (or Royal Welsh Fuzileers) | 15th May 1821 |
| | The South Wales Borderers | 2nd Bn. 24th (2nd Warwickshire) Regt. of Foot | 20th September 1824 |
| | 1st Bn. The Royal Inniskilling Fusiliers | 3rd Bn. 27th (Inniskilling) Regt. of Foot | 22nd October 1821 |
| | 1st Bn. The Gloucestershire Regt. | 1st Bn. 28th (North Gloucestershire) Regt. of Foot | 30th November 1816 |
| | 2nd Bn. The East Lancashire Regt. | 2nd Bn. 59th (2nd Nottinghamshire) Regt. of Foot | 16th April 1818 |
| | 1st Bn. The East Surrey Regt. | 2nd Bn. 31st (Huntingdonshire) Regt. of Foot | 4th January 1823 |
| | 1st Bn. The Border Regt. | 2nd Bn. 34th (Cumberland) Regt. of Foot | 3rd July 1817 |
| | 1st Bn. The South Staffordshire Regt. | 1st Bn. 38th (1st Staffordshire) Regt. of Foot | 29th August 1831 |
| | 1st Bn. The Dorsetshire Regt. | 1st Bn. 39th (Dorsetshire) Regt. of Foot | 29th May 1824 |
| | 1st Bn. P.W.V. (South Lancashire Regt.) | 1st Bn. 40th (2nd Somersetshire) Regt. of Foot | 6th April 1824 |
| | 2nd Bn. P.W.V. (South Lancashire Regt.) | 1st Bn. 82nd Regt. of Foot (Prince of Wales's Volunteers) | 20th September 1824 |
| | 1st Bn. Oxf & Bucks Lt. Infty. | 1st Bn. 43rd (Monmouthshire Light Infantry) Regt. | 13th February 1821 |
| | 2nd Bn. Oxf & Bucks Lt. Infty. | 1st Bn. 52nd (Oxfordshire Light Infantry) Regt. | 13th February 1821 |
| | 1st Bn. The Sherwood Foresters | 1st Bn. 45th (Nottinghamshire) Regt. of Foot | 4th December 1817 |
| | 1st Bn. The Loyal North Lancashire Regt. | 2nd Bn. 47th (Lancashire) Regt. of Foot | 28th May 1818 |
| | 1st Bn. The Northamptonshire Regt. | 1st Bn. 48th (Northamptonshire) Regt. of Foot | 22nd January 1818 |
| | 2nd Bn. The Northamptonshire Regt. | 2nd Bn. 58th (Rutlandshire) Regt. of Foot | 14th February 1821 |
| | 2nd Bn. The Royal Berkshire Regt. | 2nd Bn. 66th (Berkshire) Regt. of Foot | 11th January 1823 |
| | 1st Bn. The Queen's Own (Royal West Kent Regt.) | 1st Bn. 50th (West Kent) Regt. of Foot | 10th March 1819 |
| | 1st Bn. The King's Own Yorkshire L.I. | 51st (2nd Yorkshire, West Riding) Light Infantry Regt. | 11th December 1816 |
| | 1st Bn. The King's Shropshire L.I. | 2nd Bn. 53rd (Shropshire) Regt. of Foot | 17th February 1820 |
| | 1st Bn. The Middlesex Regt. | 1st Bn. 57th (West Middlesex) Regt. of Foot | 29th July 1817 |
| | The King's Royal Rifle Corps | 5th Bn. 60th (Royal American) Regt. of Foot | 21st September 1821 |
| | 1st Bn. The Durham L.I. | 68th (Durham) Light Infantry Regt. | 20th June 1823 |
| | 1st Bn. Highland L.I. | 1st Bn. 71st (Highland) Light Infantry Regt. | 16th April 1818 |
| | 2nd Bn. Highland L.I. | 74th (Highland) Regt. of Foot | 16th June 1817 |

| | | | |
|---|---|---|---|
| **VITTORIA (Cont.)** | 2nd Bn. The Gordon Highlanders | 1st Bn. 92nd (Highland) Regt. of Foot | 16th February 1830 |
| | 1st Bn. The Royal Irish Rifles | 2nd Bn. 83rd Regt. of Foot | 4th August 1819 |
| | 1st Bn. The Royal Irish Fusiliers | 2nd Bn. 87th (Prince of Wales's Own Irish) Regt. of Foot | 27th January 1824 |
| | 1st Bn. The Connaught Rangers | 1st Bn. 88th Regt. of Foot (or Connaught Rangers) | 2nd October 1818 |
| | 2nd Bn. The Connaught Rangers | 94th Regt. of Foot | 22nd January 1818 |
| | The Rifle Brigade | 95th Regt. of Foot (or Rifle Corps) | 4th January 1821 |
| **PYRENEES** | 14th Hussars | 14th (Duchess of York's Own) Regt. of (Light) Dragoons | Army Order 218/1910 |
| | The Queen's (Royal West Surrey Regt.) | 2nd (Queen's Royal) Regt. of Foot | 4th August 1819 |
| | The Buffs (East Kent Regt.) | 1st Bn. 3rd (East Kent) Regt. of Foot or the Buffs | 4th January 1823 |
| | The Royal Warwickshire Regt. | 1st Bn. 6th (1st Warwickshire) Regt. of Foot | 22nd January 1818 |
| | The Royal Fusiliers | 1st Bn. 7th Regt. of Foot (or Royal Fuzileers) | 12th November 1819 |
| | The Devonshire Regt. | 1st Bn. 11th (North Devonshire) Regt. of Foot | 3rd October 1823 |
| | The Lancashire Fusiliers | 20th (East Devonshire) Regt. of Foot | 29th August 1817 |
| | The Royal Welsh Fusiliers | 1st Bn. 23rd Regt. of Foot (or Royal Welsh Fuzileers) | 15th May 1821 |
| | The South Wales Borderers | 2nd Bn. 24th (2nd Warwickshire) Regt. of Foot | 29th July 1817 |
| | 1st Bn. The Royal Inniskilling Fusiliers | 2nd Bn. 27th (Inniskilling) Regt. of Foot | 22nd October 1821 |
| | 1st Bn. The Gloucestershire Regt. | 1st Bn. 28th (North Gloucestershire) Regt. of Foot | 28th May 1819 |
| | 2nd Bn. The Gloucestershire Regt. | 1st Bn. 61st (South Gloucestershire) Regt. of Foot | 7th June 1823 |
| | 2nd Bn. The Worcestershire Regt. | 1st Bn. 36th (Herefordshire) Regt. of Foot | 12th November 1825 |
| | 1st Bn. The East Surrey Regt. | 2nd Bn. 31st (Huntingdonshire) Regt. of Foot | 4th January 1823 |
| | 1st Bn. The Duke of Cornwall's L.I. | 1st Bn. 32nd (Cornwall) Regt. of Foot | 23rd January 1826 |
| | 1st Bn. The Border Regt. | 2nd Bn. 34th (Cumberland) Regt. of Foot | 16th August 1823 |
| | 1st Bn. The Dorsetshire Regt. | 1st Bn. 39th (Dorsetshire) Regt. of Foot | 29th May 1824 |
| | 1st Bn. P.W.V. (South Lancashire Regt.) | 1st Bn. 40th (2nd Somersetshire) Regt. of Foot | 6th April 1824 |
| | 2nd Bn. P.W.V. (South Lancashire Regt.) | 1st Bn. 82nd Regt. of Foot (Prince of Wales's Volunteers) | 20th September 1824 |
| | 1st Bn. The Black Watch | 1st Bn. 42nd (Royal Highland) Regt. of Foot | 4th December 1817 |
| | 1st Bn. Oxf & Bucks Lt. Infty. | 43rd (Monmouthshire Light Infantry) Regt. | Army Order 218/1910 |
| | 2nd Bn. Oxf & Bucks Lt. Infty. | 52nd (Oxfordshire Light Infantry) Regt. | Army Order 218/1910 |

| | | | |
|---|---|---|---|
| **PYRENEES (Cont.)** | 1st Bn. The Sherwood Foresters | 1st Bn. 45th (Nottinghamshire) Regt. of Foot | 4th December 1817 |
| | 1st Bn. The Northamptonshire Regt. | 1st Bn. 48th (Northamptonshire) Regt. of Foot | 22nd January 1818 |
| | 2nd Bn. The Northamptonshire Regt. | 2nd Bn. 58th (Rutlandshire) Regt. of Foot | 14th February 1821 |
| | 2nd Bn. The Royal Berkshire Regt. | 2nd Bn. 66th (Berkshire) Regt. of Foot | 11th January 1823 |
| | 1st Bn. The Queen's Own (Royal West Kent Regt.) | 1st Bn. 50th (West Kent) Regt. of Foot | 10th March 1819 |
| | 1st Bn. The King's Own Yorkshire L.I. | 51st (2nd Yorkshire, West Riding) Regt. (Light Infantry) | 9th August 1834 |
| | 1st Bn. The King's Shropshire L.I. | 2nd Bn. 53rd (Shropshire) Regt. of Foot | 17th February 1820 |
| | 1st Bn. The Middlesex Regt. | 1st Bn. 57th (West Middlesex) Regt. of Foot | 29th July 1817 |
| | The King's Royal Rifle Corps | 5th Bn. 60th (Royal American) Regt. of Foot | 12th January 1825 |
| | 1st Bn. The Durham L.I. | 68th (Durham) Regt. of Foot (Light Infantry) | 20th June 1823 |
| | 1st Bn. The Highland L.I. | 1st Bn. 71st (Highland) Regt. of Foot (Light Infantry) | 16th April 1818 |
| | 2nd Bn. The Highland L.I. | 74th (Highland) Regt. of Foot | 16th June 1817 |
| | 2nd Bn. The Gordon Highlanders | 1st Bn. 92nd (Highland) Regt. of Foot | 16th February 1830 |
| | The Queen's Own Cameron Highlanders. | 1st Bn. 79th Regt. of Foot (Cameron Highlanders) | 16th April 1818 |
| | 1st Bn. The Connaught Rangers | 1st Bn. 88th Regt. of Foot (or Connaught Rangers) | Army Order 218/1910 |
| | 1st Bn. The Argyll & Sutherland Highlanders | 1st Bn. 91st Regt. of Foot | 17th July 1818 |
| | The Rifle Brigade | 95th Regt. of Foot (or Rifle Corps) | Army Order 218/1910 |
| **SAN SEBASTIAN** | The Royal Scots | 1st (Royal Scots) Regt. of Foot | 21st June 1817 |
| | The King's Own (Royal Lancaster Regt.) | 4th (King's Own) Regt. of Foot | 4th January 1823 |
| | The Norfolk Regt. | 9th (East Norfolk) Regt. of Foot | 18th February 1819 |
| | 2nd Bn. The East Lancashire Regt. | 59th (2nd Nottinghamshire) Regt. of Foot | 16th April 1818 |
| | 1st Bn. The South Staffordshire Regt. | 38th (1st Staffordshire) Regt. of Foot | 19th March 1817 |
| | 1st Bn. The Loyal North Lancashire Regt. | 47th (Lancashire) Regt. of Foot | 28th May 1818 |
| **NIVELLE** | The Queen's (Royal West Surrey Regt.) | 2nd (Queen's Royal) Regt. of Foot | 4th August 1819 |
| | The Buffs (East Kent Regt.) | 1st Bn. 3rd (East Kent) Regt. of Foot The Buffs | 4th January 1823 |
| | The Northumberland Fusiliers | 1st Bn. 5th (Northumberland) Regt. of Foot | 25th September 1817 |
| | The Royal Warwickshire Regt. | 1st Bn. 6th (1st Warwickshire) Regt. of Foot | 26th April 1827 |

| | | | |
|---|---|---|---|
| **NIVELLE (Cont.)** | The Devonshire Regt. | 1st Bn. 11th (North Devonshire) Regt. of Foot | 9th July 1816 |
| | The Royal Welsh Fusiliers | 1st Bn. 23rd Regt. of Foot (or Royal Welsh Fusiliers) | 15th May 1821 |
| | The South Wales Borderers | 2nd Bn. 24th (2nd Warwickshire) Regt. of Foot | 24th July 1824 |
| | 1st Bn. The Royal Inniskilling Fusiliers | 3rd Bn. 27th (Inniskilling) Regt. of Foot | 22nd October 1821 |
| | 1st Bn. The Gloucestershire Regt. | 1st Bn. 28th (North Gloucestershire) Regt. of Foot | 28th May 1819 |
| | 2nd Bn. The Gloucestershire Regt. | 1st Bn. 61st (South Gloucestershire) Regt. of Foot | 9th July 1816 |
| | 2nd Bn. The Worcestershire Regt. | 1st Bn. 36th (Herefordshire) Regt. of Foot | 9th July 1816 |
| | 1st Bn. The East Surrey Regt. | 2nd Bn. 31st (Huntingdonshire) Regt. of Foot | 4th January 1823 |
| | 1st Bn. The Duke of Cornwall's L.I. | 1st Bn. 32nd (Cornwall) Regt. of Foot | 9th July 1816 |
| | 1st Bn. The Border Regt. | 2nd Bn. 34th (Cumberland) Regt. of Foot | 16th August 1823 |
| | 1st Bn. The Dorsetshire Regt. | 1st Bn. 39th (Dorsetshire) Regt. of Foot | 29th May 1824 |
| | 1st Bn. P.W.V. (South Lancashire Regt.) | 1st Bn. 40th (2nd Somersetshire) Regt. of Foot | 6th April 1824 |
| | 2nd Bn. P.W.V. (South Lancashire Regt.) | 1st Bn. 82nd Regt. of Foot (or Prince of Wales's Volunteers) | 20th September 1824 |
| | 1st Bn. The Black Watch | 1st Bn. 42nd (Royal Highland) Regt. of Foot | 4th December 1817 |
| | 1st Bn. Oxf & Bucks Lt. Infty. | 1st Bn. 43rd (Monmouthshire Light Infantry) Regt. | 13th February 1821 |
| | 2nd Bn. Oxf & Bucks Lt. Infty. | 1st Bn. 52nd (Oxfordshire Light Infantry) Regt. | 13th February 1821 |
| | 1st Bn. Sherwood Foresters | 1st Bn. 45th (Nottinghamshire) Regt. of Foot | 4th December 1817 |
| | 1st Bn. The Northamptonshire Regt. | 1st Bn. 48th (Northamptonshire) Regt. of Foot | 22nd January 1818 |
| | 2nd Bn. The Northamptonshire Regt. | 2nd Bn. 58th (Rutlandshire) Regt. of Foot | 14th February 1821 |
| | 2nd Bn. The Royal Berkshire Regt. | 2nd Bn. 66th (Berkshire) Regt. of Foot | 11th January 1823 |
| | 1st Bn. The King's Own Yorkshire L.I. | 51st (2nd Yorkshire, West Riding) Light Infantry Regt. | 11th December 1816 |
| | 1st Bn. The King's Shropshire L.I. | 2nd Bn. 53rd (Shropshire) Regt. of Foot | 17th February 1820 |
| | 1st Bn. The Middlesex Regt. | 1st Bn. 57th (West Middlesex) Regt. of Foot | 29th July 1817 |
| | The King's Royal Rifle Corps | 5th Bn. 60th (Royal American) Regt. of Foot | 21st September 1821 |
| | 1st Bn. The Durham L.I. | 68th (Durham Light Infantry) Regt. | 20th June 1823 |
| | 2nd Bn. The Highland L.I. | 74th (Highland) Regt. of Foot | 16th June 1817 |
| | The Queen's Own Cameron Highlanders | 79th Regt. of Foot (or Cameron Highlanders) | 16th April 1818 |
| | 1st Bn. The Royal Irish Rifles | 2nd Bn. 83rd Regt. of Foot | 4th August 1819 |
| | 1st Bn. The Royal Irish Fusiliers | 1st Bn. 87th (Prince of Wales's Own Irish) Regt. of Foot | 27th January 1824 |
| | 1st Bn. The Connaught Rangers | 1st Bn. 88th Regt. of Foot (or Connaught Rangers) | 2nd October 1818 |

| | | | |
|---|---|---|---|
| NIVELLE (Cont.) | 2nd Bn. The Connaught Rangers | 1st Bn. 94th Regt. of Foot | 22nd January 1818 |
| | 1st Bn. The Argyll & Sutherland Highlanders | 1st Bn. 91st Regt. of Foot | 17th July 1818 |
| | The Rifle Brigade | 95th Regt. of Foot (or Rifle Corps) | 4th January 1821 |
| NIVE | 16th Lancers | 16th (the Queen's) Regt. of (Light) Dragoons | 16th April 1818 |
| | Grenadier Guards | 1st & 3rd Bns. 1st Regt. of Foot Guards | Army Order 218/1910 |
| | Coldstream Guards | 1st Bn. Coldstream Regt. of Foot Guards | Army Order 218/1910 |
| | Scots Guards | 1st Bn. 3rd Regt. of Foot Guards | Army Order 218/1910 |
| | The Royal Scots | 3rd Bn. 1st (Royal Scots) Regt. of Foot | 21st June 1817 |
| | The Buffs (East Kent Regt.) | 1st Bn. 3rd (East Kent) Regt. of Foot (or the Buffs) | 4th January 1823 |
| | The King's Own (Royal Lancaster Regt.) | 1st Bn. 4th (King's Own) Regt. of Foot | 4th January 1823 |
| | The Norfolk Regt. | 1st Bn. 9th (East Norfolk) Regt. of Foot | 18th February 1819 |
| | The Devonshire Regt. | 1st Bn. 11th (North Devonshire) Regt. of Foot | 3rd October 1823 |
| | 1st Bn. The Gloucestershire Regt. | 1st Bn. 28th (North Gloucestershire) Regt. of Foot | 28th May 1819 |
| | 2nd Bn. The Gloucestershire Regt. | 1st Bn. 61st (South Gloucestershire) Regt. of Foot | 7th June 1823 |
| | 2nd Bn. The Worcestershire Regt. | 1st Bn. 36th (Herefordshire) Regt. of Foot | 12th November 1825 |
| | 2nd Bn. The East Lancashire Regt. | 2nd Bn. 59th (2nd Nottinghamshire) Regt. of Foot | 16th April 1818 |
| | 1st Bn. The East Surrey Regt. | 2nd Bn. 31st (Huntingdonshire) Regt. of Foot | 4th January 1823 |
| | 1st Bn. The Duke of Cornwall's L.I. | 1st Bn. 32nd (Cornwall) Regt. of Foot | 14th November 1831 |
| | 2nd Bn. The Duke of Wellington's Regt. | 76th Regt. of Foot | 1st January 1845 |
| | 1st Bn. The Border Regt. | 2nd Bn. 34th (Cumberland) Regt. of Foot | 16th August 1823 |
| | 1st Bn. South Staffordshire Regt. | 1st Bn. 38th (1st Staffordshire) Regt. of Foot | 29th August 1831 |
| | 1st Bn. The Dorsetshire Regt. | 1st Bn. 39th (Dorsetshire) Regt. of Foot | 29th May 1824 |
| | 1st Bn. The Black Watch | 1st Bn. 42nd (Royal Highland) Regt. of Foot | 4th December 1817 |
| | 1st Bn. Oxf & Bucks Lt. Infty. | 1st Bn. 43rd (Monmouthshire Light Infantry) Regt. | 13th February 1821 |
| | 2nd Bn. Oxf & Bucks Lt. Infty. | 1st Bn. 52nd (Oxfordshire Light Infantry) Regt. | 13th February 1821 |
| | 1st Bn. The Loyal North Lancashire Regt. | 2nd Bn. 47th (Lancashire) Regt. of Foot | Army Order 218/1910 |
| | 2nd Bn. The Royal Berkshire Regt. | 2nd Bn. 66th (Berkshire) Regt. of Foot | 11th January 1823 |
| | 1st Bn. The Queen's Own (Royal West Kent Regt.) | 1st Bn. 50th (West Kent) Regt. of Foot | 10th March 1819 |
| | 2nd Bn. The King's Shropshire L.I. | 85th Regt. of Foot (Bucks Volunteers) Light Infantry | 8th July 1826 |

| | | | |
|---|---|---|---|
| **NIVE (Cont.)** | 1st Bn. The Middlesex Regt. | 1st Bn. 57th (West Middlesex) Regt. of Foot | 29th July 1817 |
| | The King's Royal Rifle Corps | 5th Bn. 60th (Royal American) Regt. of Foot | 12th January 1825 |
| | 1st Bn. The Wiltshire Regt. | 2nd Bn. 62nd (Wiltshire) Regt. of Foot | 1st February 1844 |
| | 2nd Bn. The York & Lancaster Regt. | 2nd Bn. 84th (York & Lancaster) Regt. of Foot | 5th February 1818 |
| | 1st Bn. The Highland L.I. | 1st Bn. 71st (Highland) Regt. of Foot (Light Infantry) | 16th April 1818 |
| | 2nd Bn. The Gordon Highlanders | 1st Bn. 92nd (Highland) Regt. of Foot | 16th February 1830 |
| | The Queen's Own Cameron Highlanders | 1st Bn. 79th Regt. of Foot (or Cameron Highlanders) | 16th April 1818 |
| | 1st Bn. The Argyll & Sutherland Highlanders | 1st Bn. 91st Regt. of Foot | 17th July 1818 |
| | The Rifle Brigade | 95th Regt. of Foot (or Rifle Corps) | 4th January 1821 |
| **ORTHES** | 7th Hussars | 7th (Queen's Own) Regt. of (Light) Dragoons (Hussars) | 21st April 1893 |
| | 13th Hussars | 13th Regt. of Light Dragoons | Army Order 38/1890 |
| | 14th Hussars | 14th (Duchess of York's Own) Regt. of (Light) Dragoons | 17th February 1820 |
| | The Buffs (East Kent Regt.) | 1st Bn. 3rd (East Kent) Regt. of Foot (or the Buffs) | 19th August 1890 |
| | The Northumberland Fusiliers | 1st Bn. 5th (Northumberland) Regt. of Foot | 28th May 1818 |
| | The Royal Warwickshire Regt. | 1st Bn. 6th (1st Warwickshire) Regt. of Foot | 22nd January 1818 |
| | The Royal Fusiliers | 1st Bn. 7th Regt. of Foot (or Royal Fuzileers) | 12th November 1819 |
| | The Devonshire Regt. | 1st Bn. 11th (North Devonshire) Regt. of Foot | 3rd October 1823 |
| | The Lancashire Fusiliers | 20th (East Devonshire) Regt. of Foot | 29th August 1817 |
| | The Royal Welsh Fusiliers | 1st Bn. 23rd Regt. of Foot (or Royal Welsh Fuzileers) | 15th May 1821 |
| | The South Wales Borderers | 2nd Bn. 24th (2nd Warwickshire) Regt. of Foot | 29th July 1817 |
| | 1st Bn. The Royal Inniskilling Fusiliers | 3rd Bn. 27th (Inniskilling) Regt. of Foot | 22nd October 1821 |
| | 1st Bn. The Gloucestershire Regt. | 1st Bn. 28th (North Gloucestershire) Regt. of Foot | 28th May 1819 |
| | 2nd Bn. The Gloucestershire Regt. | 61st (South Gloucestershire) Regt. of Foot | 7th June 1823 |
| | 2nd Bn. The Worcestershire Regt. | 1st Bn. 36th (Herefordshire) Regt. of Foot | 5th February 1836 |
| | 1st Bn. The East Surrey Regt. | 2nd Bn. 31st (Huntingdonshire) Regt. of Foot | 7th June 1847 |
| | 1st Bn. The Duke of Cornwall's Lt. Infty. | 1st Bn. 32nd (Cornwall) Regt. of Foot | 23rd January 1826 |
| | 1st Bn. The Border Regt. | 2nd Bn. 34th (Cumberland) Regt. of Foot | 16th August 1823 |
| | 1st Bn. The Dorsetshire Regt. | 1st Bn. 39th (Dorsetshire) Regt. of Foot | 29th May 1824 |
| | 1st Bn. P.W.V. (South Lancashire Regt.) | 1st Bn. 40th (2nd Somersetshire) Regt. of Foot | 6th April 1824 |

| | | | |
|---|---|---|---|
| **ORTHES (Cont.)** | 2nd Bn. P.W.V. (South Lancashire Regt.) | 1st Bn. 82nd Regt. of Foot (or Prince of Wales's Volunteers) | 20th September 1824 |
| | 1st Bn. The Black Watch | 1st Bn. 42nd (Royal Highland) Regt. of Foot | 4th December 1817 |
| | 2nd Bn. Oxf & Bucks Lt. Infty. | 1st Bn. 52nd (Oxfordshire Light Infantry) Regt. | 13th February 1821 |
| | 1st Bn. The Sherwood Foresters | 1st Bn. 45th (Nottinghamshire) Regt. of Foot | 4th December 1817 |
| | 1st Bn. The Northamptonshire Regt. | 1st Bn. 48th (Northamptonshire) Regt. of Foot | 22nd January 1818 |
| | 2nd Bn. The Northamptonshire Regt. | 2nd Bn. 58th (Rutlandshire) Regt. of Foot | 14th February 1821 |
| | 2nd Bn. The Royal Berkshire Regt. | 2nd Bn. 66th (Berkshire) Regt. of Foot | 11th January 1823 |
| | 1st Bn. The Queen's Own (Royal West Kent Regt.) | 1st Bn. 50th (West Kent) Regt. of Foot | 10th March 1819 |
| | 1st Bn. The King's Own Yorkshire L.I. | 51st (2nd Yorkshire, West Riding) Light Infantry Regt. | 9th August 1834 |
| | The King's Royal Rifle Corps | 5th Bn. 60th (Royal American) Regt. of Foot | 21st September 1821 |
| | 1st Bn. The Durham L.I. | 68th (Durham Light Infantry) Regt. | 20th June 1823 |
| | 1st Bn. The Highland L.I. | 1st Bn. 71st (Highland) Light Infantry Regt. | 16th April 1818 |
| | 2nd Bn. The Highland L.I. | 1st Bn. 74th (Highland) Regt. of Foot | 16th June 1817 |
| | 2nd Bn. The Gordon Highlanders | 1st Bn. 92nd (Highland) Regt. of Foot | 16th February 1830 |
| | 1st Bn. The Royal Irish Rifles | 2nd Bn. 83rd Regt. of Foot | 4th August 1819 |
| | 1st Bn. The Royal Irish Fusiliers | 2nd Bn. 87th (Prince of Wales's Own Irish) Regt. of Foot | 27th January 1824 |
| | 1st Bn. The Connaught Rangers | 1st Bn. 88th Regt. of Foot (or Connaught Rangers) | 28th August 1817 |
| | 2nd Bn. The Connaught Rangers | 94th Regt. of Foot | 22nd January 1818 |
| | 1st Bn. The Argyll & Sutherland Highlanders | 1st Bn. 91st Regt. of Foot | 17th July 1818 |
| | The Rifle Brigade | 95th Regt. of Foot (or Rifle Corps) | 4th January 1821 |
| **TOULOUSE** | 5th Dragoon Guards | 5th (Princess Charlotte of Wales's) Regt. of Dragoon Guards | 14th February 1820 |
| | 3rd Hussars | 3rd (King's Own) Regt. of Dragoons | 7th September 1821 |
| | 4th Hussars | 4th (Queen's Own) Regt. of Dragoons | 6th April 1819 |
| | 13th Hussars | 13th Regt. of (Light) Dragoons | Army Order 38/1890 |
| | The Queen's (Royal West Surrey Regt.) | 2nd (Queen's Royal) Regt. of Foot | 4th August 1819 |
| | The Buffs (East Kent Regt.) | 1st Bn. 3rd (East Kent) Regt. of Foot (or the Buffs) | 19th August 1890 |

| | | | |
|---|---|---|---|
| **TOULOUSE (Cont.)** | The Northumberland Fusiliers | 1st Bn. 5th (Northumberland) Regt. of Foot | 28th May 1818 |
| | The Royal Fusiliers | 1st Bn. 7th Regt. of Foot (or Royal Fuzileers) | 12th November 1819 |
| | The Devonshire Regt. | 1st Bn. 11th (North Devonshire) Regt. of Foot | 9th July 1816 |
| | The Lancashire Fusiliers | 1st Bn. 20th (East Devonshire) Regt. of Foot | 12th May 1826 |
| | The Royal Welsh Fusiliers | 1st Bn. 23rd Regt. of Foot (or Royal Welsh Fuzileers) | 15th May 1821 |
| | 1st Bn. The Royal Inniskilling Fusiliers | 3rd Bn. 27th (Inniskilling) Regt. of Foot | 22nd October 1821 |
| | 1st Bn. The Gloucestershire Regt. | 1st Bn. 28th (North Gloucestershire) Regt. of Foot | 28th May 1820 |
| | 2nd Bn. The Gloucestershire Regt. | 1st Bn. 61st (South Gloucestershire) Regt. of Foot | 9th July 1816 |
| | 2nd Bn. The Worcestershire Regt. | 1st Bn. 36th (Herefordshire) Regt. of Foot | 9th July 1816 |
| | 1st Bn. P.W.V. (South Lancashire Regt.) | 1st Bn. 40th (2nd Somersetshire) Regt. of Foot | 6th April 1824 |
| | 1st Bn. The Black Watch | 1st Bn. 42nd (Royal Highland) Regt. of Foot | 26th July 1816 |
| | 1st Bn. Oxf & Bucks Lt. Infty. | 1st Bn. 43rd (Monmouthshire Light Infantry) Regt. | 13th February 1821 |
| | 2nd Bn. Oxf & Bucks Lt. Infty. | 1st Bn. 52nd (Oxfordshire Light Infantry) Regt. | 13th February 1821 |
| | 1st Bn. The Sherwood Foresters | 1st Bn. 45th (Nottinghamshire) Regt. of Foot | 4th December 1817 |
| | 1st Bn. The Northamptonshire Regt. | 1st Bn. 48th (Northamptonshire) Regt. of Foot | 22nd January 1818 |
| | 1st Bn. The King's Shropshire L.I. | 53rd (Shropshire) Regt. of Foot | 17th February 1820 |
| | The King's Royal Rifle Corps | 5th Bn. 60th (Royal American) Regt. of Foot | 21st September 1821 |
| | 2nd Bn. The Highland L.I. | 74th (Highland) Regt. of Foot | 16th June 1817 |
| | The Queen's Own Cameron Highlanders | 1st Bn. 79th Regt. of Foot (or Cameron Highlanders) | 9th July 1816 |
| | 1st Bn. The Royal Irish Rifles | 2nd Bn. 83rd Regt. of Foot | 15th January 1827 |
| | 1st Bn. The Royal Irish Fusiliers | 2nd Bn. 87th (Prince of Wales's Own Irish) Regt. of Foot | 27th January 1824 |
| | 1st Bn. The Connaught Rangers | 1st Bn. 88th Regt. of Foot (or Connaught Rangers) | 28th August 1817 |
| | 2nd Bn. The Connaught Rangers | 94th Regt. of Foot | 22nd January 1818 |
| | 1st Bn. The Argyll & Sutherland Highlanders | 1st Bn. 91st Regt. of Foot | 9th July 1816 |
| | The Rifle Brigade | 95th Regt. of Foot (or Rifle Corps) | 4th January 1821 |
| **PENINSULA** | 1st Life Guards | 1st Regt. of Life Guards | This distinction was granted to all regiments on 29th March 1815, and the regiments advised 6th April 1815. |
| | 2nd Life Guards | 2nd Regt. of Life Guards | |
| | Royal Horse Guards | Royal Regt. of Horse Guards (Blue) | |

| | | | |
|---|---|---|---|
| PENINSULA (Cont.) | 3rd Dragoon Guards | 3rd (Prince of Wales's) Regt. of Dragoon Guards | |
| | 4th Dragoon Guards | 4th (Royal Irish) Regt. of Dragoon Guards | |
| | 5th Dragoon Guards | 5th (Princess Charlotte of Wales's) Regt. of Dragoon Guards | |
| | 1st Royal Dragoons | 1st (Royal) Regt. of Dragoons | |
| | 3rd Hussars | 3rd (King's Own) Regt. of Dragoons | |
| | 4th Hussars | 4th (Queen's Own) Regt. of Dragoons | |
| | 7th Hussars | 7th (Queen's Own) Regt. of (Light) Dragoons (Hussars) | |
| | 9th Lancers | 9th Regt. of (Light) Dragoons | |
| | 10th Hussars | 10th (Prince of Wales's Own Royal) Regt. of (Light) Dragoons (Hussars) | |
| | 11th Hussars | 11th Regt. of (Light Dragoons) | |
| | 12th Lancers | 12th (Prince of Wales's) Regt. of (Light) Dragoons | |
| | 13th Hussars | 13th Regt. of (Light) Dragoons | |
| | 14th Hussars | 14th (Duchess of York's Own) Regt. of (Light) Dragoons | |
| | 15th Hussars | 15th (The King's) Regt. of (Light) Dragoons (Hussars) | |
| | 16th Lancers | 16th (The Queen's) Regt. of (Light) Dragoons | |
| | 18th Hussars | 18th Regt. of (Light) Dragoons (Hussars) | |
| | 20th Hussars | 20th Regt. of (Light) Dragoons | |
| | Grenadier Guards | 1st Regt. of Foot Guards | |
| | Coldstream Guards | Coldstream Regt. of Foot Guards | |
| | Scots Guards | 3rd Regt. of Foot Guards | |
| | The Royal Scots | 3rd Bn. 1st (Royal Scots) Regt. of Foot<br>Distinction to Regiment | 21st June 1817 |
| | The Queen's (Royal West Surrey) Regt. | 2nd (Queen's Royal) Regt. of Foot | |
| | The Buffs (East Kent Regt.) | 3rd (East Kent) Regt. of Foot or the Buffs | |
| | The King's Own (Royal Lancaster Regt.) | 4th (King's Own) Regt. of Foot | |
| | The Northumberland Fusiliers | 5th (Northumberland) Regt. of Foot | |
| | The Royal Warwickshire Regt. | 6th (1st Warwickshire) Regt. of Foot | |
| | The Royal Fusiliers | 7th Regt. of Foot (Royal Fuzileers) | |

| | | | |
|---|---|---|---|
| **PENINSULA (Cont.)** | The Norfolk Regt. | 9th (East Norfolk) Regt. of Foot | |
| | The Lincolnshire Regt. | 10th (North Lincolnshire) Regt. of Foot | |
| | The Devonshire Regt. | 11th (North Devonshire) Regt. of Foot | |
| | The Lancashire Fusiliers | 20th (East Devonshire) Regt. of Foot | |
| | The Royal Welsh Fusiliers | 23rd Regt. of Foot (Royal Welsh Fuzileers) | |
| | The South Wales Borderers | 2nd Bn. 24th (2nd Warwickshire) Regt. of Foot | |
| | | Distinction to Regiment | **15th February 1825** |
| | 1st Bn. The Royal Inniskilling Fusiliers | 27th (Inniskilling) Regt. of Foot | |
| | 1st Bn. The Gloucestershire Regt. | 28th (North Gloucestershire) Regt. of Foot | |
| | 2nd Bn. The Gloucestershire Regt. | 61st (South Gloucestershire) Regt. of Foot | |
| | 1st Bn. The Worcestershire Regt. | 29th (Worcestershire) Regt. of Foot | |
| | 2nd Bn. The Worcestershire Regt. | 36th (Herefordshire) Regt. of Foot | |
| | 1st Bn. The East Lancashire Regt. | 2nd Bn. 30th (Cambridgeshire) Regt. of Foot | |
| | | Distinction to Regiment | **10th April 1827** |
| | 2nd Bn. The East Lancashire Regt. | 2nd Bn. 59th (2nd Nottinghamshire) Regt. of Foot | |
| | | Distinction to Regiment | **5th June 1816** |
| | 1st Bn. The East Surrey Regt. | 2nd Bn. 31st (Huntingdonshire) Regt. of Foot | |
| | | Distinction to Regiment | **29th January 1825** |
| | 1st Bn. The Duke of Cornwall's L.I. | 32nd (Cornwall) Regt. of Foot | |
| | 2nd Bn. The Duke of Wellington's Regt. | 76th Regt. of Foot | |
| | 1st Bn. The Border Regt. | 2nd Bn. 34th (Cumberland) Regt. of Foot | |
| | | Distinction to Regiment | **18th September 1817** |
| | 1st Bn. The Hampshire Regt. | 37th (North Hampshire) Regt. of Foot | |
| | 2nd Bn. The Hampshire Regt. | 67th (South Hampshire) Regt. of Foot | |
| | 1st Bn. The South Staffordshire Regt. | 38th (1st Staffordshire) Regt. of Foot | |
| | 1st Bn. The Dorsetshire Regt. | 39th (Dorsetshire) Regt. of Foot | |
| | 1st Bn. P.W.V. (South Lancashire Regt.) | 40th (2nd Somersetshire) Regt. of Foot | |
| | 2nd Bn. P.W.V. (South Lancashire Regt.) | 82nd Regt. of Foot (Prince of Wales's Volunteers) | |
| | 1st Bn. The Black Watch | 42nd (Royal Highland) Regt. of Foot | |
| | 1st Bn. Oxf & Bucks Lt. Infty. | 43rd (Monmouthshire Light Infantry) Regt. | |
| | 2nd Bn. Oxf & Bucks Lt. Infty | 52nd (Oxfordshire Light Infantry) Regt. | |
| | 1st Bn. The Essex Regt. | 44th (East Essex) Regt. of Foot | |

| | | | |
|---|---|---|---|
| **PENINSULA (Cont.)** | 2nd Bn. The Essex Regt. | 56th (West Essex) Regt. of Foot | |
| | 1st Bn. The Sherwood Foresters | 45th (Nottinghamshire) Regt. of Foot | |
| | 1st Bn. The Loyal North Lancashire Regt. | 47th (Lancashire) Regt. of Foot | |
| | | Distinction to Regiment | 13th June 1816 |
| | 2nd Bn. The Loyal North Lancashire Regt. | 81st Regt. of Foot | |
| | 1st Bn. The Northamptonshire Regt. | 48th (Northamptonshire) Regt. of Foot | |
| | 2nd Bn. The Northamptonshire Regt. | 58th (Rutlandshire) Regt. of Foot | |
| | 2nd Bn. The Royal Berkshire Regt. | 66th (Berkshire) Regt. of Foot | |
| | | Distinction to Regiment | 30th July 1823 |
| | 1st Bn. The Queen's Own (Royal West Kent Regt.) | 50th (West Kent) Regt. of Foot | |
| | 1st Bn. The King's Own Yorkshire L.I. | 51st (2nd Yorkshire, West Riding) Regt. of Foot | |
| | 1st Bn. The King's Shropshire L.I. | 2nd Bn. 53rd (Shropshire) Regt. of Foot | |
| | | Distinction to Regiment | 28th March 1829 |
| | 2nd Bn. The King's Shropshire L.I. | 85th Regt. of Foot (Bucks Volunteers) (Light Infantry) | |
| | 1st Bn. The Middlesex Regt. | 57th (West Middlesex) Regt. of Foot | |
| | 2nd Bn. The Middlesex Regt. | 77th (East Middlesex) Regt. of Foot | |
| | The King's Royal Rifle Corps | 5th Bn. 60th (Royal American) Regt. of Foot | |
| | 1st Bn. The Wiltshire Regt. | 2nd Bn. 62nd (Wiltshire) Regt. of Foot | |
| | | Distinction to Regiment | 26th May 1829 |
| | 2nd Bn. The Manchester Regt. | *97th (Queen's Own) Regt. of Foot | 16th June 1874 |
| | 2nd Bn. The York & Lancaster Regt. | 2nd Bn. 84th (York & Lancaster) Regt. of Foot | |
| | | Distinction to Regiment | 5th February 1818 |
| | 1st Bn. The Durham L.I. | 68th (Durham) Regt. of Foot (Light Infantry) | |
| | 1st Bn. The Highland L.I. | **71st (Highland) Regt. of Foot (Light Infantry) | |
| | 2nd Bn. The Highland L.I. | 74th (Highland) Regt. of Foot | |
| | 2nd Bn. The Gordon Highlanders | 92nd Regt. of Foot | |
| | The Queen's Own Cameron Highlanders | 79th Regt. of Foot (Cameron Highlanders) | |
| | 1st Bn. The Royal Irish Rifles | 83rd Regt. of Foot (2nd Bn.) | |
| | 1st Bn. The Royal Irish Fusiliers | 87th (Prince of Wales's Own Irish) Regt. of Foot | |
| | 1st Bn. The Connaught Rangers | 88th Regt. of Foot (Connaught Rangers) | |
| | 2nd Bn. The Connaught Rangers | 94th Regt. of Foot | |

| | | | |
|---|---|---|---|
| **PENINSULA (Cont.)** | 1st Bn. Argyll & Sutherland Highlanders | 91st Regt. of Foot | |
| | 2nd Bn. Argyll & Sutherland Highlanders | 93rd Regt. of Foot | |
| | The Rifle Brigade | 95th Regt. of Foot (Rifle Corps) | |

* Disbanded 1818. Authorised to resume 16th June 1874.

** Between 1808-1814 this regiment was called:
1808 71st (Highland) Regt. of Foot
1808-09 71st (Glasgow Highland) Regt. of Foot
1809-10 71st (Glasgow Highland) Light Infantry Regt.

| | | | |
|---|---|---|---|
| **WATERLOO** | 1st Life Guards | 1st Regt. of Life Guards | This distinction was granted to all Regiments on 23rd November 1815, and the Regiments advised on 8th December 1815. |
| | 2nd Life Guards | 2nd Regt. of Life Guards | |
| | Royal Horse Guards | Royal Regt. of Horse Guards (Blue) | |
| | 1st King's Dragoon Guards | 1st (King's) Regt. of Dragoon Guards | |
| | 1st Royal Dragoons | 1st (Royal) Regt. of Dragoons | |
| | 2nd Dragoons (Royal Scots Greys) | 2nd (Royal North British) Regt. of Dragoons | |
| | 6th (Inniskilling) Dragoons | 6th (Inniskilling) Regt. of Dragoons | |
| | 7th Hussars | 7th (Queen's Own) Regt. of Light Dragoons (Hussars) | |
| | 10th Hussars | 10th (Prince of Wales's Own Royal) Regt. of Light Dragoons (Hussars) | |
| | 11th Hussars | 11th Regt. of Light Dragoons | |
| | 12th Lancers | 12th (Prince of Wales's) Regt. of Light Dragoons | |
| | 13th Hussars | 13th Regt. of Light Dragoons | |
| | 15th Hussars | 15th (The King's) Regt. of Light Dragoons (Hussars) | |
| | 16th Lancers | 16th (Queen's) Regt. of Light Dragoons | |
| | 18th Hussars | *18th Regt. of Light Dragoons (Hussars) | |
| | Grenadier Guards | 2nd & 3rd Bns. 1st Regt. of Foot Guards | |
| | Coldstream Guards | 2nd Bn. Coldstream Regt. of Foot Guards | |
| | Scots Guards | 2nd Bn. 3rd Regt. of Foot Guards | |
| | The Royal Scots | 3rd Bn. 1st (Royal Scots) Regt. of Foot | |
| | | Distinction to 1st and 2nd Battalions | 21st June 1817 |

| | | | |
|---|---|---|---|
| **WATERLOO (Cont.)** | The King's Own (Royal Lancaster Regt.) | 1st Bn. 4th (King's Own) Regt. of Foot | |
| | The West Yorkshire Regt. | 3rd Bn. 14th (Buckinghamshire) Regt. of Foot | |
| | | Distinction to 1st and 2nd Battalions | 23rd November 1845 |
| | The Royal Welsh Fusiliers | 23rd Regt. of Foot (Royal Welsh Fuzileers) | |
| | 1st Bn. The Royal Inniskilling Fusiliers | 1st Bn. 27th (Inniskilling) Regt. of Foot | |
| | 1st Bn. The Gloucestershire Regt. | 28th (North Gloucestershire) Regt. of Foot | |
| | 1st Bn. The East Lancashire Regt. | 2nd Bn. 30th (Cambridgeshire) Regt. of Foot | |
| | | Distinction to Regiment | 10th April 1827 |
| | 1st Bn. The Duke of Cornwall's L.I. | 32nd (Cornwall) Regt. of Foot | |
| | 1st Bn. The Duke of Wellington's Regt. | 33rd (1st Yorkshire, West Riding) Regt. of Foot | |
| | 1st Bn. P.W.V. (South Lancashire Regt.) | 1st Bn. 40th (2nd Somersetshire) Regt. of Foot | |
| | 2nd Bn. The Welsh Regt. | 2nd Bn. 69th (South Lincolnshire) Regt. of Foot | |
| | | Distinction to Regiment | 22nd January 1818 |
| | 1st Bn. The Black Watch | 42nd (Royal Highland) Regt. of Foot | |
| | 2nd Bn. The Black Watch | 2nd Bn. 73rd (Highland) Regt. of Foot | |
| | 1st Bn. The Essex Regt. | 2nd Bn. 44th (East Essex) Regt. of Foot | |
| | | Distinction to Regiment | 26th July 1816 |
| | 2nd Bn. Oxf & Bucks Lt. Infty. | 1st Bn. 52nd (Oxfordshire) Light Infantry Regt. | |
| | 1st Bn. The King's Own Yorkshire L.I. | 51st (2nd Yorkshire, West Riding) Regt. of Foot | |
| | 1st Bn. The Highland L.I. | 1st Bn. 71st (Highland) Regt. of Foot (Light Infantry) | |
| | The Queen's Own Cameron Highlanders | 1st Bn. 79th Regt. of Foot (Cameron Highlanders) | |
| | 2nd Bn. The Gordon Highlanders | 92nd Regt. of Foot (Gordon Highlanders) | |
| | The Rifle Brigade | 1st, 2nd & 3rd Bns. 95th Regt. of Foot (or Rifle Corps) | |

* Disbanded 1821. Authorised to resume 20th November 1858.

| | | | |
|---|---|---|---|
| **ALMA** | 4th Hussars | 4th (The Queen's Own) Regt. of (Light) Dragoons | 16th October 1855 |
| | 8th Hussars | 8th (The King's Royal Irish) Regt. of (Light) Dragoons (Hussars) | 16th October 1855 |
| | 11th Hussars | 11th (or Prince Albert's Own) Hussars | 16th October 1855 |
| | 13th Hussars | 13th Regt. of (Light) Dragoons | 16th October 1855 |
| | 17th Lancers | 17th Regt. of (Light) Dragoons (Lancers) | 16th October 1855 |
| | Grenadier Guards | 1st (or Grenadier) Regt. of Foot Guards | 16th October 1855 |

| | | | |
|---|---|---|---|
| **ALMA (Cont.)** | Coldstream Guards | Coldstream Regt. of Foot Guards | 16th October 1855 |
| | Scots Guards | Scots Fusilier Guards | 16th October 1855 |
| | The Royal Scots | 1st (The Royal) Regt. of Foot | 16th October 1855 |
| | The King's Own (Royal Lancaster Regt.) | 4th (The King's Own) Regt. of Foot | 16th October 1855 |
| | The Royal Fusiliers | 7th Regt. of Foot (Royal Fusiliers) | 16th October 1855 |
| | The Yorkshire Regt. | 19th (1st Yorkshire, North Riding) Regt. of Foot | 16th October 1855 |
| | The Lancashire Fusiliers | 20th (East Devonshire) Regt. of Foot | 16th October 1855 |
| | The Royal Scots Fusiliers | 21st Regt. of Foot (Royal North British Fusiliers) | 16th October 1855 |
| | The Royal Welsh Fusiliers | 23rd Regt. of Foot (Royal Welsh Fusiliers) | 16th October 1855 |
| | 1st Bn. The Gloucestershire Regt. | 28th (North Gloucestershire) Regt. of Foot | 16th October 1855 |
| | 1st Bn. The East Lancashire Regt. | 30th (Cambridgeshire) Regt. of Foot | 16th October 1855 |
| | 1st Bn. The Duke of Wellington's Regt. | 33rd (Duke of Wellington's) Regt. of Foot | 16th October 1855 |
| | 2nd Bn. The Border Regt. | 55th (Westmoreland) Regt. of Foot | 16th October 1855 |
| | 1st Bn. The South Staffordshire Regt. | 38th (1st Staffordshire) Regt. of Foot | 16th October 1855 |
| | 1st Bn. The Welsh Regt. | 41st (The Welch) Regt. of Foot | 16th October 1855 |
| | 1st Bn. The Black Watch | 42nd (Royal Highland) Regt. of Foot | 16th October 1855 |
| | 1st Bn. The Essex Regt. | 44th (East Essex) Regt. of Foot | 16th October 1855 |
| | 2nd Bn. The Sherwood Foresters | 95th (Derbyshire) Regt. of Foot | 16th October 1855 |
| | 1st Bn. The Loyal North Lancashire Regt. | 47th (Lancashire) Regt. of Foot | 16th October 1855 |
| | 1st Bn. The Royal Berkshire Regt. | 49th (The Princess Charlotte of Wales's or Hertfordshire) Regt. of Foot | 16th October 1855 |
| | 1st Bn. The Queen's Own (Royal West Kent Regt.) | 50th (The Queen's Own) Regt. of Foot | 16th October 1855 |
| | 2nd Bn. The Middlesex Regt. | 77th (East Middlesex) Regt. of Foot | 16th October 1855 |
| | 1st Bn. The Manchester Regt. | 63rd (West Suffolk) Regt. of Foot | 16th October 1855 |
| | 1st Bn. The Durham L.I. | 68th (Durham) Regt. of Foot (Light Infantry) | 16th October 1855 |
| | The Queen's Own Cameron Highlanders | 79th Regt. of Foot (Cameron Highlanders) | 16th October 1855 |
| | 1st Bn. The Connaught Rangers | 88th Regt. of Foot (Connaught Rangers) | 16th October 1855 |
| | 2nd Bn. The Argyll & Sutherland Highlanders | 93rd (Highland) Regt. of Foot | 16th October 1855 |
| | The Rifle Brigade | Rifle Brigade | 16th October 1855 |

| | | | |
|---|---|---|---|
| **BALAKLAVA** | 4th Dragoon Guards | 4th (Royal Irish) Regt. of Dragoon Guards | 16th October 1855 |
| | 5th Dragoon Guards | 5th (Princess Charlotte of Wales's) Regt. of Dragoon Guards | 16th October 1855 |
| | 1st Royal Dragoons | 1st (Royal) Regt. of Dragoons | 16th October 1855 |
| | 2nd Dragoons (Royal Scots Greys) | 2nd (Royal North British) Regt. of Dragoons | 16th October 1855 |
| | 4th Hussars | 4th (The Queen's Own) Regt. of (Light) Dragoons | 16th October 1855 |
| | 6th (Inniskilling) Dragoons | 6th (Inniskilling) Regt. of Dragoons | 16th October 1855 |
| | 8th Hussars | 8th (The King's Royal Irish) Regt. of (Light) Dragoons (Hussars) | 16th October 1855 |
| | 11th Hussars | 11th (or Prince Albert's Own) Hussars | 16th October 1855 |
| | 13th Hussars | 13th Regt. of (Light) Dragoons | 16th October 1855 |
| | 17th Lancers | 17th Regt. of (Light) Dragoons (Lancers) | 16th October 1855 |
| | 2nd Bn. The Argyll & Sutherland Highlanders | 93rd (Highland) Regt. of Foot | 16th October 1855 |
| **INKERMAN** | 4th Hussars | 4th (The Queen's Own) Regt. of (Light) Dragoons | 16th October 1855 |
| | 8th Hussars | 8th (The King's Royal Irish) Regt. of (Light) Dragoons (Hussars) | 16th October 1855 |
| | 11th Hussars | 11th (or Prince Albert's Own) Hussars | 16th October 1855 |
| | 13th Hussars | 13th Regt. of (Light) Dragoons | 16th October 1855 |
| | 17th Lancers | 17th Regt. of (Light) Dragoons (Lancers) | 16th October 1855 |
| | Grenadier Guards | 1st (or Grenadier) Regt. of Foot Guards | 16th October 1855 |
| | Coldstream Guards | Coldstream Regt. of Foot Guards | 16th October 1855 |
| | Scots Guards | Scots Fusilier Guards | 16th October 1855 |
| | The Royal Scots | 1st (The Royal) Regt. of Foot | 16th October 1855 |
| | The King's Own (Royal Lancaster Regt.) | 4th (The King's Own) Regt. of Foot | 16th October 1855 |
| | The Royal Fusiliers | 7th Regt. of Foot (Royal Fusiliers) | 16th October 1855 |
| | The Yorkshire Regt. | 19th (1st Yorkshire, North Riding) Regt. of Foot | 16th October 1855 |
| | The Lancashire Fusiliers | 20th (East Devonshire) Regt. of Foot | 16th October 1855 |
| | The Royal Scots Fusiliers | 21st Regt. of Foot (Royal North British Fusiliers) | 16th October 1855 |
| | The Royal Welsh Fusiliers | 23rd Regt. of Foot (Royal Welsh Fusiliers) | 16th October 1855 |
| | 1st Bn. The Gloucestershire Regt. | 28th (North Gloucestershire) Regt. of Foot | 16th October 1855 |

| | | | |
|---|---|---|---|
| **INKERMAN (Cont.)** | 1st Bn. The East Lancashire Regt. | 30th (Cambridgeshire) Regt. of Foot | 16th October 1855 |
| | 1st Bn. The Duke of Wellington's Regt. | 33rd (Duke of Wellington's) Regt. of Foot | 16th October 1855 |
| | 2nd Bn. The Border Regt. | 55th (Westmoreland) Regt. of Foot | 16th October 1855 |
| | 1st Bn. The South Staffordshire Regt. | 38th (1st Staffordshire) Regt. of Foot | 16th October 1855 |
| | 1st Bn. The Welsh Regt. | 41st (The Welch) Regt. of Foot | 16th October 1855 |
| | 1st Bn. The Essex Regt. | 44th (East Essex) Regt. of Foot | 16th October 1855 |
| | 2nd Bn. The Sherwood Foresters | 95th (Derbyshire) Regt. of Foot | 16th October 1855 |
| | 1st Bn. The Loyal North Lancashire Regt. | 47th (Lancashire) Regt. of Foot | 16th October 1855 |
| | 1st Bn. The Royal Berkshire Regt. | 49th (The Princess Charlotte of Wales's or Hertfordshire) Regt. of Foot | 16th October 1855 |
| | 1st Bn. The Queen's Own (Royal West Kent Regt.) | 50th (The Queen's Own) Regt. of Foot | 16th October 1855 |
| | 1st Bn. The Middlesex Regt. | 57th (West Middlesex) Regt. of Foot | 16th October 1855 |
| | 2nd Bn. The Middlesex Regt. | 77th (East Middlesex) Regt. of Foot | 16th October 1855 |
| | 1st Bn. The Manchester Regt. | 63rd (West Suffolk) Regt. of Foot | 16th October 1855 |
| | 1st Bn. The Durham L.I. | 68th (Durham) Regt. of Foot (Light Infantry) | 16th October 1855 |
| | 1st Bn. The Connaught Rangers | 88th Regt. of Foot (Connaught Rangers) | 16th October 1855 |
| | The Rifle Brigade | Rifle Brigade | 16th October 1855 |
| **SEVASTOPOL** | 1st King's Dragoon Guards | 1st (The King's) Regt. of Dragoon Guards | 16th October 1855 |
| | 4th Dragoon Guards | 4th (Royal Irish) Regt. of Dragoon Guards | 16th October 1855 |
| | 5th Dragoon Guards | 5th (Princess Charlotte of Wales's) Regt. of Dragoon Guards | 16th October 1855 |
| | 6th Dragoon Guards | 6th Regt. of Dragoon Guards (Carabiniers) | 16th October 1855 |
| | 1st Royal Dragoons | 1st (Royal) Regt. of Dragoons | 16th October 1855 |
| | 2nd Dragoons (Royal Scots Greys) | 2nd (Royal North British) Regt. of Dragoons | 16th October 1855 |
| | 4th Hussars | 4th (The Queen's Own) Regt. of (Light) Dragoons | 16th October 1855 |
| | 6th (Inniskilling) Dragoons | 6th (Inniskilling) Regt. of Dragoons | 16th October 1855 |
| | 8th Hussars | 8th (The King's Royal Irish) Regt. of (Light) Dragoons (Hussars) | 16th October 1855 |
| | 10th Hussars | 10th (The Prince of Wales's Own) Royal Regt. of (Light) Dragoons (Hussars) | 16th October 1855 |

| | | | |
|---|---|---|---|
| **SEVASTOPOL (Cont.)** | 11th Hussars | 11th (or Prince Albert's Own) Hussars | 16th October 1855 |
| | 12th Lancers | 12th (The Prince of Wales's) Royal Regt. of Lancers | 16th October 1855 |
| | 13th Hussars | 13th Regt. of (Light) Dragoons | 16th October 1855 |
| | 17th Lancers | 17th Regt. of (Light) Dragoons (Lancers) | 16th October 1855 |
| | Grenadier Guards | 1st (or Grenadier) Regt. of Foot Guards | 16th October 1855 |
| | Coldstream Guards | Coldstream Regt. of Foot Guards | 16th October 1855 |
| | Scots Guards | Scots Fusilier Guards | 16th October 1855 |
| | The Royal Scots | 1st (The Royal) Regt. of Foot | 16th October 1855 |
| | The Buffs (East Kent Regt.) | 3rd (East Kent) Regt. of Foot (The Buffs) | 16th October 1855 |
| | The King's Own (Royal Lancaster Regt.) | 4th (The King's Own) Regt. of Foot | 16th October 1855 |
| | The Royal Fusiliers | 7th Regt. of Foot (Royal Fusiliers) | 16th October 1855 |
| | The Norfolk Regt. | 9th (East Norfolk) Regt. of Foot | 16th October 1855 |
| | The Somerset Light Infantry | 13th (1st Somersetshire) (or Prince Albert's) Regt. of Light Infantry | 16th October 1855 |
| | The West Yorkshire Regt. | 14th (Buckinghamshire) Regt. of Foot | 16th October 1855 |
| | The Leicestershire Regt. | 17th (Leicestershire) Regt. of Foot | 16th October 1855 |
| | The Royal Irish Regt. | 18th (Royal Irish) Regt. of Foot | 16th October 1855 |
| | The Yorkshire Regt. | 19th (1st Yorkshire, North Riding) Regt. of Foot | 16th October 1855 |
| | The Lancashire Fusiliers | 20th (East Devonshire) Regt. of Foot | 16th October 1855 |
| | The Royal Scots Fusiliers | 21st Regt. of Foot (Royal North British Fusiliers) | 16th October 1855 |
| | The Royal Welsh Fusiliers | 23rd Regt. of Foot (Royal Welsh Fusiliers) | 16th October 1855 |
| | 2nd Bn. The Cameronians | 90th Regt. of Foot (Perthshire Volunteers) (Light Infantry) | 16th October 1855 |
| | 1st Bn. The Gloucestershire Regt. | 28th (North Gloucestershire) Regt. of Foot | 16th October 1855 |
| | 1st Bn. The East Lancashire Regt. | 30th (Cambridgeshire) Regt. of Foot | 16th October 1855 |
| | 1st Bn. The East Surrey Regt. | 31st (Huntingdonshire) Regt. of Foot | 16th October 1855 |
| | 2nd Bn. The Duke of Cornwall's L.I. | 46th (South Devonshire) Regt. of Foot | 16th October 1855 |
| | 1st Bn. The Duke of Wellington's Regt. | 33rd (Duke of Wellington's) Regt. of Foot | 16th October 1855 |
| | 1st Bn. The Border Regt. | 34th (Cumberland) Regt. of Foot | 16th October 1855 |
| | 2nd Bn. The Border Regt. | 55th (Westmoreland) Regt. of Foot | 16th October 1855 |
| | 1st Bn. The South Staffordshire Regt. | 38th (1st Staffordshire) Regt. of Foot | 16th October 1855 |
| | 1st Bn. The Dorsetshire Regt. | 39th (Dorsetshire) Regt. of Foot | 16th October 1855 |

| | | | |
|---|---|---|---|
| **SEVASTOPOL (Cont.)** | 2nd Bn. P.W.V. (South Lancashire Regt.) | 82nd Regt. of Foot (The Prince of Wales's Volunteers) | 16th October 1855 |
| | 1st Bn. The Welsh Regt. | 41st (The Welch) Regt. of Foot | 16th October 1855 |
| | 1st Bn. The Black Watch | 42nd (Royal Highland) Regt. of Foot | 16th October 1855 |
| | 1st Bn. The Essex Regt. | 44th (East Essex) Regt. of Foot | 16th October 1855 |
| | 2nd Bn. The Essex Regt. | 56th (West Essex) Regt. of Foot | 16th October 1855 |
| | 2nd Bn. The Sherwood Foresters | 95th (Derbyshire) Regt. of Foot | 16th October 1855 |
| | 1st Bn. The Loyal North Lancashire Regt. | 47th (Lancashire) Regt. of Foot | 16th October 1855 |
| | 1st Bn. The Northamptonshire Regt. | 48th (Northamptonshire) Regt. of Foot | 16th October 1855 |
| | 1st Bn. The Royal Berkshire Regt. | 49th (The Princess Charlotte of Wales's or Hertfordshire) Regt. of Foot | 16th October 1855 |
| | 1st Bn. The Queen's Own (Royal West Kent Regt.) | 50th (The Queen's Own) Regt. of Foot | 16th October 1855 |
| | 2nd Bn. The Queen's Own (Royal West Kent Regt.) | 97th (Earl of Ulster's) Regt. of Foot | 16th October 1855 |
| | 1st Bn. The Middlesex Regt. | 57th (West Middlesex) Regt. of Foot | 16th October 1855 |
| | 2nd Bn. The Middlesex Regt. | 77th (East Middlesex) Regt. of Foot | 16th October 1855 |
| | 1st Bn. The Wiltshire Regt. | 62nd (Wiltshire) Regt. of Foot | 16th October 1855 |
| | 1st Bn. The Manchester Regt. | 63rd (West Suffolk) Regt. of Foot | 16th October 1855 |
| | 1st Bn. The Durham L.I. | 68th (Durham) Regt. of Foot (Light Infantry) | 16th October 1855 |
| | 1st Bn. The Highland L.I. | 71st (Highland) Regt. of Foot (Light Infantry) | 16th October 1855 |
| | 1st Bn. Seaforth Highlanders | 72nd (The Duke of Albany's Own Highlanders) Regt. of Foot | 16th October 1855 |
| | The Queen's Own Cameron Highlanders | 79th Regt. of Foot (Cameron Highlanders) | 16th October 1855 |
| | 2nd Bn. The Royal Irish Fusiliers | 89th Regt. of Foot | 16th October 1855 |
| | 1st Bn. The Connaught Rangers | 88th Regt. of Foot (Connaught Rangers) | 16th October 1855 |
| | 2nd Bn. The Argyll & Sutherland Highlanders | 93rd (Highland) Regt. of Foot | 16th October 1855 |
| | The Rifle Brigade | Rifle Brigade | 16th October 1855 |
| ***MEDITERRANEAN** | 3rd Bn. The Royal Berkshire Regt. | Royal Berkshire Militia | 9th June 1856 |
| | 3rd Bn. The Buffs (East Kent Regt.) | East Kent Militia | 9th June 1856 |
| | 3rd Bn. The King's Own (Royal Lancaster Regt.) | 1st Royal Lancashire Militia (Duke of Lancaster's Own) | 9th June 1856 |

| | | | |
|---|---|---|---|
| *MEDITERRANEAN (Cont.) | 3rd Bn. The Loyal North Lancashire Regt. | 3rd Royal Lancashire Militia (Duke of Lancaster's Own) | 9th June 1856 |
| | 3rd Bn. The Northamptonshire Regt. | Northamptonshire Militia | 9th June 1856 |
| | 3rd Bn. Oxf & Bucks Lt. Infty. | Oxfordshire Militia | 9th June 1856 |
| | 3rd & 4th Bns. The South Staffordshire Regt. | The King's Own 1st Staffordshire Militia | 9th June 1856 |
| | 3rd Bn. The Wiltshire Regt. | Royal Wiltshire Militia | 9th June 1856 |
| | 3rd Bn. The West Yorkshire Regt. | 2nd West Yorkshire Militia | 9th June 1856 |
| | 5th Bn. The Royal Fusiliers | 3rd or Royal Westminster, Middlesex Militia | 9th June 1856 |

* This honour disappeared when the Militia became Special Reserve.

# ASIA
# (India & the Far East)

## ASIA
## (India and the Far East)

| | | | |
|---|---|---|---|
| ARCOT | War in the Carnatic | | 31st August to 14th November 1751 |
| PLASSEY | Overthrow of Siraj-ud-Dowlah | | 23rd June 1757 |
| CONDORE | Expedition to Northern Circars | | 8th December 1758 |
| MASULIPATAM | War in the Carnatic | | 8th April 1759 |
| BADARA | Defeat of the Dutch | | 25th November 1759 |
| WANDIWASH | Seven Years War (Defeat of Lally) | | 22nd January 1760 |
| PONDICHERRY | " " | | 10th January 1761 |
| BUXAR | Campaign against Nawabs of Bengal & Oudh | | 23rd October 1764 |
| ROHILCUND 1774 | 1st Rohilla War (Battle of Kutra) | | 23rd April 1774 |
| GUZERAT | Operations in Western India | | 1776-1782 |
| CARNATIC | | | Various dates |
| SHOLINGHUR | 2nd Mysore War | | 27th September 1781 |
| MANGALORE | " | Capture | 9th March 1783 |
| NUNDY DROOG | 3rd Mysore War | | 18th October 1791 |
| MYSORE | | | 1789-1791 |
| ROHILCUND 1794 | 2nd Rohilla War (Battle of Bitaura) | | 26th October 1794 |
| AMBOYNA | Expedition against Dutch in East Indies | | 17th February 1796 & 1810 |
| TERNATE | " " " | | 1801 |
| BANDA | " " " | | 1796 & 1810 |
| SEEDASEER | 4th Mysore War | | 8th March 1799 |
| SERINGAPATAM | " | | 5th April to 4th May 1799 |
| ARABIA | Operations in the Persian Gulf | | 1809, 1819, 1820 |
| BOURBON | Operations against French, Capture of Island | | 8th July 1810 |
| INDIA | | | Various dates |
| HINDOOSTAN | | | Various dates |
| ALLY GHUR | 2nd Maratha War 1803-1805 | | 4th September 1803 |
| DELHI 1803 | " | | 11th September 1803 |
| ASSAYE | " | | 23rd September 1803 |
| LESWARREE | " | | 1st November 1803 |

| | | | |
|---|---|---|---|
| **DEIG** | 2nd Maratha War 1803-1805 | | 13th November to 25th December 1804 |
| **COCHIN** | Rebellion in Travancore | | 1809 |
| **JAVA** | Operations against Dutch in East Indies | | 4th to 26th August 1811 |
| **KIRKEE** | 3rd Maratha & Pindari War | | 5th November 1817 |
| **SEETABULDEE** | " | | 26th to 27th November 1817 |
| **NAGPORE** | " | | 19th to 29th December 1817 |
| **MAHEIDPOOR** | " | | 21st December 1817 |
| **CORYGAUM** | " | | 1st & 2nd January 1818 |
| **NOWAH** | " | | 21st January 1818 |
| **PERSIAN GULF** | Operations against Pirates | | 1819 |
| **BENI BOO ALI** | " | | 2nd March 1821 |
| **BHURTPORE** | Revolt of Rajah | Capture | 18th January 1826 |
| **ADEN** | Expedition to establish Garrison | Capture | 19th January 1839 |
| **AVA** | 1st Burmese War | | 1824-1826 |
| **KEMMENDINE** | " | | 1st to 9th December 1824 |
| **ARRACAN** | " | | 1825 |
| **BURMAH** | " | | 1825 |
| **GHUZNEE 1839** | 1st Afghan War | | 23rd July 1839 |
| **KHELAT** | " | Capture | 13th November 1839 |
| **KAHUN** | " | Defence | May to September 1840 |
| **JELLALABAD** | " | Defence | January to April 1842 |
| **KELAT-I-GHILZIE** | " | Defence | November to May 1842 |
| **CANDAHAR 1842** | " | | 10th March 1842 |
| **GHUZNEE 1842** | " | | 6th September 1842 |
| **CABOOL 1842** | " | | 1839 to 1842 |
| **AFFGHANISTAN** | " | | 1842 |
| **CUTCHEE** | Operations in Scinde | | 1839 to 1842 |
| **CHINA** (with Dragon) | 1st Chinese War (The Opium War) | | 1842 |
| **MEEANEE** | Conquest of Scinde | | 17th February 1843 |
| **HYDERABAD** | " | | 24th March 1843 |
| **SCINDE** | " | | 1843 |
| **MAHARAJPORE** | The Gwalior Campaign (Right Wing) | | 29th December 1843 |

| | | | |
|---|---|---|---|
| PUNNIAR | The Gwalior Campaign (Left Wing) | | 29th December 1843 |
| MOODKEE | 1st Sikh War | | 18th December 1845 |
| FEROZESHAH | ” | | 21st-22nd December 1845 |
| ALIWAL | ” | | 28th January 1846 |
| SOBRAON | ” | | 10th February 1846 |
| MOOLTAN | 2nd Sikh War | | September 1848–January 1849 |
| CHILLIANWALLAH | ” | | 13th January 1849 |
| GOOJERAT | ” | | 21st February 1849 |
| PUNJAUB | ” | | 1848-1849 |
| PEGU | 2nd Burmese War | | 1852-1853 |
| RESHIRE | The Persian War | | 9th December 1856 |
| BUSHIRE | ” | | 10th December 1856 |
| KOOSH-AB | ” | | 8th February 1857 |
| PERSIA | ” | | 1856-1857 |
| DELHI 1857 | The Indian Mutiny | | June to September 1857 |
| LUCKNOW | ” | Defence & Relief | 1857-1858 |
| DEFENCE OF ARRAH | ” | | July to August 1857 |
| BEHAR | ” | | 1857-1858 |
| CENTRAL INDIA | ” | | 1857-1858 |
| CANTON | 2nd China War | | 29th December 1857 |
| TAKU FORTS | ” | | 21st August 1860 |
| PEKIN | ” | | 5th October 1860 |
| CHINA | ” | | 1857-1860 |
| ALI MASJID | 2nd Afghan War | | 21st November 1878 |
| PEIWAR KOTAL | ” | | 2nd December 1878 |
| CHARASIAH | ” | | 6th October 1879 |
| KABUL | ” | | December 1879 |
| AHMAD KHEL | ” | | 19th April 1880 |
| KANDAHAR | ” | | 1st September 1880 |
| AFGHANISTAN 1878-1880 | ” | | 1878-1880 |
| BURMA 1885-1887 | 3rd Burmese War | | 1885-1887 |
| DEFENCE OF CHITRAL | The Chitral Campaign | | March to April 1895 |

| | | |
|---|---|---|
| **CHITRAL** | The Chitral Campaign | 1895 |
| **MALAKAND** | Tochi Valley Expedition | 26th July 1897 |
| **SAMANA** | Tirah Campaign | 12th to 14th September 1897 |
| **TIRAH** | " | 1897-1898 |
| **PUNJAB FRONTIER** | | 1897-1898 |
| **PEKIN** | The Boxer Rising | 1900 |
| **CHINA** | " | 1900 |

| | ABBREVIATED TITLE | FORMER TITLE | DATE OF AWARD |
|---|---|---|---|
| **ARCOT** | 1st Bn. The Royal Dublin Fusiliers | H.E.I.C. Madras European Regt. | Madras GO 12th March 1841 |
| **PLASSEY** | 1st Bn. The Dorset Regt. | 39th Regt. of Foot | 17th November 1835 |
| | 1st Bn. The Royal Munster Fusiliers | H.E.I.C. Bengal (European) Regt. | GGO 23rd February 1829 |
| | 1st Bn. The Royal Dublin Fusiliers | *H.E.I.C. 1st Madras European Regt. | Madras GO 12th March 1841 |
| | 2nd Bn. The Royal Dublin Fusiliers | H.E.I.C. Bombay European Regt. | 6th November 1844 |
| | * With Royal Tiger inscribed 'Plassey' & 'Buxar' | | |
| **CONDORE** | 1st Bn. The Royal Munster Fusiliers | H.E.I.C. Bengal (European) Regt. | Army Order 79/1894 |
| | 1st Bn. The Royal Dublin Fusiliers | **H.E.I.C. 1st Madras European Regt. | Madras GO 12th March 1841 |
| | ** Granted to Regiment in error, no details of the Regiment were present. | | |
| **MASULIPATAM** | 1st Bn. The Royal Munster Fusiliers | H.E.I.C. Bengal (European) Regt. | Army Order 79/1894 |
| **BADARA** | 1st Bn. The Royal Munster Fusiliers | H.E.I.C. Bengal (European) Regt. | Army Order 79/1894 |
| **WANDIWASH** | 1st Bn. The Royal Dublin Fusiliers | H.E.I.C. Madras European Regt. | Madras GO 12th March 1841 |
| **PONDICHERRY** | 1st Bn. The Royal Dublin Fusiliers | H.E.I.C. Madras European Regt. | Madras GO 12th March 1841 |
| **BUXAR** | 1st Bn. The Royal Munster Fusiliers | H.E.I.C. Bengal (European) Regt. | GGO 23rd February 1829 |
| | 2nd Bn. The Royal Dublin Fusiliers | H.E.I.C. Bombay European Regt. | Bombay GO 6th November 1844 |
| **ROHILCUND 1774** | 1st Bn. The Royal Munster Fusiliers | (a)H.E.I.C. Bengal (European) Regt. | Army Order 79/1894 |
| | (a) Originally granted to 2nd Bengal European Regt. and inherited by 1st Bn. in 1803. Later withdrawn. Regranted 1894. | | |
| **GUZERAT** | 1st Bn. The Royal Munster Fusiliers | (b)H.E.I.C. 1st Bengal European Regt. | GGO 23rd February 1829 |
| | 2nd Bn. The Royal Dublin Fusiliers | (c)H.E.I.C. Bombay European Regt. | c.1845 |
| | (b) For Services 1803-1804. | | |
| | (c) For Services 1778 & 1782. | | |

| | | | |
|---|---|---|---|
| **CARNATIC (For services 1780-1784 & 1790-1792)** | 1st Bn. The Highland L.I. | (d)73rd (Highland) Regt. of Foot | 12th February 1889 |
| | 1st Bn. Seaforth Highlanders | (e)78th (Highland) Regt. of Foot | 12th February 1889 |
| | 1st Bn. The Royal Munster Fusiliers | H.E.I.C. Bengal (European) Regt. | 12th February 1889 |
| | | INDIAN ARMY | |
| | 27th Light Cavalry | (f)3rd Regt. Madras Native Cavalry | 12th February 1889 |
| | 2nd Q.V.O. Sappers & Miners | Madras Pioneers | 12th February 1889 |
| | 61st K.G.O. Pioneers | (g)1st Carnatic Battalion | 12th February 1889 |
| | 62nd Punjabis | 2nd Carnatic Battalion | 12th February 1889 |
| | 63rd Palamcottah L.I. | 3rd Carnatic Battalion | 12th February 1889 |
| | 64th Pioneers | 4th Carnatic Battalion | 12th February 1889 |
| | 66th Punjabis | 6th Carnatic Battalion | 12th February 1889 |
| | 67th Punjabis | 7th Carnatic Battalion | 12th February 1889 |
| | 69th Punjabis | 9th Carnatic Battalion | 12th February 1889 |
| | 72nd Punjabis | 12th Carnatic Battalion | 12th February 1889 |
| | 73rd Carnatic Infantry | 13th Carnatic Battalion | 12th February 1889 |
| | 74th Punjabis | 14th Carnatic Battalion | 12th February 1889 |
| | 75th Carnatic Infantry | 15th Carnatic Battalion | 12th February 1889 |
| | 76th Punjabis | 16th Carnatic Battalion | 12th February 1889 |
| | 79th Carnatic Infantry | 20th Carnatic Battalion | 12th February 1889 |
| | 80th Carnatic Infantry | 21st Carnatic Battalion | 12th February 1889 |

(d) Became 71st in 1786.

(e) Became 72nd in 1786.

(f) 1st Regt. Madras Cavalry 1784; 4th Regt. 1786; 2nd Regt. 1788.

(g) The Carnatic Battalions became Madras Battalions in 1784.

(h) Bombay European Regt. Elephant superscribed Carnatic & Mysore 6th November 1844

| | | | |
|---|---|---|---|
| **SHOLINGHUR** | 1st Bn. The Highland L.I. | 73rd (Highland) Regt. of Foot | 12th February 1889 |
| | 1st Bn. The Royal Munster Fusiliers | H.E.I.C. Bengal (European) Regt. | Madras GO 12th March 1841 |
| | 1st Bn. The Royal Dublin Fusiliers | H.E.I.C. Madras European Regt. | 12th February 1889 |
| | | INDIAN ARMY | |
| | 27th Light Cavalry | (a)3rd Regt. Nawab of Arcot's Cavalry | Madras GO 48/1841 |
| | 2nd Q.V.O. Sappers & Miners | Madras Pioneers | Madras GO 48/1841 |
| | 63rd Palamcottah L.I. | 3rd Carnatic Battalion | Madras GO 48/1841 |

| | | | |
|---|---|---|---|
| SHOLINGHUR (Cont.) | 64th Pioneers | 4th Carnatic Battalion | Madras GO 48/1841 |
| | 66th Punjabis | 6th Carnatic Battalion | Madras GO 48/1841 |
| | 69th Punjabis | 9th Carnatic Battalion | Madras GO 48/1841 |
| | 72nd Punjabis | 12th Carnatic Battalion | Madras GO 48/1841 |
| | 73rd Carnatic Infantry | 13th Carnatic Battalion | Madras GO 48/1841 |
| | 74th Punjabis | 14th Carnatic Battalion | Madras GO 48/1841 |
| | 75th Carnatic Infantry | 15th Carnatic Battalion | Madras GO 48/1841 |
| | 76th Punjabis | 16th Carnatic Battalion | Madras GO 48/1841 |
| | 79th Carnatic Infantry | 20th Carnatic Battalion | Madras GO 48/1841 |
| | 80th Carnatic Infantry | 21st Carnatic Battalion | Madras GO 48/1841 |
| | (a) Entered service of H.E.I.C. in 1784. | | |
| MANGALORE | 2nd Bn. The Black Watch | 2nd Bn. 42nd (Royal Highland) Regt. of Foot | Awarded after Gen. G. Lake was appointed Colonel in 1796 |
| | The 101st Grenadiers | (b)8th Bombay Battalion, Sepoys | |
| | (b) Became Bombay Grenadiers in 1784. | | |
| NUNDY DROOG (With Royal Tiger) | 1st Bn. The Royal Dublin Fusiliers | H.E.I.C. Madras European Regt. | G.G.O. 12th March 1841 |
| MYSORE | 19th Hussars | 19th Light Dragoons | 12th February 1889 |
| | 2nd Bn. The Worcestershire Regt. | 36th (Herefordshire) Regt. of Foot | 12th February 1889 |
| | 2nd Bn. The Duke of Wellington's Regt. | 76th Regt. of Foot | 12th February 1889 |
| | 2nd Bn. The Black Watch | 73rd (Highland) Regt. of Foot | 12th February 1889 |
| | 2nd Bn. Oxf & Bucks Lt. Infty. | 52nd (Oxfordshire) Regt. of Foot | 12th February 1889 |
| | 2nd Bn. The Middlesex Regt. | 77th Regt. of Foot | 12th February 1889 |
| | 1st Bn. The Highland L.I. | 71st (Highland) Regt. of Foot | 12th February 1889 |
| | 2nd Bn. The Highland L.I. | 74th (Highland) Regt. of Foot | 12th February 1889 |
| | 1st Bn. Seaforth Highlanders | 72nd (Highland) Regt. of Foot | 12th February 1889 |
| | 1st Bn. The Gordon Highlanders | 75th (Highland) Regt. of Foot | 12th February 1889 |
| | | INDIAN ARMY | |
| | 26th K.G.O. Light Cavalry | 1st Regt. Madras Native Cavalry | 12th February 1889 |
| | 27th Light Cavalry | 2nd Regt. Madras Native Cavalry | 12th February 1889 |

| | | | |
|---|---|---|---|
| **MYSORE (Cont.)** | 28th Light Cavalry | 3rd Regt. Madras Native Cavalry | 12th February 1889 |
| | 2nd Q.V.O. Sappers & Miners | Madras Pioneer Battalion | 12th February 1889 |
| | 61st K.G.O. Pioneers | 1st Madras Battalion | 12th February 1889 |
| | 62nd Punjabis | 2nd Madras Battalion | 12th February 1889 |
| | 63rd Palamcottah L.I. | 3rd Madras Battalion | 12th February 1889 |
| | 64th Pioneers | 4th Madras Battalion | 12th February 1889 |
| | 66th Punjabis | 6th Madras Battalion | 12th February 1889 |
| | 67th Punjabis | 7th Madras Battalion | 12th February 1889 |
| | 69th Punjabis | 9th Madras Battalion | 12th February 1889 |
| | 73rd Carnatic Infantry | 13th Madras Battalion | 12th February 1889 |
| | 74th Punjabis | 14th Madras Battalion | 12th February 1889 |
| | 75th Carnatic Infantry | 15th Madras Battalion | 12th February 1889 |
| | 76th Punjabis | 16th Madras Battalion | 12th February 1889 |
| | 79th Carnatic Infantry | 20th Madras Battalion | 12th February 1889 |
| | 80th Carnatic Infantry | 21st Madras Battalion | 12th February 1889 |
| | 81st Pioneers | 28th Madras Battalion | 12th February 1889 |
| | 82nd Punjabis | 29th Madras Battalion | 12th February 1889 |
| | The 101st Grenadiers | 1st Bombay Battalion or Bombay Grenadiers | 12th February 1889 |
| | 103rd Mahratta L.I. | 2nd Bn. Bombay Sepoys | 12th February 1889 |
| | 104th Wellesley's Rifles | 9th Bn. Bombay Sepoys | 12th February 1889 |
| | 105th Mahratta L.I. | 3rd Bn. Bombay Sepoys | 12th February 1889 |
| | 107th Pioneers | 4th Bn. Bombay Sepoys | 12th February 1889 |
| | 108th Infantry | 7th Bn. Bombay Sepoys | 12th February 1889 |
| | 109th Infantry | 5th Bn. Bombay Sepoys | 12th February 1889 |
| **ROHILCUND 1794** | 2nd Bn. The Royal Munster Fusiliers | H.E.I.C. 2nd Bengal European Regt. | Army Order 79/1894 |
| **AMBOYNA** | 1st Bn. The Royal Dublin Fusiliers | H.E.I.C. Madras European Regt. | 12th March 1841 |
| **TERNATE** | 1st Bn. The Royal Dublin Fusiliers | H.E.I.C. Madras European Regt. | 12th March 1841 |
| **BANDA** | 1st Bn. The Royal Dublin Fusiliers | H.E.I.C. Madras European Regt. | 12th March 1841 |

| Honour | Present Unit | Original Unit | Date of Grant |
|---|---|---|---|
| **SEEDASEER** | 103rd Mahratta L.I. | 1st Bn. 2nd Regt. Bombay Native Infantry | 20th May 1823 |
| | 105th Mahratta L.I. | 1st Bn. 3rd Regt. Bombay Native Infantry | 20th May 1823 |
| | 107th Pioneers | 1st Bn. 4th Regt. Bombay Native Infantry | 20th May 1823 |
| **SERINGAPATAM** | 19th Hussars | (a)19th Light Dragoons | 28th May 1818 |
| | The Suffolk Regt. | 12th (East Suffolk) Regt. of Foot | 28th May 1818 |
| | 1st Bn. The Duke of Wellington's Regt. | 33rd (1st Yorkshire, West Riding) Regt. of Foot | 28th May 1818 |
| | 2nd Bn. The Black Watch | 73rd (Highland) Regt. of Foot | 28th May 1818 |
| | 2nd Bn. The Middlesex Regt. | 77th Regt. of Foot | 28th May 1818 |
| | 2nd Bn. The Highland L.I. | 74th (Highland) Regt. of Foot | 28th May 1818 |
| | 1st Bn. The Gordon Highlanders | 75th (Highland) Regt. of Foot | 28th May 1818 |
| | 2nd Bn. The Connaught Rangers | The Scotch Brigade | 28th May 1818 |
| | 2nd Bn. The Royal Dublin Fusiliers | (b)H.E.I.C. 1st Bn. Bombay (European) Regt. | 11th April 1822 |
| | | INDIAN ARMY | |
| | 26th K.G.O. Light Cavalry | 1st Regt. Madras Native Cavalry | 26th December 1820 |
| | 27th Light Cavalry | 2nd Regt. Madras Native Cavalry | 26th December 1820 |
| | 28th Light Cavalry | 3rd Regt. Madras Native Cavalry | 26th December 1820 |
| | 2nd Q.V.O. Sappers & Miners | Madras Pioneer Battalion | 26th December 1820 |
| | 61st K.G.O. Pioneers | 1st Bn. 1st Regt. Madras Native Infantry | 26th December 1820 |
| | 66th Punjabis | 1st Bn. 6th Regt. Madras Native Infantry | 26th December 1820 |
| | 73rd Carnatic Infantry | 2nd Bn. 3rd Regt. Madras Native Infantry | 26th December 1820 |
| | 76th Punjabis | 2nd Bn. 5th Regt. Madras Native Infantry | 26th December 1820 |
| | 79th Carnatic Infantry | 2nd Bn. 7th Regt. Madras Native Infantry | 26th December 1820 |
| | 80th Carnatic Infantry | 2nd Bn. 2nd Regt. Madras Native Infantry | 26th December 1820 |
| | 81st Pioneers | 1st Bn. 11th Regt. Madras Native Infantry | 26th December 1820 |
| | 82nd Punjabis | 2nd Bn. 11th Regt. Madras Native Infantry | 26th December 1820 |
| | 83rd Wallajahbad L.I. | 1st Bn. 12th Regt. Madras Native Infantry | 26th December 1820 |
| | 84th Punjabis | 2nd Bn. 12th Regt. Madras Native Infantry | 26th December 1820 |
| | 103rd Mahratta L.I. | 1st Bn. 2nd Regt. Bombay Native Infantry | 20th May 1823 |
| | 104th Wellesley's Rifles | 2nd Bn. 2nd Regt. Bombay Native Infantry | 20th May 1823 |
| | 105th Mahratta L.I. | 1st Bn. 3rd Regt. Bombay Native Infantry | 20th May 1823 |
| | 107th Pioneers | 1st Bn. 4th Regt. Bombay Native Infantry | 20th May 1823 |
| | 109th Infantry | 1st Bn. 5th Regt. Bombay Native Infantry | 20th May 1823 |

(a) Disbanded 1821. Reformed 1858 Honour regranted 27th November 1912.

(b) Elephant caparisoned with SERINGAPATAM 16.4.1807. Regranted 18.3.1874.

| | | | |
|---|---|---|---|
| **ARABIA** | 1st Bn. The York & Lancaster Regt. | 65th (2nd Yorkshire, North Riding) Regt. of Foot | 24th February 1823 |
| **BOURBON** | 2nd Bn. The Welsh Regt. | 69th (South Lincolnshire) Regt. of Foot | 13th June 1826 |
| | 2nd Bn. The Royal Irish Rifles | 86th (Leinster) Regt. of Foot | 3rd October 1823 |
| | | INDIAN ARMY | |
| | 66th Punjabis | 1st Bn. 6th Regt. Madras Native Infantry | Madras GO 1838 |
| | 84th Punjabis | 2nd Bn. 12th Regt. Madras Native Infantry | Madras GO 1838 |
| | 104th Wellesley's Rifles | 2nd Bn. 2nd Regt. Bombay Native Infantry | Bombay GO 167/1855 |
| **INDIA** | The Suffolk Regt. | 12th (East Suffolk) Regt. of Foot (For services 1797 to 1809) | 11th June 1836 |
| | 2nd Bn. The York & Lancaster Regt. | 84th Regt. of Foot (For services 1796 to 1819) | 12th December 1826 |
| | 2nd Bn. The Royal Irish Rifles | (c)86th Regt. of Foot (For services 1799 to 1819) | 3rd October 1823 |
| | 2nd Bn. The Welsh Regt. | 69th (South Lincolnshire) Regt. of Foot (For services 1805 to 1825) | 13th April 1826 |

(c) Became 86th (Royal County Down) Regt. of Foot in 1812.

| | | | |
|---|---|---|---|
| **INDIA (With Royal Tiger)** | The West Yorkshire Regt. | 14th (Bedfordshire) Regt. of Foot (For services 1807 to 1831) | 1st November 1838 |
| | 1st Bn. The York & Lancaster Regt. | 65th (2nd Yorkshire, North Riding) Regt. of Foot (For services 1802 to 1822) | 24th February 1823 |
| | 2nd Bn. The Hampshire Regt. | 67th (South Hampshire) Regt. of Foot (For services 1805 to 1826) | 20th December 1826 |
| | 1st Bn. The Gordon Highlanders | 75th (Highland) Regt. of Foot (For services 1791 to 1806) | 6th July 1807 |

| Battle Honour | Present Unit | Unit at Time of Award | Date of Award |
|---|---|---|---|
| **HINDOOSTAN** | 8th Hussars | 8th (The King's Royal Irish) Regt. of Light Dragoons (For services 1802 to 1822) | 14th March 1825 |
| | 2nd Bn. The Worcestershire Regt. | 36th (Herefordshire) Regt. of Foot (For services 2nd Bn. Sept. 1790 to Sept. 1793) | 16th October 1835 |
| | 2nd Bn. Oxf & Bucks Lt. Infty. | 52nd (Oxfordshire) Regt. of Foot (For services Sept. 1790 to Sept. 1793) | 20th February 1821 |
| | 1st Bn. The Highland L.I. | 71st (Highland) Regt. of Foot (For services 1780 to 1798) | 23rd May 1821 |
| | 1st Bn. Seaforth Highlanders | 72nd (Highland) Regt. of Foot | 10th January 1837 |
| **HINDOOSTAN (With Royal Tiger)** | The Leicestershire Regt. | 17th (Leicestershire) Regt. of Foot (For services 1804 to 1823) | 18th May 1825 |
| **HINDOOSTAN (With Elephant & Howdah)** | 2nd Bn. The Duke of Wellington's Regt. | 76th Regt. of Foot<br>(Elephant added) | 20th October 1806<br>7th February 1807 |
| **ALLY GHUR** | 2nd Bn. The Duke of Wellington's Regt. | 76th Regt. of Foot | 1st October 1886 |
| **DELHI 1803** | 2nd Bn. The Duke of Wellington's Regt. | 76th Regt. of Foot | 1st October 1886 |
| | | INDIAN ARMY | |
| | 2nd Q.V.O. Rajput Light Infantry | 2nd Bn. 15th Regt. Bengal Native Infantry | 23rd February 1829 |
| **ASSAYE (With Elephant)** | 19th Hussars | 19th Regt. of Light Dragoons | 16th April 1807 |
| | 2nd Bn. Highland L.I. | 74th (Highland) Regt. of Foot | 16th April 1807 |
| | 2nd Bn. Seaforth Highlanders | 78th (Highland) Regt. of Foot (or Ross-shire Buffs) | 16th April 1807 |
| | | INDIAN ARMY | |
| | 2nd Q.V.O. Sappers & Miners | Madras Pioneers | 30th October 1803 |
| | 62nd Punjabis | 1st Bn. 2nd Regt. Madras Native Infantry | 30th October 1803 |
| | 64th Pioneers | 1st Bn. 4th Regt. Madras Native Infantry | 30th October 1803 |
| | 84th Punjabis | 2nd Bn. 12th Regt. Madras Native Infantry | 30th October 1803 |

| | | | |
|---|---|---|---|
| **LESWARREE** | 8th Hussars | 8th (The King's Royal Irish) Regt. of (Light) Dragoons | 14th March 1825 |
| | 2nd Bn. The Duke of Wellington's Regt. | 76th Regt. of Foot | 1st October 1886 |
| | | INDIAN ARMY | |
| | 1st Brahmans | 2nd Bn. 9th Regt. Bengal Native Infantry | 23rd February 1829 |
| | 2nd Q.V.O. Rajput Light Infantry | 2nd Bn. 15th Regt. Bengal Native Infantry | 23rd February 1829 |
| | 4th P.A.V. Rajputs | 2nd Bn. 16th Regt. Bengal Native Infantry | 23rd February 1829 |
| **DEIG** | 2nd Bn. The Duke of Wellington's Regt. | 76th Regt. of Foot | 1st October 1886 |
| | 1st Bn. The Royal Munster Fusiliers | H.E.I.C. 1st Bengal (European) Regt. | 23rd February 1829 |
| | | INDIAN ARMY | |
| | 2nd Q.V.O. Rajput Light Infantry | 2nd Bn. 15th Regt. Bengal Native Infantry | 23rd February 1829 |
| **COCHIN** | 93rd Burma Infantry | (a)17th Regt. Madras Native Infantry | Madras GO 4th February 1840 |

(a) In 1824 renumbered 33rd Madras N.I. This distinction is not shown in Army Lists from 1905-1929. Now borne by 8th Punjab Regiment.

| | | | |
|---|---|---|---|
| **JAVA** | The West Yorkshire Regt. | 14th (Buckinghamshire) Regt. of Foot | 28th May 1818 |
| | 2nd Bn. The East Lancashire Regt. | 59th (2nd Nottinghamshire) Regt. of Foot | 28th May 1818 |
| | 2nd Bn. The Welsh Regt. | 69th (South Lincolnshire) Regt. of Foot | 28th May 1818 |
| | 2nd Bn. Seaforth Highlanders | 78th (Highland) Regt. of Foot (Ross-shire Buffs) | 28th May 1818 |
| | 2nd Bn. The Royal Irish Fusiliers | 89th Regt. of Foot | 28th May 1818 |
| | | INDIAN ARMY | |
| | Governor General's Body Guard | Governor General's Body Guard | GGO 43/1829 |
| | 2nd Q.V.O. Sappers & Miners | Madras Pioneers | 20th December 1820 |
| **KIRKEE** | 2nd Bn. The Royal Dublin Fusiliers | H.E.I.C. 1st Bombay (European) Regt. | Bombay GO 20th May 1823 |
| | | INDIAN ARMY | |
| | 102nd K.E.O. Grenadiers | 2nd Bn. 1st Regt. Bombay Native Infantry | Bombay GO 20th May 1823 |
| | 112th Infantry | 2nd Bn. 6th Regt. Bombay Native Infantry | Bombay GO 20th May 1823 |
| | 113th Infantry | 1st Bn. 7th Regt. Bombay Native Infantry | Bombay GO 20th May 1823 |
| | 123rd Outram's Rifles | Dapuri Brigade, Poona Auxiliary Force | Bombay GO 20th May 1823 |
| **SEETABULDEE** | Governor's Body Guard, Madras | Governor's Body Guard | 27th September 1819 |
| | 61st K.G.O Pioneers | (b)1st Bn. 24th Regt. Madras Native Infantry | 27th September 1819 |

(b) Restored to original position as 1st/1st Madras N.I. in 1818.

| | | | |
|---|---|---|---|
| **NAGPORE** | The Royal Scots | 1st (or Royal) Regt. of Foot | 26th February 1823 |
| | | INDIAN ARMY | |
| | 2nd Q.V.O. Sappers & Miners | Madras Pioneers | 10th March 1826 |
| | 6th Jat Light Infantry | 1st Bn. 22nd Regt. Bengal Native Infantry | GGO 592/1882 |
| | 61st K.G.O. Pioneers | 1st Bn. 24th Regt. Madras Native Infantry | 10th March 1826 |
| | 62nd Punjabis | 1st Bn. 2nd Regt. Madras Native Infantry | 10th March 1826 |
| | 81st Pioneers | 1st Bn. 11th Regt. Madras Native Infantry | 10th March 1826 |
| | 83rd Wallajahbad L.I. | 1st Bn. 12th Reg. Madras Native Infantry (Wallajahbad L.I.) | 10th March 1826 |
| | 86th Carnatic Infantry | 2nd Bn. 13th Regt. Madras Native Infantry | 10th March 1826 |
| | 88th Carnatic Infantry | 2nd Bn. 14th Regt. Madras Native Infantry | 10th March 1826 |
| | 97th Deccan Infantry | 3rd Bn. Berar Infantry | 10th March 1826 |
| **MAHEIDPOOR** | The Royal Scots | 1st (or Royal Scots) Regt. of Foot | 26th February 1823 |
| | 1st Bn. The Royal Dublin Fusiliers | H.E.I.C. Madras (European) Regt. | 29th September 1819 |
| | | INDIAN ARMY | |
| | 28th Light Cavalry | 3rd Regt. Madras Native Cavalry | 29th September 1819 |
| | 2nd Q.V.O. Sappers & Miners | Madras Pioneers | 29th September 1819 |
| | 63rd Palamcottah Light Infantry | 1st Bn. 3rd Regt. Madras Native Infantry or Palamcottah L.I. | 29th September 1819 |
| | 74th Punjabis | 2nd Bn. 6th Regt. Madras Native Infantry | 29th September 1819 |
| | 87th Punjabis | 1st Bn. 14th Regt. Madras Native Infantry | 29th September 1819 |
| | 88th Carnatic Infantry | 2nd Bn. 14th Regt. Madras Native Infantry | 29th September 1819 |
| | 91st Punjabis (Light Infantry) | 1st Bn. 16th Regt. Madras Native Infantry or Trichinopoly L.I. | 29th September 1819 |
| | 94th Russell's Infantry | 1st Bn. Russell's Brigade | c.1864 |
| | 95th Russell's Infantry | 2nd Bn. Russell's Brigade | c.1864 |
| **CORYGAUM** | 34th P.A.V.O. Poona Horse | Poona Auxiliary Horse | 29th September 1819 |
| | 102nd K.E.O. Grenadiers | 2nd Bn. 1st or Grenadier Regt. Bombay Native Infantry | 7th February 1818 |

| | | | |
|---|---|---|---|
| **NOWAH** | 94th Russell's Infantry | 1st Bn. Russell's Brigade | 1864 |
| | 95th Russell's Infantry | 2nd Bn. Russell's Brigade | 1864 |
| | 96th Berar Infantry | 2nd Bn. Berar Infantry | 1864 |
| **PERSIAN GULF** | 121st Pioneers | 1st (or Marine) Bn. 11th Regt. Bombay Native Infantry | c.1854 |
| **BENI BOO ALI** | 2nd Bn. The Royal Dublin Fusiliers | H.E.I.C. 1st Bombay European Regt. | Bombay GO 11th February 1831 |
| | | INDIAN ARMY | |
| | 3rd Sappers & Miners | Bombay Engineer Company | Bombay GO 22nd September 1877 |
| | 103rd Mahratta Light Infantry | 1st Bn. 2nd Regt. Bombay Native Infantry | Bombay GO 11th February 1831 |
| | 104th Wellesley's Rifles | 2nd Bn. 2nd Regt. Bombay Native Infantry | Bombay GO 11th February 1831 |
| | 105th Mahratta Light Infantry | 1st Bn. 3rd Regt. Bombay Native Infantry | Bombay GO 11th February 1831 |
| | 107th Pioneers | 1st Bn. 4th Regt. Bombay Native Infantry | Bombay GO 11th February 1831 |
| | 113th Infantry | 1st Bn. 7th Regt. Bombay Native Infantry | Bombay GO 11th February 1831 |
| | 121st Pioneers | 1st (or Marine) Bn. 11th Regt. Bombay Native Infantry | Bombay GO 11th February 1831 |
| **BHURTPORE** | 11th Hussars | 11th Regt. of Light Dragoons | 6th December 1826 |
| | 16th Lancers | 16th (The Queen's) Regt. of Light Dragoons (Lancers) | 6th December 1826 |
| | The West Yorkshire Regt. | 14th (Buckinghamshire) Regt. of Foot | 6th December 1826 |
| | 2nd Bn. The East Lancashire Regt. | 59th (2nd Nottinghamshire) Regt. of Foot | 6th December 1826 |
| | 1st Bn. The Royal Munster Fusiliers | H.E.I.C. 1st Bengal (European) Regt. | GGO 85/1826 |
| | | INDIAN ARMY | |
| | 1st D.Y.O. Lancers (Skinner's Horse) | 1st Regt. of Local Horse | GGO 85/1826 |
| | 1st K.G.O. Sappers & Miners | Corps of Bengal Sappers & Miners | GGO 58/1852 |
| | 1st Brahmans | 21st Regt. Bengal Native Infantry | GGO 85/1826 |
| | 2nd Q.V.O. Rajput Light Infantry | 31st Regt. Bengal Native Infantry | GGO 85/1826 |
| | 3rd Brahmans | 32nd Regt. Bengal Native Infantry | GGO 85/1826 |
| | 4th P.A.V. Rajputs | 33rd Regt. Bengal Native Infantry | GGO 85/1826 |
| | 1st K.G.O. Gurkha Rifles (The Malaun Regt.) | 4th Local 1st Nasiri Battalion | GGO 580/1874 |

| | | | |
|---|---|---|---|
| **BHURTPORE (Cont.)** | 2nd K.E.O. Gurkha Rifles (The Sirmoor Rifles) | 6th (or Sirmoor) Local Battalion | GOCC 25th November 1859 |
| | 9th Gurkha Rifles | 63rd Regt. Bengal Native Infantry | GGO 85/1826 |
| **ADEN** | 2nd Bn. The Royal Dublin Fusiliers | H.E.I.C. 1st Bombay European Regt. | c.1841 |
| | 121st Pioneers | The Marine Battalion | c.1841 |
| | 124th D.C.O. Baluchistan Infantry | 24th Regt. Bombay Native Infantry | c.1841 |
| **AVA** | The Royal Scots | 2nd Bn. 1st (or Royal) Regt. of Foot | 6th December 1826 |
| | The Somerset L.I. | 13th (1st Somersetshire) Regt. of Foot (Light Infantry) | 6th December 1826 |
| | 1st Bn. The South Staffordshire Regt. | 38th (1st Staffordshire) Regt. of Foot | 6th December 1826 |
| | 1st Bn. The Welsh Regt. | 41st Regt. of Foot | 6th December 1826 |
| | 1st Bn. The Essex Regt. | 44th (East Essex) Regt. of Foot | 6th December 1826 |
| | 1st Bn. The Sherwood Foresters | 45th (Nottinghamshire) Regt. of Foot | 6th December 1826 |
| | 2nd Bn. The Dorsetshire Regt. | 54th (West Norfolk) Regt. of Foot | 6th December 1826 |
| | 1st Bn. The Loyal North Lancashire Regt. | 47th (Lancashire) Regt. of Foot | 6th December 1826 |
| | 1st Bn. The Royal Irish Fusiliers | 87th (Prince of Wales's Own Irish) Regt. of Foot | 6th December 1826 |
| | 2nd Bn. The Royal Irish Fusiliers | 89th Regt. of Foot | 6th December 1826 |
| | 1st Bn. The Royal Dublin Fusiliers | H.E.I.C. Madras European Regt. | 12th March 1841 |
| | | INDIAN ARMY | |
| | Governor General's Body Guard | Governor General's Body Guard | GGO 84/1826 |
| | 26th K.G.O. Light Cavalry | 1st Regt. Madras Light Cavalry | 22nd April 1826 |
| | 2nd Q.V.O. Sappers & Miners | Madras Pioneers | 22nd April 1826 |
| | 61st K.G.O. Pioneers | 1st Regt. Madras Native Infantry | 22nd April 1826 |
| | 63rd Palamcottah L.I. | 3rd Regt. Madras Native Infantry, Palamcottah L.I. | 22nd April 1826 |
| | 67th Punjabis | 7th Regt. Madras Native Infantry | 22nd April 1826 |
| | 69th Punjabis | 9th Regt. Madras Native Infantry | 22nd April 1826 |
| | 72nd Punjabis | 12th Regt. Madras Native Infantry | 22nd April 1826 |
| | 76th Punjabis | 16th Regt. Madras Native Infantry | 22nd April 1826 |
| | 82nd Punjabis | 22nd Regt. Madras Native Infantry | 22nd April 1826 |
| | 86th Carnatic Infantry | 26th Regt. Madras Native Infantry | 22nd April 1826 |
| | 88th Carnatic Infantry | 28th Regt. Madras Native Infantry | 22nd April 1826 |
| | 90th Punjabis | 30th Regt. Madras Native Infantry | 22nd April 1826 |
| | 92nd Punjabis | 32nd Regt. Madras Native Infantry | 22nd April 1826 |

| | | | |
|---|---|---|---|
| **KEMMENDINE** | 86th Carnatic Infantry | 26th Regt. Madras Native Infantry | 21st January 1825 |
| **ARRACAN** | 2nd Lancers | 2nd Regt. of Local Horse (Gardner's) | GGO 22nd April 1826 |
| | 5th Light Infantry | 42nd Regt. Bengal Native Infantry | GGO 22nd April 1826 |
| **BURMAH** | 121st Pioneers | The Marine Battalion | c.1854 |
| **GHUZNEE 1839** | 4th Hussars | 4th (The Queen's Own) Regt. of (Light) Dragoons | 18th July 1840 |
| **(Date added A.O. 208/1907)** | 16th Lancers | 16th (The Queen's) Regt. of (Light) Dragoons | 18th July 1840 |
| | The Queen's (Royal West Surrey Regt.) | 2nd (The Queen's Royal) Regt. of Foot | 18th July 1840 |
| | The Somerset L.I. | 13th (1st Somersetshire) Regt. of Foot (Light Infantry) | 18th July 1840 |
| | The Leicestershire Regt. | 17th (Leicestershire) Regt. of Foot | 18th July 1840 |
| | 1st Bn. The Royal Munster Fusiliers | H.E.I.C. 1st Bengal European Regt. (Light Infantry) | 19th November 1839 |
| | | INDIAN ARMY | |
| | 3rd Skinner's Horse | 4th Regt. of Local Horse | GOGG 19th November 1839 |
| | 31st D.C.O. Lancers | 1st Regt. Bombay Light Cavalry | GOGG 19th November 1839 |
| | 34th P.A.V.O. Poona Horse | Poona Auxiliary Horse | GOGG 19th November 1839 |
| | 3rd Sappers & Miners | Corps of Bombay Sappers & Miners | GOGG 19th November 1839 |
| | 119th Infantry (The Mooltan Regt.) | 19th Regt. Bombay Native Infantry | GOGG 19th November 1839 |
| **KHELAT** | The Queen's (Royal West Surrey Regt.) | 2nd (The Queen's Royal) Regt. of Foot | 18th July 1840 |
| | The Leicestershire Regt. | 17th (Leicestershire) Regt. of Foot | 18th July 1840 |
| | | INDIAN ARMY | |
| | 3rd Skinners Horse | 4th Regt. of Local Horse | 15th February 1840 |
| | 3rd Sappers & Miners | Corps of Bombay Sappers & Miners | 15th February 1840 |
| | 2nd Q.V.O. Rajput Light Infantry | 31st Regt. Bengal Native Infantry | 15th February 1840 |
| **KAHUN** | 105th Mahratta Light Infantry | 5th Regt. Bombay Native Infantry | GO 1841 |
| **JELLALABAD (With Mural Crown)** | The Somerset L.I. | 13th (1st Somersetshire) Regt. of Foot (Light Infantry) | 20th August 1842 |

| Battle Honour | Present Unit | Unit at time of award | Date of award |
|---|---|---|---|
| **KELAT I GHILZIE (With Mural Crown 'Invicta')** | 12th Pioneers | The Regiment of Kelat-i-Ghilzie (Formerly 3rd Infantry, Shah Shuja's Contingent) | GOGG 4th October 1842 |
| **CANDAHAR 1842 (Date added A.O. 208/1907)** | 1st Bn. P.W.V. (South Lancashire Regt.) | 40th (2nd Somersetshire) Regt. of Foot | 20th March 1844 |
| | 1st Bn. The Welsh Regt. | 41st (Welsh) Regt. of Foot | 28th July 1843 |
| | | INDIAN ARMY | |
| | 1st D.Y.O. Lancers (Skinner's Horse) | 1st Regt. Bengal Irregular Cavalry | GOGG 4th October 1842 |
| | 34th P.A.V.O. Poona Horse | Poona Auxiliary Horse | GOGG 4th October 1842 |
| | 5th Light Infantry | *42nd Regt. Bengal Native Infantry | GOGG 4th October 1842 |
| | 6th Jat Light Infantry | *43rd Regt. Bengal Native Infantry | GOGG 4th October 1842 |
| | 12th Pioneers | The Regiment of Kelat-i-Ghilzie | GOGG 4th October 1842 |
| | * Made Light Infantry 4th October 1843. | | |
| **GHUZNEE 1842 (Date added A.O. 208/1907)** | 1st Bn. P.W.V. (South Lancashire Regt.) | 40th (2nd Somersetshire) Regt. of Foot | 20th March 1844 |
| | 1st Bn. The Welsh Regt. | 41st (Welsh) Regt. of Foot | 22nd June 1844 |
| | | INDIAN ARMY | |
| | 33rd Q.V.O. Light Cavalry | 3rd Regt. Bombay Light Cavalry | GOGG 4th October 1842 |
| | 5th Light Infantry | 42nd Regt. Bengal Native Infantry | GOGG 4th October 1842 |
| | 6th Jat Light Infantry | 43rd Regt. Bengal Native Infantry | GOGG 4th October 1842 |
| | 12th Pioneers | The Regiment of Kelat-i-Ghilzie | GOGG 4th October 1842 |
| **CABOOL 1842** | 3rd Hussars | 3rd (King's Own) Regt. of Light Dragoons | 22nd June 1844 |
| | The Norfolk Regt. | 9th (East Norfolk) Regt. of Foot | 22nd June 1844 |
| | The Somerset L.I. | 13th (1st Somersetshire) Regt. of Foot (Light Infantry) | 22nd June 1844 |
| | 1st Bn. The East Surrey Regt. | 31st (Huntingdonshire) Regt. of Foot | 22nd June 1844 |
| | 1st Bn. P.W.V. (South Lancashire Regt.) | 40th (2nd Somersetshire) Regt. of Foot | 20th March 1844 |
| | 1st Bn. The Welsh Regt. | 41st (Welsh) Regt. of Foot | 22nd June 1844 |
| | | INDIAN ARMY | |
| | 33rd Q.V.O. Light Cavalry | 3rd Regt. Bombay Light Cavalry | GOGG 4th October 1842 |
| | 1st K.G.O. Sappers & Miners | Corps of Bengal Sappers & Miners | GOGG 4th October 1842 |
| | 4th P.A.V. Rajputs | 33rd Regt. Bengal Native Infantry | GOGG 4th October 1842 |
| | 5th Light Infantry | 42nd Regt. Bengal Native Infantry | GOGG 4th October 1842 |

| | | | |
|---|---|---|---|
| **CABOOL 1842** | 6th Jat Light Infantry | 43rd Regt. Bengal Native Infantry | GOGG 4th October 1842 |
| **(Cont.)** | 12th Pioneers | The Regiment of Kelat-i-Ghilzie | GOGG 4th October 1842 |
| ***AFFGHANISTAN 1839** | 4th Hussars | 4th (The Queen's Own) Regt. of (Light) Dragoons | 18th July 1840 |
| **(Date added A.O. 208/1914)** | 16th Lancers | 16th (The Queen's) Regt. of (Light) Dragoons | 18th July 1840 |
| | The Queen's (Royal West Surrey Regt.) | 2nd (The Queen's Royal) Regt. of Foot | 18th July 1840 |
| | The Somerset L.I. | 13th (1st Somersetshire) Regt. of Foot (Light Infantry) | 18th July 1840 |
| | The Leicestershire Regt. | 17th (Leicestershire) Regt. of Foot | 18th July 1840 |
| | 1st Bn. The Royal Munster Fusiliers | H.E.I.C. 1st Bengal European Regt. (Light Infantry) | 19th November 1842 |
| | | INDIAN ARMY | |
| | 3rd Skinner's Horse | 4th Regt. of Local Horse | 19th November 1842 |
| | 31st D.C.O. Lancers | 1st Regt. Bombay Light Cavalry | 19th November 1842 |
| | 34th P.A.V.O. Poona Horse | Poona Auxiliary Horse | 19th November 1842 |
| | 3rd Sappers & Miners | Corps of Bombay Sappers & Miners | 19th November 1842 |
| | 2nd Q.V.O. Rajput Light Infantry | 31st Regt. Bengal Native Infantry | 19th November 1842 |
| | 5th Light Infantry | 42nd Regt. Bengal Native Infantry | 19th November 1842 |
| | 6th Jat Light Infantry | 43rd Regt. Bengal Native Infantry | 19th November 1842 |
| | 119th Infantry (The Mooltan Regt.) | 19th Regt. Bombay Native Infantry | 19th November 1842 |

* The distinction for the Indian Army is AFGHANISTAN in some cases.

| | | | |
|---|---|---|---|
| **CUTCHEE** | 35th Scinde Horse | 1st Regt. Scinde Irregular Horse | 1855 |
| | 36th Jacob's Horse | 2nd Regt. Scinde Irregular Horse | 1855 |
| **CHINA** | The Royal Irish Regiment | 18th (Royal Irish) Regt. of Foot | 12th January 1843 |
| **(With Dragon)** | 1st Bn. The Cameronians | 26th (Cameronian) Regt. of Foot | 12th January 1843 |
| | 2nd Bn. The Border Regt. | 55th (Westmoreland) Regt. of Foot | 12th January 1843 |
| | 1st Bn. The Royal Berkshire Regt. | 49th (Princess Charlotte of Wales's or Hertfordshire) Regt. of Foot | 12th January 1843 |
| | 2nd Bn. The North Staffordshire Regt. | 98th Regt. of Foot | 12th January 1843 |
| | | INDIAN ARMY | |
| | 2nd Q.V.O. Sappers & Miners | Corps of Madras Sappers & Miners | 30th October 1843 |
| | 62nd Punjabis | 2nd Regt. Madras Native Infantry | 30th October 1843 |

| | | | |
|---|---|---|---|
| **CHINA (With Dragon) (Cont.)** | 66th Punjabis | 6th Regt. Madras Native Infantry | 30th October 1843 |
| | 74th Punjabis | 14th Regt. Madras Native Infantry | 30th October 1843 |
| **MEEANEE** | The Cheshire Regt. | 22nd (Cheshire) Regt. of Foot | 2nd July 1844 |
| | | INDIAN ARMY | |
| | 34th P.A.V.O. Poona Horse | Poona Auxiliary Horse | GGO 246/1843 |
| | 35th Scinde Horse | 1st Regt. Scinde Irregular Horse | GGO 246/1843 |
| | 36th Jacob's Horse | 2nd Regt. Scinde Irregular Horse | GGO 246/1843 |
| | 2nd Q.V.O. Sappers & Miners | Corps of Madras Sappers & Miners | GGO 246/1843 |
| | 112th Infantry | 12th Regt. Bombay Native Infantry | GGO 246/1843 |
| | 125th Napier's Rifles | 25th Regt. Bombay Native Infantry | GGO 246/1843 |
| **HYDERABAD** | The Cheshire Regt. | 22nd (Cheshire) Regt. of Foot | 2nd July 1844 |
| | | INDIAN ARMY | |
| | 33rd Q.V.O. Light Cavalry | 3rd Regt. Bombay Light Cavalry | GGO 246/1843 |
| | 34th P.A.V.O. Poona Horse | Poona Auxiliary Horse | GGO 246/1843 |
| | 35th Scinde Horse | 1st Regt. Scinde Irregular Horse | GGO 246/1843 |
| | 36th Jacob's Horse | 2nd Regt. Scinde Irregular Horse | GGO 246/1843 |
| | 2nd Q.V.O. Sappers & Miners | Corps of Madras Sappers & Miners | GGO 246/1843 |
| | The 101st Grenadiers | 1st or Grenadier Regt. Bombay Native Infantry | GGO 246/1843 |
| | 108th Infantry | 8th Regt. Bombay Native Infantry | GGO 246/1843 |
| | 112th Infantry | 12th Regt. Bombay Native Infantry | GGO 246/1843 |
| | 121st Pioneers | 21st Regt. Bombay Native Infantry (The Marine Battalion) | GGO 246/1843 |
| | 125th Napier's Rifles | 25th Regt. Bombay Native Infantry | GGO 246/1843 |
| **SCINDE** | The Cheshire Regt. | 22nd (Cheshire) Regt. of Foot | 18th August 1843 |
| **MAHARAJPORE** | 16th Lancers | 16th (The Queen's) Regt. of Light Dragoons (Lancers) | 22nd June 1844 |
| | 1st Bn. The Dorsetshire Regt. | 39th (Dorsetshire) Regt. of Foot | 22nd June 1844 |
| | 1st Bn. P.W.V. (South Lancashire Regt.) | 40th (2nd Somersetshire) Regt. of Foot | 22nd June 1844 |

| Battle | Present Title | Former Title | Date of Grant |
|---|---|---|---|
| **MAHARAJPORE (Cont.)** | | INDIAN ARMY | |
| | Governor General's Body Guard | Governor General's Body Guard | 4th January 1844 |
| | 3rd Skinner's Horse | 4th Regt. Bengal Irregular Cavalry | 4th January 1844 |
| | 2nd Q.V.O. Rajput Light Infantry | 31st Regt. Bengal Native Infantry | 4th January 1844 |
| | 6th Jat Light Infantry | 43rd Regt. Bengal Native (Light) Infantry | 4th January 1844 |
| | 12th Pioneers | The Regiment of Kelat-i-Ghilzie | 4th January 1844 |
| **PUNNIAR** | 9th Lancers | 9th (The Queen's) Regt. of Light Dragoons (Lancers) | 22nd June 1844 |
| | The Buffs (East Kent Regt.) | 3rd (East Kent) Regt. of Foot (The Buffs) | 22nd June 1844 |
| | 1st Bn. The Queen's Own (Royal West Kent Regt.) | 50th (The Queen's Own) Regt. of Foot | 22nd June 1844 |
| | | INDIAN ARMY | |
| | 6th K.E.O. Cavalry | 8th Regt. Bengal Irregular Cavalry | 4th January 1844 |
| **MOODKEE** | 3rd Hussars | 3rd (King's Own) Regt. of Light Dragoons | 8th June 1847 |
| | The Norfolk Regt. | 9th (East Norfolk) Regt. of Foot | 8th June 1847 |
| | 1st Bn. The East Surrey Regt. | 31st (Huntingdonshire) Regt. of Foot | 8th June 1847 |
| | 2nd Bn. The South Staffordshire Regt. | 80th (Staffordshire Volunteers) Regt. of Foot | 8th June 1847 |
| | 1st Bn. The Queen's Own (Royal West Kent Regt.) | 50th (The Queen's Own) Regt. of Foot | 8th June 1847 |
| | | INDIAN ARMY | |
| | Governor General's Body Guard | Governor General's Body Guard | 12th December 1846 |
| | 3rd Skinner's Horse | 4th Regt. Bengal Irregular Cavalry | 12th December 1846 |
| | 6th K.E.O. Cavalry | 8th Regt. Bengal Irregular Cavalry | 12th December 1846 |
| | 5th Light Infantry | 42nd Regt. Bengal Native (Light) Infantry | 12th December 1846 |
| | 7th D.C.O. Rajputs | 47th Regt. Bengal Native Infantry | 12th December 1846 |
| **FEROZESHAH** | 3rd Hussars | 3rd (King's Own) Regt. of Light Dragoons | 8th June 1847 |
| | The Norfolk Regt. | 9th (East Norfolk) Regt. of Foot | 8th June 1847 |
| | 1st Bn. The Worcestershire Regt. | 29th (Worcestershire) Regt. of Foot | 8th June 1847 |
| | 1st Bn. The East Surrey Regt. | 31st (Huntingdonshire) Regt. of Foot | 8th June 1847 |
| | 2nd Bn. The South Staffordshire Regt. | 80th (Staffordshire Volunteers) Regt. of Foot | 8th June 1847 |
| | 1st Bn. The Queen's Own (Royal West Kent Regt.) | 50th (The Queen's Own) Regt. of Foot | 8th June 1847 |

| Battle | Present Unit | Unit at the Time | Date of Award |
|---|---|---|---|
| **FEROZESHAH (Cont.)** | 1st Bn. The Wiltshire Regt. | 62nd (Wiltshire) Regt. of Foot | 8th June 1847 |
| | 1st Bn. The Royal Munster Fusiliers | H.E.I.C. 1st Bengal European Regt. (Light Infantry) | 12th December 1846 |
| | | INDIAN ARMY | |
| | Governor General's Body Guard | Governor General's Body Guard | 12th December 1846 |
| | 3rd Skinner's Horse | 4th Regt. Bengal Irregular Cavalry | 12th December 1846 |
| | 6th K.E.O. Cavalry | 8th Regt. Bengal Irregular Cavalry | 12th December 1846 |
| | 1st K.G.O. Sappers & Miners | Corps of Bengal Sappers & Miners | 12th December 1846 |
| | 4th P.A.V. Rajputs | 33rd Regt. Bengal Native Infantry | 12th December 1846 |
| | 5th Light Infantry | 42nd Regt. Bengal Native (Light) Infantry | 12th December 1846 |
| | 7th D.C.O. Rajputs | 47th Regt. Bengal Native Infantry | 12th December 1846 |
| **ALIWAL** | 16th Lancers | 16th (The Queen's) Light Dragoons (Lancers) | 8th June 1847 |
| | 1st Bn. The East Surrey Regt. | 31st (Huntingdonshire) Regt. of Foot | 8th June 1847 |
| | 1st Bn. The Queen's Own (Royal West Kent Regt.) | 50th (The Queen's Own) Regt. of Foot | 8th June 1847 |
| | 1st Bn. The King's Shropshire L.I. | 53rd (Shropshire) Regt. of Foot | 8th June 1847 |
| | | INDIAN ARMY | |
| | Governor General's Body Guard | Governor General's Body Guard | GGO 12th August 1846 |
| | 3rd Skinner's Horse | 4th Regt. Bengal Irregular Cavalry | GGO 12th August 1846 |
| | 7th D.C.O. Rajputs | 47th Regt. Bengal Native Infantry | GGO 12th August 1846 |
| | 13th Rajputs | The Shekhawati Brigade | GGO 12th August 1846 |
| | 1st K.G.O. Gurkha Rifles (The Malaun Regt.) | 4th or Nasiri Local Battalion | GGO 12th August 1846 |
| | 2nd K.E.O. Gurkha Rifles (The Sirmoor Rifles) | 6th or Sirmoor Local Battalion | GGO 12th August 1846 |
| **SOBRAON** | 3rd Hussars | 3rd (King's Own) Regt. of Light Dragoons | 8th June 1847 |
| | 9th Lancers | 9th (Queen's Royal) Regt. of Light Dragoons (Lancers) | 8th June 1847 |
| | 16th Lancers | 16th (The Queen's) Light Dragoons (Lancers) | 8th June 1847 |
| | The Norfolk Regt. | 9th (East Norfolk) Regt. of Foot | 8th June 1847 |
| | The Lincolnshire Regt. | 10th (North Lincolnshire) Regt. of Foot | 8th June 1847 |
| | 1st Bn. The Worcestershire Regt. | 29th (Worcestershire) Regt. of Foot | 8th June 1847 |

| | | | |
|---|---|---|---|
| **SOBRAON (Cont.)** | 1st Bn. The East Surrey Regt. | 31st (Huntingdonshire) Regt. of Foot | 8th June 1847 |
| | 2nd Bn. The South Staffordshire Regt. | 80th (Staffordshire Volunteers) Regt. of Foot | 8th June 1847 |
| | 1st Bn. The Queen's Own (Royal West Kent Regt.) | 50th (The Queen's Own) Regt. of Foot | 8th June 1847 |
| | 1st Bn. The King's Shropshire L.I. | 53rd (Shropshire) Regt. of Foot | 8th June 1847 |
| | 1st Bn. The Wiltshire Regt. | 62nd (Wiltshire) Regt. of Foot | 8th June 1847 |
| | 1st Bn. The Royal Munster Fusiliers | H.E.I.C. 1st Bengal European Regt. (Light Infantry) | GGO 12th August 1846 |
| | | INDIAN ARMY | |
| | Governor General's Body Guard | Governor General's Body Guard | GGO 12th August 1846 |
| | 2nd Lancers | 2nd Regt. Bengal Irregular Cavalry | GGO 12th August 1846 |
| | 6th K.E.O. Cavalry | 8th Regt. Bengal Irregular Cavalry | GGO 12th August 1846 |
| | 1st K.G.O. Sappers & Miners | Corps of Bengal Sappers & Miners | GGO 12th August 1846 |
| | 4th P.A.V. Rajputs | 33rd Regt. Bengal Native Infantry | GGO 12th August 1846 |
| | 5th Light Infantry | 42nd Regt. Bengal Native (Light) Infantry | GGO 12th August 1846 |
| | 6th Jat Light Infantry | 43rd Regt. Bengal Native (Light) Infantry | GGO 12th August 1846 |
| | 7th D.C.O. Rajputs | 47th Regt. Bengal Native Infantry | GGO 12th August 1846 |
| | 8th Rajputs | 59th Regt. Bengal Native Infantry | GGO 12th August 1846 |
| | 1st K.G.O. Gurkha Rifles (The Malaun Regt.) | 4th or Nasiri Local Battalion | GGO 12th August 1846 |
| | 2nd K.E.O. Gurkha Rifles (The Sirmoor Rifles) | 6th or Sirmoor Local Battalion | GGO 12th August 1846 |
| | 9th Gurkha Rifles | 63rd Regt. Bengal Native Infantry | GGO 12th August 1846 |
| **MOOLTAN** | The Lincolnshire Regt. | 10th (North Lincolnshire) Regt. of Foot | 14th December 1852 |
| | 1st Bn. The Duke of Cornwall's L.I. | 32nd (Cornwall) Regt. of Foot | 14th December 1852 |
| | The King's Royal Rifle Corps | 1st Bn. 60th (The King's Royal Rifle Corps) | 14th December 1852 |
| | 2nd Bn. The Royal Dublin Fusiliers | H.E.I.C. 1st Bombay (European) Fusiliers | 7th October 1853 |
| | | INDIAN ARMY | |
| | 5th Cavalry | 7th Regt. Bengal Irregular Cavalry | 7th October 1853 |
| | 31st D.C.O. Lancers | 1st Regt. Bombay Light Cavalry (Lancers) | 7th October 1853 |
| | 35th Scinde Horse | 1st Regt. Scinde Irregular Horse | 7th October 1853 |
| | 36th Jacob's Horse | 2nd Regt. Scinde Irregular Horse | 7th October 1853 |

| | | | |
|---|---|---|---|
| **MOOLTAN (Cont.)** | Q.V.O. Corps of Guides (F.F.) | Corps of Guides | 7th October 1853 |
| | 25th Mountain Battery | 1st Co. 4th Battalion, Bombay Foot Artillery | 7th October 1853 |
| | 1st K.G.O. Sappers & Miners | Corps of Bengal Sappers & Miners | 7th October 1853 |
| | 3rd Sappers & Miners | Corps of Bombay Sappers & Miners | 7th October 1853 |
| | 103rd Mahratta Light Infantry | 3rd Regt. Bombay Native Infantry | 7th October 1853 |
| | 104th Wellesley's Rifles | 4th Regt. Bombay Native Infantry (or Rifle Corps) | 7th October 1853 |
| | 109th Infantry | 9th Regt. Bombay Native Infantry | 7th October 1853 |
| | 119th Infantry (The Mooltan Regt.) | 19th Regt. Bombay Native Infantry | 7th October 1853 |
| **CHILLIANWALLAH** | 3rd Hussars | 3rd (King's Own) Regt. of Light Dragoons | 14th December 1852 |
| | 9th Lancers | 9th (Queen's Royal) Regt. of Light Dragoons (Lancers) | 14th December 1852 |
| | 14th Hussars | 14th (The King's) Regt. of Light Dragoons | 14th December 1852 |
| | The South Wales Borderers | 24th (2nd Warwickshire) Regt. of Foot | 14th December 1852 |
| | 2nd Bn. The Gloucestershire Regt. | 61st (South Gloucestershire) Regt. of Foot | 14th December 1852 |
| | 1st Bn. The Worcestershire Regt. | 29th (Worcestershire) Regt. of Foot | 14th December 1852 |
| | 2nd Bn. The Royal Munster Fusiliers | H.E.I.C. 2nd Bengal (European)Regt. | 7th October 1853 |
| | | INDIAN ARMY | |
| | 2nd Q.V.O. Rajput Light Infantry | 31st Regt. Bengal Native Infantry | 7th October 1853 |
| | 11th Rajputs | 70th Regt. Bengal Native Infantry | 7th October 1853 |
| **GOOJERAT** | 3rd Hussars | 3rd (King's Own) Regt. of Light Dragoons | 14th December 1852 |
| | 9th Lancers | 9th (Queen's Royal) Regt. of Light Dragoons (Lancers) | 14th December 1852 |
| | 14th Hussars | 14th (The King's) Regt. of Light Dragoons | 14th December 1852 |
| | The Lincolnshire Regt. | 10th (North Lincolnshire) Regt. of Foot | 14th December 1852 |
| | The South Wales Borderers | 24th (2nd Warwickshire) Regt. of Foot | 14th December 1852 |
| | 2nd Bn. The Gloucestershire Regt. | 61st (South Gloucestershire) Regt. of Foot | 14th December 1852 |
| | 1st Bn. The Worcestershire Regt. | 29th (Worcestershire) Regt. of Foot | 14th December 1852 |
| | 1st Bn. The Duke of Cornwall's L.I. | 32nd (Cornwall) Regt. of Foot | 14th December 1852 |
| | 1st Bn. The King's Shropshire L.I. | 53rd (Shropshire) Regt. of Foot | 14th December 1852 |
| | The King's Royal Rifle Corps | 1st Bn. 60th (The King's Royal Rifle Corps) | 14th December 1852 |
| | 2nd Bn. The Royal Munster Fusiliers | H.E.I.C. 2nd Bengal (European) Fusiliers | 7th October 1853 |
| | 2nd Bn. The Royal Dublin Fusiliers | H.E.I.C. 1st Bombay (European) Fusiliers | 7th October 1853 |

| Battle | Present-day unit | Unit at the time | Date |
|---|---|---|---|
| **GOOJERAT (Cont.)** | | INDIAN ARMY | |
| | 35th Scinde Horse | 1st Regt. Scinde Irregular Horse | 7th October 1853 |
| | 36th Jacob's Horse | 2nd Regt. Scinde Irregular Horse | 7th October 1853 |
| | Q.V.O. Corps of Guides (F.F.) | Corps of Guides | 7th October 1853 |
| | 1st K.G.O. Sappers & Miners | Corps of Bengal Sappers & Miners | 7th October 1853 |
| | 3rd Sappers & Miners | Corps of Bombay Sappers & Miners | 7th October 1853 |
| | 2nd Q.V.O. Rajput Light Infantry | 31st Regt. Bengal Native Infantry | 7th October 1853 |
| | 11th Rajputs | 70th Regt. Bengal Native Infantry | 7th October 1853 |
| | 103rd Mahratta Light Infantry | 3rd Regt. Bombay Native Infantry | 7th October 1853 |
| | 119th Infantry (The Mooltan Regt.) | 19th Regt. Bombay Native Infantry | 7th October 1853 |
| **PUNJAUB** | 3rd Hussars | 3rd (King's Own) Regt. of Light Dragoons | 14th December 1852 |
| | 9th Lancers | 9th (Queen's Royal) Regt. of Light Dragoons (Lancers) | 14th December 1852 |
| | 14th Hussars | 14th (The King's) Regt. of Light Dragoons | 14th December 1852 |
| | The Lincolnshire Regt. | 10th (North Lincolnshire) Regt. of Foot | 14th December 1852 |
| | The South Wales Borderers | 24th (2nd Warwickshire) Regt. of Foot | 14th December 1852 |
| | 2nd Bn. The Gloucestershire Regt. | 61st (South Gloucestershire) Regt. of Foot | 14th December 1852 |
| | 1st Bn. The Worcestershire Regt. | 29th (Worcestershire) Regt. of Foot | 14th December 1852 |
| | 1st Bn. The Duke of Cornwall's L.I. | 32nd (Cornwall) Regt. of Foot | 14th December 1852 |
| | 1st Bn. The King's Shropshire L.I. | 53rd (Shropshire) Regt. of Foot | 14th December 1852 |
| | The King's Royal Rifle Corps | 1st Bn. 60th (The King's Royal Rifle Corps) | 14th December 1852 |
| | 2nd Bn. The North Staffordshire Regt. | 98th (The Prince of Wales's) Regt. of Foot | 14th December 1852 |
| | 2nd Bn. The Royal Munster Fusiliers | H.E.I.C. 2nd Bengal (European) Fusiliers | 7th October 1853 |
| | 2nd Bn. The Royal Dublin Fusiliers | H.E.I.C. 1st Bombay (European) Fusiliers | 7th October 1853 |
| | | INDIAN ARMY | |
| | 2nd Lancers | 2nd Regt. Bengal Irregular Cavalry | 7th October 1853 |
| | 5th Cavalry | 7th Regt. Bengal Irregular Cavalry | 7th October 1853 |
| | 7th Hariana Lancers | 17th Regt. Bengal Irregular Cavalry | 7th October 1853 |
| | 31st D.C.O. Lancers | 1st Regt. Bombay Light Cavalry (Lancers) | 7th October 1853 |
| | 35th Scinde Horse | 1st Regt. Scinde Irregular Horse | 7th October 1853 |
| | 36th Jacob's Horse | 2nd Regt. Scinde Irregular Horse | 7th October 1853 |
| | Q.V.O. Corps of Guides (F.F.) | Corps of Guides | 7th October 1853 |

| | | | |
|---|---|---|---|
| PUNJAUB (Cont.) | 25th Mountain Battery | 1st Co. 4th Battalion, Bombay Foot Artillery | 7th October 1853 |
| | 1st K.G.O. Sappers & Miners | Corps of Bengal Sappers & Miners | 7th October 1853 |
| | 3rd Sappers & Miners | Corps of Bombay Sappers & Miners | 7th October 1853 |
| | 2nd Q.V.O. Rajput Light Infantry | 31st Regt. Bengal Native Infantry | 7th October 1853 |
| | 11th Rajputs | 70th Regt. Bengal Native Infantry | 7th October 1853 |
| | 51st Sikhs (F.F.) | 1st Regt. Sikh Local Infantry | 7th October 1853 |
| | 52nd Sikhs (F.F.) | 2nd (or Hill) Regt. Sikh Local Infantry | 7th October 1853 |
| | 103rd Mahratta Light Infantry | 3rd Regt. Bombay Native Infantry | 7th October 1853 |
| | 104th Wellesley's Rifles | 4th Regt. Bombay Native Infantry | 7th October 1853 |
| | 109th Infantry | 9th Regt. Bombay Native Infantry | 7th October 1853 |
| | 119th Infantry (The Mooltan Regt.) | 19th Regt. Bombay Native Infantry | 7th October 1853 |
| | 121st Pioneers | The Marine Battalion | 7th October 1853 |
| PEGU | The Royal Irish Regt. | 18th (Royal Irish) Regt. of Foot | 20th September 1853 |
| | 2nd Bn. The South Staffordshire Regt. | 80th (Staffordshire Volunteers) Regt. of Foot | 20th September 1853 |
| | 1st Bn. The King's Own Yorkshire L.I. | 51st (2nd Yorkshire, West Riding) or the King's Own Light Infantry Regt. | 20th September 1853 |
| | 1st Bn. The Royal Munster Fusiliers | H.E.I.C. 1st European Bengal Fusiliers | 18th May 1855 |
| | 1st Bn. The Royal Dublin Fusiliers | H.E.I.C. 1st Madras (European) Fusiliers | 18th May 1855 |
| | | INDIAN ARMY | |
| | 2nd Q.V.O. Sappers & Miners | Corps of Madras Sappers & Miners | 18th May 1855 |
| | 54th Sikhs (F.F.) | 4th Regt. Sikh Local Infantry | 18th May 1855 |
| | 61st Pioneers | 1st Regt. Madras Native Infantry | 18th May 1855 |
| | 69th Punjabis | 9th Regt. Madras Native Infantry | 18th May 1855 |
| | 79th Carnatic Infantry | 19th Regt. Madras Native Infantry | 18th May 1855 |
| | 86th Carnatic Infantry | 26th Regt. Madras Native Infantry | 18th May 1855 |
| RESHIRE | 1st Bn. The North Staffordshire Regt. | 64th (2nd Staffordshire) Regt. of Foot | 21st January 1859 |
| | 2nd Bn. Durham L.I. | H.E.I.C. 2nd Bombay European Light Infantry | GGO 332/1861 |
| | | INDIAN ARMY | |
| | 33rd Q.V.O. Light Cavalry | 3rd Regt. Bombay Light Cavalry | Bombay GO 997/1858 |
| | 34th P.A.V.O. Poona Horse | Poona Irregular Horse | Bombay GO 997/1858 |

| | | | |
|---|---|---|---|
| RESHIRE (Cont.) | 3rd Sappers & Miners | Corps of Bombay Sappers & Miners | Bombay GO 997/1858 |
| | 104th Wellesley's Rifles | 4th Regt. Bombay Native Infantry or Rifle Corps | Bombay GO 997/1858 |
| | 120th Rajputana Infantry | 20th Regt. Bombay Native Infantry | Bombay GO 997/1858 |
| | 129th D.C.O. Baluchis | 2nd Baluch Battalion | Bombay GO 997/1858 |
| BUSHIRE | 1st Bn. The North Staffordshire Regt. | 64th (2nd Staffordshire) Regt. of Foot | 21st January 1859 |
| | 2nd Bn. The Durham L.I. | H.E.I.C. 2nd Bombay European Light Infantry | GGO 332/1861 |
| | | INDIAN ARMY | |
| | 33rd Q.V.O. Light Cavalry | 3rd Regt. Bombay Light Cavalry | Bombay GO 191/1861 |
| | 34th P.A.V.O. Poona Horse | Poona Irregular Horse | Bombay GO 191/1861 |
| | 3rd Sappers & Miners | Corps of Bombay Sappers & Miners | Bombay GO 191/1861 |
| | 104th Wellesley's Rifles | 4th Regt. Bombay Native Infantry or Rifle Corps | Bombay GO 191/1861 |
| | 120th Rajputana Infantry | 20th Regt. Bombay Native Infantry | Bombay GO 191/1861 |
| | 129th D.C.O. Baluchis | 2nd Baluch Battalion | Bombay GO 191/1861 |
| KOOSH-AB | 1st Bn. The North Staffordshire Regt. | 64th (2nd Staffordshire) Regt. of Foot | 21st January 1859 |
| | 2nd Bn. Seaforth Highlanders | 78th (Highland) Regt. of Foot (Ross-shire Buffs) | 21st January 1859 |
| | 2nd Bn. Durham L.I. | H.E.I.C. 2nd Bombay European Light Infantry | GGO 332/1861 |
| | | INDIAN ARMY | |
| | 33rd Q.V.O. Light Cavalry | 3rd Regt. Bombay Light Cavalry | Bombay GO 997/1858 |
| | 34th P.A.V.O. Poona Horse | Poona Irregular Horse | Bombay GO 997/1858 |
| | 3rd Sappers & Miners | Corps of Bombay Sappers & Miners | Bombay GO 997/1858 |
| | 104th Wellesley's Rifles | 4th Regt. Bombay Native Infantry or Rifle Corps | Bombay GO 997/1858 |
| | 120th Rajputana Infantry | 20th Regt. Bombay Native Infantry | Bombay GO 997/1858 |
| | 126th Baluchistan Infantry | 26th Regt. Bombay Native Infantry | Bombay GO 997/1858 |
| | 129th D.C.O. Baluchis | 2nd Baluch Battalion | Bombay GO 997/1858 |
| PERSIA | 14th Hussars | 14th (The King's) Regt. of (Light) Dragoons | 21st January 1859 |
| | 1st Bn. The North Staffordshire Regt. | 64th (2nd Staffordshire) Regt. of Foot | 21st January 1859 |
| | 2nd Bn. Seaforth Highlanders | 78th (Highland) Regt. of Foot (or Ross-shire Buffs) | 21st January 1859 |
| | 2nd Bn. The Durham L.I. | H.E.I.C. 2nd Bombay European Light Infantry | GGO 332/1861 |

| | | | |
|---|---|---|---|
| **PERSIA (Cont.)** | | INDIAN ARMY | |
| | 33rd Q.V.O. Light Cavalry | 3rd Regt. Bombay Light Cavalry | GGO 997/1858 |
| | 34th P.A.V.O. Poona Horse | Poona Irregular Horse | GGO 997/1858 |
| | 35th Scinde Horse | 1st Regt. Scinde Irregular Horse | GGO 997/1858 |
| | 2nd Q.V.O. Sappers & Miners | Corps of Madras Sappers & Miners | GGO 997/1858 |
| | 3rd Sappers & Miners | Corps of Bombay Sappers & Miners | GGO 997/1858 |
| | 104th Wellesley's Rifles | 4th Regt. Bombay Native Infantry or Rifle Corps | GGO 997/1858 |
| | 120th Rajputana Infantry | 20th Regt. Bombay Native Infantry | GGO 997/1858 |
| | 123rd Outram's Rifles | 23rd Regt. Bombay Native (Light) Infantry | GGO 997/1858 |
| | 126th Baluchistan Infantry | 26th Regt. Bombay Native Infantry | GGO 997/1858 |
| | 129th D.C.O. Baluchis | 2nd Baluch Battalion | GGO 997/1858 |
| **DELHI 1857** | 6th Dragoon Guards | 6th Dragoon Guards (Carabiniers) | 3rd September 1863 |
| | 9th Lancers | 9th (The Queen's Royal) Regt. of (Light) Dragoons (Lancers) | 3rd September 1863 |
| | The King's (Liverpool Regt.) | 8th (The King's) Regt. of Foot | 3rd September 1863 |
| | 2nd Bn. The Gloucestershire Regt. | 61st (South Gloucestershire) Regt. of Foot | 3rd September 1863 |
| | 2nd Bn. Oxf & Bucks Lt. Infty. | 52nd (Oxfordshire) Regt. of Foot (Light Infantry) | 3rd September 1863 |
| | The King's Royal Rifle Corps | 1st Bn. 60th (The King's Royal Rifle Corps) | 3rd September 1863 |
| | 1st Bn. The Gordon Highlanders | 75th Regt. of Foot | 3rd September 1863 |
| | 1st Bn. The Royal Munster Fusiliers | H.E.I.C. 1st Bengal (European) Regt. (Fusiliers) | 3rd September 1863 |
| | 2nd Bn. The Royal Munster Fusiliers | H.E.I.C. 2nd Bengal (European) Regt. (Fusiliers) | 3rd September 1863 |
| | | INDIAN ARMY | |
| | 9th Hodson's Horse | Hodson's Horse 1st Regt. | GGO 4/1864 |
| | 10th D.C.O. Lancers | Hodson's Horse 2nd Regt. | GGO 4/1864 |
| | 21st P.A.V.O. Cavalry (F.F.) | 1st Regt. of Cavalry, Punjab Irregular Force | GGO 4/1864 |
| | 22nd Sam Browne's Cavalry (F.F.) | 2nd Regt. of Cavalry, Punjab Irregular Force | GGO 4/1864 |
| | 25th Cavalry (F.F.) | 5th Regt. of Cavalry, Punjab Irregular Force | GGO 4/1864 |
| | Q.V.O. Corps of Guides | The Corps of Guides | GGO 4/1864 |
| | 1st K.G.O. Sappers & Miners | Corps of Bengal Sappers & Miners | GGO 4/1864 |
| | 32nd Sikh Pioneers | Punjab Sappers (Punjab Pioneers) | GGO 4/1864 |
| | 54th Sikhs (F.F.) | 4th Regt. Sikh Infantry, Punjab Irregular Force | GGO 4/1864 |

| | | | |
|---|---|---|---|
| **DELHI 1857 (Cont.)** | 55th Coke's Rifles (F.F.) | 1st Regt. Punjab Infantry, Punjab Irregular Force | GGO 4/1864 |
| | 56th Punjabi Rifles (F.F.) | 2nd Regt. Punjab Infantry, Punjab Irregular Force | GGO 4/1864 |
| | 57th Wilde's Rifles (F.F.) | 4th Regt. Punjab Infantry, Punjab Irregular Force | GGO 4/1864 |
| | 127th Q.M.O. Baluch Light Infantry | 1st Belooch Battalion, Bombay Native Infantry | GGO 4/1864 |
| | 2nd K.E.O. Gurkha Rifles | The Sirmoor Battalion | GGO 4/1864 |
| | 3rd Q.A.O. Gurkha Rifles | 7th (or Kamaon) Local Battalion | GGO 4/1864 |
| **LUCKNOW (For Defence)** | The Northumberland Fusiliers | 5th Regt. of Foot (Northumberland Fusiliers) | 3rd September 1863 |
| | 1st Bn. The Duke of Cornwall's L.I. | 32nd (Cornwall) Regt. of Foot | 3rd September 1863 |
| | 1st Bn. The North Staffordshire Regt. | 64th (2nd Staffordshire) Regt. of Foot | 3rd September 1863 |
| | 2nd Bn. Seaforth Highlanders | 78th (Highland) Regt. of Foot (or Ross-shire Buffs) | 3rd September 1863 |
| | 2nd Bn. The York & Lancaster Regt. | 84th (York & Lancaster) Regt. of Foot | 3rd September 1863 |
| | 2nd Bn. The Cameronians | 90th Regt. of Foot (Perthshire Volunteers) (Light Infantry) | 3rd September 1863 |
| | 1st Bn. The Royal Dublin Fusiliers | H.E.I.C. 1st Madras (European) Regt. (Fusiliers) | 3rd September 1863 |
| | | INDIAN ARMY | |
| | 14th K.G.O. Ferozepore Sikhs | The Regiment of Ferozepore | GGO 4/1864 |
| | 16th Rajputs * | The Regiment of Lucknow | GGO 4/1864 |
| **LUCKNOW (For Relief)** | 9th Lancers | 9th (The Queen's Royal) Regt. of (Light) Dragoons (Lancers) | 3rd September 1963 |
| | The Northumberland Fusiliers | 5th Regt. of Foot (Northumberland Fusiliers) | 3rd September 1863 |
| | The King's (Liverpool Regt.) | 8th (The King's) Regt. of Foot | 3rd September 1863 |
| | The Royal Welsh Fusiliers | 23rd (Royal Welsh Fusiliers) Regt. of Foot | 3rd September 1863 |
| | 1st Bn. The King's Shropshire L.I. | 53rd (Shropshire) Regt. of Foot | 3rd September 1863 |
| | 1st Bn. The Gordon Highlanders | 75th Regt. of Foot | 3rd September 1863 |
| | 2nd Bn. P.W.V. (South Lancashire Regt.) | 82nd Regt. of Foot (The Prince of Wales's Volunteers) | 3rd September 1863 |
| | 2nd Bn. The York & Lancaster | 84th (York & Lancaster) Regt. of Foot | 3rd September 1863 |
| | 2nd Bn. The Argyll & Sutherland Highlanders | 93rd (Highland) Regt. of Foot | 3rd September 1863 |

* With Turretted Gateway

| | | INDIAN ARMY | |
|---|---|---|---|
| **LUCKNOW (For Relief) (Cont.)** | 9th Hodson's Horse | Hodson's Horse 1st Regt. | GGO 4/1864 |
| | 10th D.C.O. Lancers | Hodson's Horse 2nd Regt. | GGO 4/1864 |
| | 11th K.E.O. Cavalry | 1st Regt. Sikh Irregular Cavalry | GGO 4/1864 |
| | 21st P.A.V.O. Cavalry (F.F.) | 1st Regt. of Cavalry, Punjab Irregular Force | GGO 4/1864 |
| | 22nd Sam Browne's Cavalry (F.F.) | 2nd Regt. of Cavalry, Punjab Irregular Force | GGO 4/1864 |
| | 25th Cavalry (F.F.) | 5th Regt. of Cavalry, Punjab Irregular Force | GGO 4/1864 |
| | 1st K.G.O. Sappers & Miners | Corps of Bengal Sappers & Miners | GGO 4/1864 |
| | 32nd Sikh Pioneers | Punjab Sappers (Punjab Pioneers) | GGO 4/1864 |
| | 56th Punjabi Rifles (F.F.) | 2nd Regt. Punjab Infantry, Punjab Irregular Force | GGO 4/1864 |
| | 57th Wilde's Rifles (F.F.) | 4th Regt. Punjab Infantry, Punjab Irregular Force | GGO 4/1864 |
| **LUCKNOW (For Capture)** | 2nd Dragoon Guards | 2nd (The Queen's) Regt. of Dragoon Guards | 3rd September 1863 |
| | 7th Hussars | 7th (The Queen's Own) Regt. of (Light) Dragoons (Hussars) | 3rd September 1863 |
| | 9th Lancers | 9th (The Queen's Royal) Regt. of (Light) Dragoons (Lancers) | 3rd September 1863 |
| | The Northumberland Fusiliers | 5th Regt. of Foot (Northumberland Fusiliers) | 3rd September 1863 |
| | The Lincolnshire Regt. | 10th (North Lincolnshire) Regt. of Foot | 3rd September 1863 |
| | The Lancashire Fusiliers | 20th (East Devonshire) Regt. of Foot | 3rd September 1863 |
| | The Royal Welsh Fusiliers | 23rd (Royal Welsh Fusiliers) Regt. of Foot | 3rd September 1863 |
| | 2nd Bn. The Cameronians | 90th Regt. of Foot (Perthshire Volunteers) (Light Infantry) | 3rd September 1863 |
| | 1st Bn. The Border Regt. | 34th (Cumberland) Regt. of Foot | 3rd September 1863 |
| | 1st Bn. The South Staffordshire Regt. | 38th (1st Staffordshire) Regt. of Foot | 3rd September 1863 |
| | 1st Bn. The Black Watch | 42nd (Royal Highland) Regt. of Foot | 3rd September 1863 |
| | 2nd Bn. The Queen's Own (Royal West Kent Regt.) | 97th (Earl of Ulster's) Regt. of Foot | 3rd September 1863 |
| | 1st Bn. The King's Shropshire L.I. | 53rd (Shropshire) Regt. of Foot | 3rd September 1863 |
| | 2nd Bn. Seaforth Highlanders | 78th (Highland) Regt. of Foot (or Ross-shire Buffs) | 3rd September 1863 |
| | The Queen's Own Cameron Highlanders | 79th Regt. of Foot (Cameron Highlanders) | 3rd September 1863 |
| | 2nd Bn. The York & Lancaster Regt. | 84th (York & Lancaster) Regt. of Foot | 3rd September 1863 |
| | 2nd Bn. The Argyll & Sutherland Highlanders | 93rd (Highland) Regt. of Foot | 3rd September 1863 |

| | | | |
|---|---|---|---|
| LUCKNOW (For Capture) (Cont.) | 1st Bn. The Royal Munster Fusiliers | H.E.I.C. 1st Bengal (European) Regt. Fusiliers | 3rd September 1863 |
| | 1st Bn. The Royal Dublin Fusiliers | H.E.I.C. 1st Madras (European) Regt. Fusiliers | 3rd September 1863 |
| | The Rifle Brigade | The Rifle Brigade | 3rd September 1863 |
| | | INDIAN ARMY | |
| | 14th K.G.O. Ferozepore Sikhs | The Regiment of Ferozepore | GGO 4/1864 |
| | 32nd Sikh Pioneers | Punjab Sappers (Punjab Pioneers) | GGO 4/1864 |
| | 56th Punjabi Rifles (F.F.) | 2nd Regt. Punjab Infantry, Punjab Irregular Force | GGO 4/1864 |
| | 57th Wilde's Rifles (F.F.) | 4th Regt. Punjab Infantry, Punjab Irregular Force | GGO 4/1864 |
| | 87th Punjabis | 27th Regt. Madras Native Infantry | GGO 4/1864 |
| DEFENCE OF ARRAH | 45th Rattray's Sikhs | Bengal Military Police Battalion | GGO 221/1874 |
| BEHAR | 45th Rattray's Sikhs | Bengal Military Police Battalion | GGO 221/1874 |
| CENTRAL INDIA | 8th Hussars | 8th (The King's Royal Irish) Regt. of (Light) Dragoons (Hussars) | 3rd September 1863 |
| | 12th Lancers | 12th (The Prince of Wales's Royal) Regt. of Lancers | 3rd September 1863 |
| | 14th Hussars | 14th (The King's) Regt. of (Light) Dragoons | 3rd September 1863 |
| | 17th Lancers | 17th Regt. of (Light) Dragoons (Lancers) | 12th March 1879 |
| | 2nd Bn. The Royal Inniskilling Fusiliers | H.E.I.C. 3rd Madras (European) Regt. | 3rd September 1863 |
| | 2nd Bn. The South Staffordshire Regt. | 80th Regt. of Foot (Staffordshire Volunteers) | 3rd September 1863 |
| | 2nd Bn. The Sherwood Foresters | 95th (Derbyshire) Regt. of Foot | 3rd September 1863 |
| | 1st Bn. The Highland L.I. | 71st (Highland) Regt. of Foot (Light Infantry) | 3rd September 1863 |
| | 1st Bn. Seaforth Highlanders | 72nd (Duke of Albany's Own Highlanders) Regt. of Foot | 3rd September 1863 |
| | 1st Bn. The Royal Irish Rifles | 83rd Regt. of Foot | 3rd September 1863 |
| | 2nd Bn. The Royal Irish Rifles | 86th (Royal County Down) Regt. of Foot | 3rd September 1863 |
| | 1st Bn. The Connaught Rangers | 88th Regt. of Foot (Connaught Rangers) | 3rd September 1863 |
| | 2nd Bn. The Leinster Regt. | H.E.I.C. 3rd Bombay (European) Regt. | 3rd September 1863 |
| | | INDIAN ARMY | |
| | 20th Deccan Horse | 1st Cavalry Regt. Hyderabad Contingent | GGO 4/1864 |
| | 30th Lancers (Gordon's Horse) | 4th Cavalry Regt. Hyderabad Contingent | GGO 4/1864 |

| | | | |
|---|---|---|---|
| **CENTRAL INDIA (Cont.)** | 31st D.C.O. Lancers | 1st Regt. Bombay Light Cavalry (Lancers) | GGO 4/1864 |
| | 32nd Lancers | 2nd Regt. Bombay Light Cavalry | GGO 4/1864 |
| | 33rd Q.V.O. Light Cavalry | 3rd Regt. Bombay Light Cavalry | GGO 4/1864 |
| | 35th Scinde Horse | 1st Regt. Scinde Irregular Horse | GGO 4/1864 |
| | 2nd Q.V.O. Sappers & Miners | Corps of Madras Sappers & Miners | GGO 4/1864 |
| | 3rd Sappers & Miners | Corps of Bombay Sappers & Miners | GGO 4/1864 |
| | 2nd Q.V.O. Rajput Light Infantry | 31st Regt. Bengal Native Infantry | GGO 4/1864 |
| | 42nd Deoli Regt. | The Meena Battalion | GGO 4/1864 |
| | 44th Merwera Infantry | The Mhairwara Battalion | GGO 4/1864 |
| | 61st K.G.O. Pioneers | 1st Regt. Madras Native Infantry | GGO 4/1864 |
| | 79th Carnatic Infantry | 19th Regt. Madras Native Infantry | GGO 4/1864 |
| | 96th Berar Infantry | 3rd Infantry Regt. Hyderabad Contingent | GGO 4/1864 |
| | 98th Infantry | 5th Infantry Regt. Hyderabad Contingent | GGO 4/1864 |
| | 104th Wellesley's Rifles | 4th Regt. Bombay Native Infantry or Rifle Corps | GGO 4/1864 |
| | 110th Mahratta Light Infantry | 10th Regt. Bombay Native Infantry | GGO 4/1864 |
| | 112th Infantry | 12th Regt. Bombay Native Infantry | GGO 4/1864 |
| | 113th Infantry | 13th Regt. Bombay Native Infantry | GGO 4/1864 |
| | 124th Duchess of Connaught's Own Baluchistan Infty. | 24th Regt. Bombay Native Infantry | GGO 4/1864 |
| | 125th Napier's Rifles | 25th Regt. Bombay Native Infantry | GGO 4/1864 |
| **CANTON** | 2nd Bn. The East Lancashire Regt. | 59th (2nd Nottinghamshire) Regt. of Foot | 4th November 1861 |
| **CHINA 1858-1859** | 7th D.C.O. Rajputs | 47th Regt. Bengal Native Infantry | GGO 592/1892 |
| | 10th Jats | 65th Regt. Bengal Native Infantry | GGO 592/1892 |
| | 11th Rajputs | 70th Regt. Bengal Native Infantry | GGO 592/1892 |
| **CHINA 1860-1862** | 15th Ludhiana Sikhs | The Regiment of Ludhiana | GGO 592/1892 |
| | 22nd Punjabis | 11th Regt. Punjab Infantry | GGO 592/1892 |
| | 27th Punjabis | 19th Regt. Punjab Infantry | GGO 592/1892 |
| | 105th Mahratta Light Infantry | 5th Regt. Bombay Native (Light) Infantry | GGO 592/1892 |

| Battle Honour | Present Title | Title at Time | Authority |
|---|---|---|---|
| **TAKU FORTS** | 1st King's Dragoon Guards | 1st (The King's) Regt. of Dragoon Guards | 4th November 1861 |
| | The Royal Scots | 2nd Bn. 1st (The Royal) Regt. of Foot | 4th November 1861 |
| | The Queen's (Royal West Surrey Regt.) | 1st Bn. 2nd (The Queen's Royal) Regt. of Foot | 4th November 1861 |
| | The Buffs (East Kent Regt.) | 1st Bn. 3rd (East Kent) Regt. of Foot (The Buffs) | 4th November 1861 |
| | 1st Bn. The East Surrey Regt. | 31st (Huntingdonshire) Regt. of Foot | 4th November 1861 |
| | 1st Bn. The Essex Regt. | 44th (East Essex) Regt. of Foot | 4th November 1861 |
| | The King's Royal Rifle Corps | 2nd Bn. 60th (The King's Royal Rifle Corps) | 4th November 1861 |
| | 2nd Bn. The Hampshire Regt. | 67th (South Hampshire) Regt. of Foot | 4th November 1861 |
| | | INDIAN ARMY | |
| | 11th K.E.O. Lancers | 1st Regt. Sikh Irregular Cavalry | GGO 132/1862 |
| | 19th Lancers | Fane's Horse | GGO 132/1862 |
| | 2nd Q.V.O. Sappers & Miners | Corps of Madras Sappers & Miners | GGO 132/1862 |
| | 20th D.C.O. Infantry | 8th Regt. Punjab Infantry | GGO 132/1862 |
| | 23rd Sikh Pioneers | 15th (Pioneer) Regt. Punjab Infantry | |
| **PEKIN 1860** (Date (1860) added 5th June 1914) | 1st King's Dragoon Guards | 1st (The King's) Regt. of Dragoon Guards | 4th November 1861 |
| | The Royal Scots | 2nd Bn. 1st (The Royal) Regt. of Foot | 4th November 1861 |
| | The Queen's (Royal West Surrey Regt.) | 1st Bn. 2nd (The Queen's Royal) Regt. of Foot | 4th November 1861 |
| | The King's Royal Rifle Corps | 2nd Bn. 60th (The King's Royal Rifle Corps) | 4th November 1861 |
| | 2nd Bn. The Hampshire Regt. | 67th (South Hampshire) Regt. of Foot | 4th November 1861 |
| | 2nd Bn. The Wiltshire Regt. | 99th Regt. of Foot | 4th November 1861 |
| **PEKIN** | 11th K.E.O. Lancers | 1st Regt. Sikh Irregular Cavalry | GGO 132/1862 |
| | 19th Lancers | Fane's Horse | GGO 132/1862 |
| | 2nd Q.V.O. Sappers & Miners | Corps of Madras Sappers & Miners | GGO 132/1862 |
| | 20th D.C.O. Infantry | * 8th Regt. Punjab Infantry | GGO 132/1862 |
| | 23rd Sikh Pioneers | ** 15th (Pioneer) Regt. Punjab Infantry | GGO 132/1862 |
| **ALI MASJID** | 10th Hussars | 10th (The Prince of Wales's Own) Royal Regt. of Hussars | GO 56/1881 |
| | The Leicestershire Regt. | 17th (Leicestershire) Regt. of Foot | GO 56/1881 |
| | 2nd Bn. The Loyal North Lancashire Regt. | 81st Regt. of Foot (Loyal Lincoln Volunteers) | GO 56/1881 |
| | 1st Bn. The King's Own Yorkshire L.I. | 51st (2nd Yorkshire, West Riding) or The King's Own Lt Infty. Regt. | GO 56/1881 |

* 24th Regt. BNI 1861 20th BNI 1861

** 27th Regt. BNI 1861 23rd BNI 1861

| | | | |
|---|---|---|---|
| **ALI MASJID (Cont.)** | The Rifle Brigade | The Rifle Brigade (The Prince Consort's Own) | GO 56/1881 |
| | | INDIAN ARMY | |
| | 11th K.E.O. Lancers | 11th (The Prince of Wales's Own) Regt. of Bengal Lancers | GGO 418/1881 |
| | Q.V.O. Corps of Guides (F.F.) | Queen's Own Corps of Guides, Punjab Frontier Force | GGO 418/1881 |
| | 24th Hazara Mountain Battery (F.F.) | No. 4 (Hazara) Mountain Battery, Punjab Frontier Force | GGO 418/1881 |
| | 1st K.G.O. Sappers & Miners | Corps of Bengal Sappers & Miners | GGO 418/1881 |
| | 6th Jat Light Infantry | 6th Regt. Bengal Native (Light) Infantry | GGO 418/1881 |
| | 14th K.G.O. Ferozepore Sikhs | 14th (the Ferozepore) Regt. Bengal Native Infantry | GGO 418/1881 |
| | 20th D.C.O. Infantry | 20th (Punjab) Regt. Bengal Native Infantry | GGO 418/1881 |
| | 27th Punjabis | 27th (Punjab) Regt. Bengal Native Infantry | GGO 418/1881 |
| | 45th Rattray's Sikhs | 45th (Rattray's Sikh) Regt. Bengal Native Infantry | GGO 418/1881 |
| | 51st Sikhs (F.F.) | 1st Regt. Sikh Infantry, Punjab Frontier Force | GGO 418/1881 |
| | 4th Gurkha Rifles | 4th Gurkha Regt. | |
| **PEIWAR KOTAL** | The King's (Liverpool Regt.) | 8th (The King's) Regt. of Foot | GO 56/1881 |
| | 1st Bn. Seaforth Highlanders | 72nd (The Duke of Albany's Own Highlanders) Regt. of Foot | GO 56/1881 |
| | | INDIAN ARMY | |
| | 12th Cavalry | 12th Regt. Bengal Cavalry | GGO 418/1881 |
| | 21st Kohat Mountain Battery (F.F.) | No. 1 (Kohat) Mountain Battery, Punjab Frontier Force | GGO 418/1881 |
| | 23rd Sikh Pioneers | 23rd (Punjab) Regt. Bengal Native Infantry (Pioneers) | GGO 418/1881 |
| | 29th Punjabis | 29th (Punjab) Regt. Bengal Native Infantry | GGO 418/1881 |
| | 56th Punjabi Rifles (F.F.) | 2nd Regt. of Infantry, Punjab Frontier Force | GGO 418/1881 |
| | 58th Vaughan's Rifles (F.F.) | 5th Regt. of Infantry, Punjab Frontier Force | GGO 418/1881 |
| | 5th Gurkha Rifles (F.F.) | 5th Gurkha Regt. or Hazara Gurkha Battalion | GGO 418/1881 |
| **CHARASIAH** | 9th Lancers | 9th (The Queen's Royal) Regt. of Lancers | GO 56/1881 |
| | 2nd Bn. The Hampshire Regt. | 67th (South Hampshire) Regt. of Foot | GO 56/1881 |
| | 1st Bn. Seaforth Highlanders | 72nd (The Duke of Albany's Own Highlanders) Regt. of Foot | GO 56/1881 |
| | 2nd Bn. The Gordon Highlanders | 92nd (Gordon Highlanders) Regt. of Foot | GO 56/1881 |

| | | INDIAN ARMY | |
|---|---|---|---|
| **CHARASIAH (Cont.)** | 12th Cavalry | 12th Regt. of Bengal Cavalry | GGO 418/1881 |
| | 14th Murray's Jat Lancers | 14th Regt. of Bengal Lancers | GGO 418/1881 |
| | 25th Cavalry (F.F.) | 5th Regt. of Cavalry, Punjab Frontier Force | GGO 418/1881 |
| | 22nd Derajat Mountain Battery (F.F.) | No. 2 Mountain Battery, Punjab Frontier Force | GGO 418/1881 |
| | 1st K.G.O. Sappers & Miners | Corps of Bengal Sappers & Miners | GGO 418/1881 |
| | 23rd Sikh Pioneers | 23rd (Punjab) Regt. of Bengal Native Infantry (Pioneers) | GGO 418/1881 |
| | 28th Punjabis | 28th (Punjab) Regt. of Bengal Native Infantry | GGO 418/1881 |
| | 58th Vaughan's Rifles (F.F.) | 5th Regt. of Infantry, Punjab Frontier Force | GGO 418/1881 |
| | 5th Gurkha Rifles (F.F.) | 5th Gurkha Regt. or Hazara Gurkha Battalion | GGO 418/1881 |
| **KABUL 1879** | 9th Lancers | 9th (The Queen's Royal) Regt. of Lancers | GO 56/1881 |
| | The Norfolk Regt. | 9th (East Norfolk) Regt. of Foot | GO 56/1881 |
| | 2nd Bn. The Hampshire Regt. | 67th (South Hampshire) Regt. of Foot | GO 56/1881 |
| | 1st Bn. Seaforth Highlanders | 72nd (The Duke of Albany's Own Highlanders) Regt. of Foot | GO 56/1881 |
| | 2nd Bn. The Gordon Highlanders | 92nd (Gordon Highlanders) Regt. of Foot | GO 56/1881 |
| | | INDIAN ARMY | |
| | 12th Cavalry | 12th Regt. of Bengal Cavalry | GGO 418/1881 |
| | 14th Murray's Jat Lancers | 14th Regt. of Bengal Lancers | GGO 418/1881 |
| | 25th Cavalry (F.F.) | 5th Regt. of Cavalry, Punjab Frontier Force | GGO 418/1881 |
| | Q.V.O. Corps of Guides (F.F.) | Queen's Own Corps of Guides, Punjab Frontier Force | GGO 418/1881 |
| | 21st Kohat Mountain Battery (F.F.) | No. 1 Mountain Battery, Punjab Frontier Force | GGO 418/1881 |
| | 22nd Derajat Mountain Battery (F.F.) | No. 2 Mountain Battery, Punjab Frontier Force | GGO 418/1881 |
| | 24th Hazara Mountain Battery (F.F.) | No. 4 (Hazara) Mountain Battery, Punjab Frontier Force | GGO 418/1881 |
| | 1st K.G.O. Sappers & Miners | Corps of Bengal Sappers & Miners | GGO 418/1881 |
| | 23rd Sikh Pioneers | 23rd (Punjab) Regt. of Bengal Native Infantry (Pioneers) | GGO 418/1881 |
| | 28th Punjabis | 28th (Punjab) Regt. of Bengal Native Infantry | GGO 418/1881 |
| | 53rd Sikhs (F.F.) | 3rd Regt. Sikh Infantry, Punjab Frontier Force | GGO 418/1881 |
| | 58th Vaughan's Rifles (F.F.) | 5th Regt. of Infantry, Punjab Frontier Force | GGO 418/1881 |
| | 2nd K.E.O. Gurkha Rifles (The Sirmoor Rifles) | 2nd (Prince of Wales's Own) Gurkha Regt. (The Sirmoor Rifles) | GGO 418/1881 |
| | 4th Gurkha Rifles | 4th Gurkha Regt. | GGO 418/1881 |
| | 5th Gurkha Rifles (F.F.) | 5th Gurkha Regt. or Hazara Gurkha Battalion | GGO 418/1881 |

| | | | |
|---|---|---|---|
| AHMAD KHEL | 2nd Bn. The East Lancashire Regt. | 59th (2nd Nottinghamshire) Regt. of Foot | GO 56/1881 |
| | The King's Royal Rifle Corps | 60th (The King's Royal Rifle Corps) | GO 56/1881 |
| | | INDIAN ARMY | |
| | 19th Lancers | 19th Regt. of Bengal Lancers | GGO 418/1881 |
| | 21st P.A.V.O. Cavalry (F.F.) | 1st Regt. of Cavalry, Punjab Frontier Force | GGO 418/1881 |
| | 22nd Sam Browne's Cavalry (F.F.) | 2nd Regt. of Cavalry, Punjab Frontier Force | GGO 418/1881 |
| | 1st K.G.O. Sappers & Miners | Corps of Bengal Sappers & Miners | GGO 418/1881 |
| | 15th Ludhiana Sikhs | 15th (The Ludhiana) Regt. Bengal Native Infantry | GGO 418/1881 |
| | 19th Punjabis | 19th (Punjab) Regt. Bengal Native Infantry | GGO 418/1881 |
| | 25th Punjabis | 25th (Punjab) Regt. Bengal Native Infantry | GGO 418/1881 |
| | 52nd Sikhs (F.F.) | 2nd (or Hill) Regt. Sikh Infantry, Punjab Frontier Force | GGO 418/1881 |
| | 3rd Q.A.O. Gurkha Rifles | 3rd (the Kumaon) Gurkha Regt. | GGO 418/1881 |
| KANDAHAR 1880 | 9th Lancers | 9th (The Queen's Royal) Regt. of Lancers | GO 56/1881 |
| | The Royal Fusiliers | 7th Regt. of Foot (Royal Fusiliers) | GO 56/1881 |
| | The King's Royal Rifle Corps | 60th (The King's Royal Rifle Corps) | GO 56/1881 |
| | 2nd Bn. The Royal Berkshire Regt. | 66th (Berkshire) Regt. of Foot | GO 56/1881 |
| | 1st Bn. Seaforth Highlanders | 72nd (The Duke of Albany's Own Highlanders) Regt. of Foot | GO 56/1881 |
| | 2nd Bn. The Gordon Highlanders | 92nd (Gordon Highlanders) Regt. of Foot | GO 56/1881 |
| | | INDIAN ARMY | |
| | 22nd Derajat Mountain Battery (F.F.) | No. 2 (Derajat) Mountain Battery, Punjab Frontier Force | GGO 418/1881 |
| | 3rd Skinner's Horse | 3rd Regt. of Bengal Cavalry | GGO 418/1881 |
| | 23rd Cavalry (F.F.) | 3rd Regt. of Cavalry, Punjab Frontier Force | GGO 418/1881 |
| | 33rd Q.V.O. Light Cavalry | 3rd (the Queen's Own) Regt. of Bombay Light Cavalry | GGO 418/1881 |
| | 34th P.A.V.O. Poona Horse | The Poona Horse | GGO 418/1881 |
| | 38th K.G.O. Central India Horse | 1st Regt. Central India Horse | GGO 418/1881 |
| | 39th K.G.O. Central India Horse | 2nd Regt. Central India Horse | GGO 418/1881 |
| | 3rd Sappers & Miners | Corps of Bombay Sappers & Miners | GGO 418/1881 |
| | 15th Ludhiana Sikhs | 15th (The Ludhiana) Regt. Bengal Native Infantry | GGO 418/1881 |

| | | | |
|---|---|---|---|
| **KANDAHAR 1880 (Cont.)** | 23rd Sikh Pioneers | 23rd (Punjab) Regt. Bengal Native Infantry | GGO 418/1881 |
| | 24th Punjabis | 24th (Punjab) Regt. Bengal Native Infantry | GGO 418/1881 |
| | 25th Punjabis | 25th (Punjab) Regt. Bengal Native Infantry | GGO 418/1881 |
| | 52nd Sikhs (F.F.) | 2nd (or Hill) Regt. Sikh Infantry, Punjab Frontier Force | GGO 418/1881 |
| | 53rd Sikhs (F.F.) | 3rd Regt. Sikh Infantry, Punjab Frontier Force | GGO 418/1881 |
| | The 101st Grenadiers | 1st or Grenadier Regt. Bombay Native Infantry | GGO 418/1881 |
| | 104th Wellesley's Rifles | 4th Regt. Bombay Native Infantry or Rifle Corps | GGO 418/1881 |
| | 119th Infantry (The Mooltan Regt.) | 19th Regt. Bombay Native Infantry | GGO 418/1881 |
| | 128th Pioneers | 28th Regt. Bombay Native Infantry | GGO 418/1881 |
| | 129th D.C.O. Baluchis | 29th Regt. Bombay Native Infantry or 2nd Baluch Bn. | GGO 418/1881 |
| | 2nd K.E.O. Gurkha Rifles (The Sirmoor Rifles) | 2nd (Prince of Wales's Own) Gurkha Regt. (The Sirmoor Rifles) | GGO 418/1881 |
| | 4th Gurkha Rifles | 4th Gurkha Regt. | GGO 418/1881 |
| | 5th Gurkha Rifles (F.F.) | 5th Gurkha Regt. or Hazara Gurkha Battalion | GGO 418/1881 |
| **AFGHANISTAN 1878-1879** | 10th Hussars | 10th (The Prince of Wales's Own) Royal Regt. of Hussars | GO 56/1881 |
| | The Leicestershire Regt. | 17th (Leicestershire) Regt. of Foot | GO 56/1881 |
| | 2nd Bn. The East Surrey Regt. | 70th (Surrey) Regt. of Foot | GO 56/1881 |
| | 2nd Bn. The Loyal North Lancashire Regt. | 81st Regt. of Foot (Loyal Lincoln Volunteers) | GO 56/1881 |
| | The Rifle Brigade | The Rifle Brigade (The Prince Consort's Own) | GO 56/1881 |
| | | INDIAN ARMY | |
| | 11th K.E.O. Lancers | 11th (The Prince of Wales's Own) Regt. of Bengal Lancers | GGO 418/1881 |
| | 35th Scinde Horse | 1st Regt. of Scinde Horse | GGO 418/1881 |
| | 23rd (Peshawar) Mountain Battery (F.F.) | No.3 (Peshawar) Mountain Battery, Punjab Frontier Force | GGO 418/1881 |
| | 6th Jat Light Infantry | 6th Regt. Bengal Native (Light) Infantry | GGO 418/1881 |

| | | | |
|---|---|---|---|
| **AFGHANISTAN 1878-1879 (Cont.)** | 9th Bhopal Infantry | The Bhopal Battalion | GGO 418/1881 |
| | 12th Pioneers | 12th (Kelat-i-Ghilzie) Regt. Bengal Native Infantry | GGO 418/1881 |
| | 14th K.G.O. Ferozepore Sikhs | 14th (The Ferozepore) Regt. Bengal Native Infantry | GGO 418/1881 |
| | 26th Punjabis | 26th (Punjab) Regt. Bengal Native Infantry | GGO 418/1881 |
| | 44th Merwera Infantry | The Mhairwarra Battalion | GGO 418/1881 |
| | 51st Sikhs (F.F.) | 1st Regt. Sikh Infantry, Punjab Frontier Force | GGO 418/1881 |
| | 55th Coke's Rifles (F.F.) | 1st Regt. Punjab Infantry, Punjab Frontier Force | GGO 418/1881 |
| | 56th Punjabi Rifles (F.F.) | 2nd Regt. of Infantry, Punjab Frontier Force | GGO 418/1881 |
| **AFGHANISTAN 1878-1880** | 9th Lancers | 9th (The Queen's Royal) Regt. of Lancers | GO 56/1881 |
| | 15th Hussars | 15th (The King's) Regt. of Hussars | GO 56/1881 |
| | The Northumberland Fusiliers | 5th (Northumberland Fusiliers) Regt. of Foot | GO 56/1881 |
| | The King's (Liverpool Regt.) | 8th (The King's) Regt. of Foot | GO 56/1881 |
| | The Suffolk Regt. | 12th (East Suffolk) Regt. of Foot | GO 56/1881 |
| | The King's Own Scottish Borderers | 25th (The King's Own Borderers) Regt. of Foot | GO 56/1881 |
| | 2nd Bn. The East Lancashire Regt. | 59th (2nd Nottinghamshire) Regt. of Foot | GO 56/1881 |
| | 2nd Bn. The Hampshire Regt. | 67th (South Hampshire) Regt. of Foot | GO 56/1881 |
| | 1st Bn. The King's Own Yorkshire L.I. | 51st (2nd Yorkshire, West Riding) Regt. of Foot | GO 56/1881 |
| | The King's Royal Rifle Corps | 60th (The King's Royal Rifle Corps) | GO 56/1881 |
| | 1st Bn. Seaforth Highlanders | 72nd (The Duke of Albany's Own Highlanders) Regt. of Foot | GO 56/1881 |
| | 2nd Bn. The Gordon Highlanders | 92nd (Gordon Highlanders) Regt. of Foot | GO 56/1881 |
| | | INDIAN ARMY | |
| | 8th Cavalry | 8th Regt. of Bengal Cavalry | GGO 418/1881 |
| | 10th D.C.O. Lancers | 10th Bengal (Duke of Cambridge's Own) Lancers | GGO 418/1881 |
| | 12th Cavalry | 12th Regt. of Bengal Cavalry | GGO 418/1881 |
| | 13th DoC Lancers | 13th Regt. of Bengal Lancers | GGO 418/1881 |
| | 14th Murray's Jat Lancers | 14th Regt. of Bengal Lancers | GGO 418/1881 |
| | 15th Lancers | 15th (Cureton's Multani) Regt. of Bengal Cavalry | GGO 418/1881 |
| | 19th Lancers | 19th Regt. of Bengal Lancers | GGO 418/1881 |
| | 21st P.A.V.O. Cavalry (F.F.) | 1st Regt. of Cavalry, Punjab Frontier Force | GGO 418/1881 |
| | 22nd Sam Browne's Cavalry (F.F.) | 2nd Regt. of Cavalry, Punjab Frontier Force | GGO 418/1881 |

| | | | |
|---|---|---|---|
| **AFGHANISTAN 1878-1880 (Cont.)** | 25th Cavalry (F.F.) | 5th Regt. of Cavalry, Punjab Frontier Force | GGO 418/1881 |
| | Q.V.O. Corps of Guides (F.F.) | The Queen's Own Corps of Guides, Punjab Frontier Force | GGO 418/1881 |
| | 21st Kohat Mountain Battery (F.F.) | No. 1 (Kohat) Mountain Battery, Punjab Frontier Force | GGO 418/1881 |
| | 22nd Derajat Mountain Battery (F.F.) | No. 2 (Derajat) Mountain Battery, Punjab Frontier Force | GGO 418/1881 |
| | 24th Hazara Mountain Battery (F.F.) | No. 4 (Hazara) Mountain Battery, Punjab Frontier Force | GGO 418/1881 |
| | 26th Jacob's Mountain Battery | No. 2 Bombay Mountain Battery | GGO 418/1881 |
| | 1st K.G.O. Sappers & Miners | Corps of Bengal Sappers & Miners | GGO 418/1881 |
| | 2nd Q.V.O. Sappers & Miners | Corps of Madras Sappers & Miners | GGO 418/1881 |
| | 3rd Sappers & Miners | Corps of Bombay Sappers & Miners | GGO 418/1881 |
| | 11th Rajputs | 11th Regt. Bengal Native Infantry | GGO 418/1881 |
| | 15th Ludhiana Sikhs | 15th (The Ludhiana) Regt. Bengal Native Infantry | GGO 418/1881 |
| | 19th Punjabis | 19th (Punjab) Regt. Bengal Native Infantry | GGO 418/1881 |
| | 20th D.C.O. Infantry | 20th (Punjab) Regt. Bengal Native Infantry | GGO 418/1881 |
| | 21st Punjabis | 21st (Punjab) Regt. Bengal Native Infantry | GGO 418/1881 |
| | 23rd Sikh Pioneers | 23rd (Punjab) Regt. Bengal Native Infantry (Pioneers) | GGO 418/1881 |
| | 24th Punjabis | 24th (Punjab) Regt. Bengal Native Infantry | GGO 418/1881 |
| | 25th Punjabis | 25th (Punjab) Regt. Bengal Native Infantry | GGO 418/1881 |
| | 27th Punjabis | 27th (Punjab) Regt. Bengal Native Infantry | GGO 418/1881 |
| | 28th Punjabis | 28th (Punjab) Regt. Bengal Native Infantry | GGO 418/1881 |
| | 29th Punjabis | 29th (Punjab) Regt. Bengal Native Infantry | GGO 418/1881 |
| | 32nd Sikh Pioneers | 32nd (Punjab) Regt. Bengal Native Infantry (Pioneers) | GGO 418/1881 |
| | 45th Rattray's Sikhs | 45th (Rattray's Sikh) Regt. Bengal Native Infantry | GGO 418/1881 |
| | 52nd Sikhs (F.F.) | 2nd (or Hill) Regt. Sikh Infantry, Punjab Frontier Force | GGO 418/1881 |
| | 58th Vaughan's Rifles (F.F.) | 5th Regt. of Infantry, Punjab Frontier Force | GGO 418/1881 |
| | 81st Pioneers | 21st Regt. Madras Native Infantry | GGO 418/1881 |
| | 90th Punjabis | 30th Regt. Madras Native Infantry | GGO 418/1881 |
| | The 101st Grenadiers | 1st or Grenadier Regt. Bombay Native Infantry | GGO 418/1881 |
| | 119th Infantry | 19th Regt. Bombay Native Infantry | GGO 418/1881 |
| | 129th D.C.O. Baluchis | 29th Regt. Bombay Native Infantry or 2nd Baluch Bn. | GGO 418/1881 |

| | | | |
|---|---|---|---|
| **AFGHANISTAN 1878-1880 (Cont.)** | 130th K.G.O. Baluchis | 30th Regt. Bombay Native Infantry or 3rd Baluch Bn. | GGO 418/1881 |
| | 1st K.G.O. Gurkha Rifles | 1st Gurkha Regt. (Light Infantry) | GGO 418/1881 |
| | 2nd K.E.O. Gurkha Rifles | 2nd (Prince of Wales's Own) Gurkha Regt. (The Sirmoor Rifles) | GGO 418/1881 |
| | 3rd Q.A.O. Gurkha Rifles | 3rd (The Kumaon) Gurkha Regt. | GGO 418/1881 |
| | 4th Gurkha Rifles | 4th Gurkha Regt. | GGO 418/1881 |
| | 5th Gurkha Rifles (F.F.) | 5th Gurkha Regt. or Hazara Gurkha Battalion | GGO 418/1881 |
| **AFGHANISTAN 1879-1880** | 6th Dragoon Guards | 6th Dragoon Guards (Carabiniers) | GO 56/1881 |
| | 8th Hussars | 8th (King's Royal Irish) Hussars | GO 56/1881 |
| | The Royal Fusiliers | 7th Regt. of Foot (Royal Fusiliers) | GO 56/1881 |
| | The Norfolk Regt. | 9th (East Norfolk) Regt. of Foot | GO 56/1881 |
| | The Devonshire Regt. | 11th (North Devonshire) Regt. of Foot | GO 56/1881 |
| | The West Yorkshire Regt. | 14th (Buckinghamshire) or Prince of Wales's Own Regt. of Foot | GO 56/1881 |
| | The East Yorkshire Regt. | 15th (Yorkshire, East Riding) Regt. of Foot | GO 56/1881 |
| | The Royal Irish Regt. | 18th (Royal Irish) Regt. of Foot | GO 56/1881 |
| | 1st Bn. The Manchester Regt. | 63rd (West Suffolk) Regt. of Foot | GO 56/1881 |
| | 2nd Bn. The Royal Berkshire Regt. | 66th (Berkshire) Regt. of Foot | GO 56/1881 |
| | 2nd Bn. Seaforth Highlanders | 78th (Highland) Regt. of Foot (or Ross-shire Buffs) | GO 56/1881 |
| | 2nd Bn. The King's Shropshire L.I. | 85th (Bucks Volunteers) The King's Light Infantry Regt. | GO 56/1881 |
| | | INDIAN ARMY | |
| | 1st D.Y.O. Lancers | 1st Regt. of Bengal Cavalry | GGO 418/1881 |
| | 3rd Skinner's Horse | 3rd Regt. of Bengal Cavalry | GGO 418/1881 |
| | 4th Cavalry | 4th Regt. of Bengal Cavalry | GGO 418/1881 |
| | 5th Cavalry | 5th Regt. of Bengal Cavalry | GGO 418/1881 |
| | 17th Cavalry | 17th Regt. of Bengal Cavalry | GGO 418/1881 |
| | 18th K.G.O. Lancers | 18th Regt. of Bengal Cavalry | GGO 418/1881 |
| | 23rd Cavalry (F.F.) | 3rd Regt. of Cavalry, Punjab Frontier Force | GGO 418/1881 |
| | 26th K.G.O. Light Cavalry | 1st Regt. Madras Light Cavalry | GGO 418/1881 |
| | 32nd Lancers | 2nd Regt. Bombay Light Cavalry | GGO 418/1881 |

| | | | |
|---|---|---|---|
| **AFGHANISTAN 1879-1880 (Cont.)** | 33rd Q.V.O. Light Cavalry | 3rd (The Queen's Own) Regt. of Bombay Light Cavalry | GGO 418/1881 |
| | 34th P.A.V.O. Poona Horse | The Poona Horse | GGO 418/1881 |
| | 36th Jacob's Horse | 2nd Regt. of Scinde Horse | GGO 418/1881 |
| | 38th K.G.O. Central India Horse | 1st Regt. Central India Horse | GGO 418/1881 |
| | 39th K.G.O. Central India Horse | 2nd Regt. Central India Horse | GGO 418/1881 |
| | 2nd Q.V.O. Rajput Light Infantry | 2nd (The Queen's Own) Regt. Bengal Native (Light) Infantry | GGO 418/1881 |
| | 3rd Brahmans | 3rd Regt. Bengal Native Infantry | GGO 418/1881 |
| | 4th P.A.V. Rajputs | 4th Regt. Bengal Native Infantry | GGO 418/1881 |
| | 5th Light Infantry | 5th Regt. Bengal Native (Light) Infantry | GGO 418/1881 |
| | 8th Rajputs | 8th Regt. Bengal Native Infantry | GGO 418/1881 |
| | 13th Rajputs (The Shekhawati Regt.) | 13th Regt. Bengal Native Infantry | GGO 418/1881 |
| | 16th Rajputs (The Lucknow Regt.) | 16th (The Lucknow) Regt. Bengal Native Infantry | GGO 418/1881 |
| | 17th Infantry (The Loyal Regt.) | 17th (The Loyal Purbiah) Regt. Bengal Native Infantry | GGO 418/1881 |
| | 22nd Punjabis | 22nd (Punjab) Regt. Bengal Native Infantry | GGO 418/1881 |
| | 30th Punjabis | 30th (Punjab) Regt. Bengal Native Infantry | GGO 418/1881 |
| | 31st Punjabis | 31st (Punjab) Regt. Bengal Native Infantry | GGO 418/1881 |
| | 42nd Deoli Regt. | Infantry of Deoli Irregular Force | GGO 418/1881 |
| | 53rd Sikhs (F.F.) | 3rd Regt. Sikh Infantry, Punjab Frontier Force | GGO 418/1881 |
| | 57th Wilde's Rifles (F.F.) | 4th Regt. of Infantry, Punjab Frontier Force | GGO 418/1881 |
| | 61st K.G.O. Pioneers | 1st Regt. Madras Native Infantry | GGO 418/1881 |
| | 64th Pioneers | 4th Regt. Madras Native Infantry | GGO 418/1881 |
| | 75th Carnatic Infantry | 15th Regt. Madras Native Infantry | GGO 418/1881 |
| | 104th Wellesley's Rifles | 4th Regt. Bombay Native Infantry or Rifle Corps | GGO 418/1881 |
| | 105th Mahratta Light Infantry | 5th Regt. Bombay Native (Light) Infantry | GGO 418/1881 |
| | 108th Infantry | 8th Regt. Bombay Native Infantry | GGO 418/1881 |
| | 109th Infantry | 9th Regt. Bombay Native Infantry | GGO 418/1881 |
| | 110th Mahratta Light Infantry | 10th Regt. Bombay Native Infantry | GGO 418/1881 |
| | 113th Infantry | 13th Regt. Bombay Native Infantry | GGO 418/1881 |
| | 116th Mahrattas | 16th Regt. Bombay Native Infantry | GGO 418/1881 |
| | 123rd Outram's Rifles | 23rd Regt. Bombay Native (Light) Infantry | GGO 418/1881 |
| | 124th Duchess of Connaught's Own Baluchistan Infantry | 24th Regt. Bombay Native Infantry | GGO 418/1881 |

| | | | |
|---|---|---|---|
| **AFGHANISTAN 1879-1880 (Cont.)** | 127th Q.M.O. Baluch Light Infantry | 27th Regt. Bombay Native (Light) Infantry or 1st Baluch Bn. | GGO 418/1881 |
| | 128th Pioneers | 28th Regt. Bombay Native Infantry | GGO 418/1881 |
| | 9th Gurkha Rifles | 9th Regt. Bengal Native Infantry | GGO 418/1881 |
| **BURMA 1885-1887** | The Queen's (Royal West Surrey Regt.) | The Queen's (Royal West Surrey Regt.) | Army Order 392/1890 |
| | The King's (Liverpool Regt.) | The King's (Liverpool Regt.) | Army Order 392/1890 |
| | The Somerset L.I. | The Prince Albert's (Somersetshire Light Infantry) | Army Order 392/1890 |
| | The Royal Scots Fusiliers | The Royal Scots Fusiliers | Army Order 392/1890 |
| | The Royal Welsh Fusiliers | The Royal Welsh Fusiliers | Army Order 392/1890 |
| | The South Wales Borderers | The South Wales Borderers | Army Order 392/1890 |
| | The Hampshire Regt. | The Hampshire Regt. | Army Order 392/1890 |
| | The King's Own Yorkshire L.I. | The King's Own Light Infantry (South Yorkshire Regt.) | Army Order 392/1890 |
| | The Royal Munster Fusiliers | The Royal Munster Fusiliers | Army Order 392/1890 |
| | The Rifle Brigade | The Rifle Brigade (The Prince Consort's Own) | Army Order 392/1890 |
| | | INDIAN ARMY | |
| | 7th Hariana Lancers | 7th Regt. of Bengal Cavalry | GGO 64/1891 |
| | 26th K.G.O. Light Cavalry | 1st Regt. Madras Lancers | GGO 64/1891 |
| | 27th Light Cavalry | 2nd Regt. Madras Lancers | GGO 64/1891 |
| | 31st D.C.O. Lancers | 1st Regt. Bombay Lancers | GGO 64/1891 |
| | 24th Hazara Mountain Battery (F.F.) | No. 4 (Hazara) Mountain Battery, Punjab Frontier Force | GGO 64/1891 |
| | 25th Mountain Battery | No. 1 (Bombay) Mountain Battery | GGO 64/1891 |
| | 27th Mountain Battery | No. 1 (Bengal) Mountain Battery | GGO 64/1891 |
| | 28th Mountain Battery | No. 2 (Bengal) Mountain Battery | GGO 64/1891 |
| | 1st K.G.O. Sappers & Miners | Corps of Bengal Sappers & Miners | GGO 64/1891 |
| | 2nd Q.V.O. Sappers & Miners | Corps of Madras Sappers & Miners (Queen's Own Corps) | GGO 64/1891 |

| | | | |
|---|---|---|---|
| **BURMA 1885-1887 (Cont.)** | 3rd Sappers & Miners | Corps of Bombay Sappers & Miners | GGO 64/1891 |
| | 1st Brahmans | 1st Regt. Bengal Infantry | GGO 64/1891 |
| | 2nd Q.V.O. Rajput Light Infantry | 2nd (The Queen's Own)Regt. of Bengal (Light) Infantry | GGO 64/1891 |
| | 4th P.A.V. Rajputs | 4th Regt. of Bengal Infantry | GGO 64/1891 |
| | 5th Light Infantry | 5th Regt. of Bengal (Light) Infantry | GGO 64/1891 |
| | 10th Jats | 10th Regt. of Bengal Infantry | GGO 64/1891 |
| | 11th Rajputs | 11th Regt. of Bengal Infantry | GGO 64/1891 |
| | 12th Pioneers | 12th (the Kelat-i-Ghilzie) Regt. of Bengal Infantry | GGO 64/1891 |
| | 16th Rajputs | 16th (The Lucknow) Regt. of Bengal Infantry | GGO 64/1891 |
| | 18th Infantry | 18th Regt. of Bengal Infantry | GGO 64/1891 |
| | 26th Punjabis | 26th (Punjab) Regt. of Bengal Infantry | GGO 64/1891 |
| | 27th Punjabis | 27th (Punjab) Regt. of Bengal Infantry | GGO 64/1891 |
| | 33rd Punjabis | 33rd (Punjab) Regt. of Bengal Infantry | GGO 64/1891 |
| | 61st K.G.O. Pioneers | 1st Regt. of Madras Infantry (Pioneers) | GGO 64/1891 |
| | 63rd Palamcottah Light Infantry | 3rd (or Palamcottah) Regt. of Madras (Light) Infantry | GGO 64/1891 |
| | 72nd Punjabis | 12th Regt. of Madras Infantry | GGO 64/1891 |
| | 73rd Carnatic Infantry | 13th Regt. of Madras Infantry | GGO 64/1891 |
| | 74th Punjabis | 14th Regt. of Madras Infantry | GGO 64/1891 |
| | 75th Carnatic Infantry | 15th Regt. of Madras Infantry | GGO 64/1891 |
| | 76th Punjabis | 16th Regt. of Madras Infantry | GGO 64/1891 |
| | 81st Pioneers | 21st Regt. of Madras Infantry | GGO 64/1891 |
| | 83rd Wallajahbad Light Infantry | 23rd or Wallajahbad Regt. of Madras (Light) Infantry | GGO 64/1891 |
| | 86th Carnatic Infantry | 26th Regt. of Madras Infantry | GGO 64/1891 |
| | 87th Punjabis | 27th Regt. of Madras Infantry | GGO 64/1891 |
| | 90th Punjabis | 30th Regt. of Madras Infantry | GGO 64/1891 |
| | 95th Russell's Infantry | 2nd Infantry, Hyderabad Contingent | GGO 64/1891 |
| | 96th Berar Infantry | 3rd Infantry, Hyderabad Contingent | GGO 64/1891 |
| | The 101st Grenadiers | 1st Regt. of Bombay Infantry (Grenadiers) | GGO 64/1891 |
| | 105th Mahratta Light Infantry | 5th Regt. of Bombay (Light) Infantry | GGO 64/1891 |
| | 107th Pioneers | 7th Regt. of Bombay Infantry | GGO 64/1891 |
| | 123rd Outram's Rifles | 23rd Regt. of Bombay (Light) Infantry | GGO 64/1891 |
| | 125th Napier's Rifles | 25th Regt. of Bombay (Light) Infantry | GGO 64/1891 |

| | | | |
|---|---|---|---|
| **BURMA 1885-1887 (Cont.)** | 127th Q.M.O. Baluch Light Infantry | 27th Regt. of Bombay (Light) Infantry (1st Baluch Regt.) | GGO 64/1891 |
| | 3rd Q.A.O. Gurkha Rifles | 3rd Gurkha Regt. | GGO 64/1891 |
| | 6th Gurkha Rifles | 42nd Regt. Gurkha Light Infantry | GGO 64/1891 |
| | 8th Gurkha Rifles | * 44th Regt. Gurkha Light Infantry | GGO 64/1891 |
| **ENCE OF CHITRAL** | 14th K.G.O. Ferozepore Sikhs | 14th Regt. of Bengal Infantry (The Ferozepore Sikhs) | 27th January 1897 |
| **CHITRAL** | The Buffs (East Kent Regt.) | 1st Bn. The Buffs (East Kent Regt.) | 27th January 1897 |
| | The Bedfordshire Regt. | 1st Bn. The Bedfordshire Regt. | 27th January 1897 |
| | The King's Own Scottish Borderers | 2nd Bn. The King's Own Scottish Borderers | 27th January 1897 |
| | The East Lancashire Regt. | 1st Bn. The East Lancashire Regt. | 27th January 1897 |
| | The King's Royal Rifle Corps | 1st Bn. The King's Royal Rifle Corps | 27th January 1897 |
| | Seaforth Highlanders | 1st Bn. Seaforth Highlanders (Ross-shire Buffs, The Duke of Albany's) | 27th January 1897 |
| | The Gordon Highlanders | 1st Bn. The Gordon Highlanders | 27th January 1897 |
| | | INDIAN ARMY | |
| | 9th Hodson's Horse | 9th Regt. of Bengal Lancers | 27th January 1897 |
| | 11th K.E.O. Lancers | 11th (The Prince of Wales's Own) Regt. of Bengal Lancers | 27th January 1897 |
| | Q.V.O. Corps of Guides (F.F.) | The Queen's Own Corps of Guides, Punjab Frontier Force | 27th January 1897 |
| | 22nd Derajat Mountain Battery (F.F.) | No. 2 (Derajat) Mountain Battery, Punjab Frontier Force | 27th January 1897 |
| | 24th Hazara Mountain Battery (F.F.) | No. 4 (Hazara) Mountain Battery, Punjab Frontier Force | 27th January 1897 |
| | 1st K.G.O. Sappers & Miners | Corps of Bengal Sappers & Miners | 27th January 1897 |
| | 2nd Q.V.O. Sappers & Miners | Queens Own Corps of Sappers & Miners | 27th January 1897 |
| | 13th Rajputs | 13th (The Shekhawati) Regt. of Bengal Infantry | 27th January 1897 |
| | 15th Ludhiana Sikhs | 15th Regt. of Bengal Infantry (The Ludhiana Sikhs) | 27th January 1897 |
| | 23rd Sikh Pioneers | 23rd (Punjab) Regt. of Bengal Infantry (Pioneers) | 27th January 1897 |
| | 25th Punjabis | 25th (Punjab) Regt. of Bengal Infantry | 27th January 1897 |

* 2nd Bn. 43rd Regt. Gurkha Light Infty. were also present

| | | | |
|---|---|---|---|
| **CHITRAL (Cont.)** | 29th Punjabis | 29th (Punjab) Regt. of Bengal Infantry | 27th January 1897 |
| | 30th Punjabis | 30th (Punjab) Regt. of Bengal Infantry | 27th January 1897 |
| | 32nd Sikh Pioneers | 32nd (Punjab) Regt. of Bengal Infantry (Pioneers) | 27th January 1897 |
| | 34th Sikh Pioneers | 34th (Punjab) Regt. of Bengal Infantry (Pioneers) | 27th January 1897 |
| | 37th Dogras | 37th (Dogra) Regt. of Bengal Infantry | 27th January 1897 |
| | 54th Sikhs (F.F.) | 4th Regt. of Sikh Infantry, Punjab Frontier Force | 27th January 1897 |
| | 3rd Q.A.O. Gurkha Rifles | 3rd Gurkha (Rifle) Regt. | 27th January 1897 |
| | 4th Gurkha Rifles | 4th Gurkha (Rifle) Regt. | 27th January 1897 |
| **MALAKAND** | 11th K.E.O. Lancers | 11th (Prince of Wales's Own) Regt. of Bengal Lancers | 15th December 1899 |
| | Q.V.O. Corps of Guides (F.F.) | The Queen's Own Corps of Guides, Punjab Frontier Force | 15th December 1899 |
| | 28th Mountain Battery | No. 8 (Bengal) Mountain Battery | 15th December 1899 |
| | 2nd Q.V.O. Sappers & Miners | Corps of Madras Sappers & Miners | 15th December 1899 |
| | 24th Punjabis | 24th (Punjab) Regt. of Bengal Infantry | 15th December 1899 |
| | 31st Punjabis | 31st (Punjab) Regt. of Bengal Infantry | 15th December 1899 |
| | 35th Sikhs | 35th (Sikh) Regt. of Bengal Infantry | 15th December 1899 |
| | 38th Dogras | 38th (Dogra) Regt. of Bengal Infantry | 15th December 1899 |
| | 45th Rattray's Sikhs | 45th (Rattray's Sikh) Regt. of Bengal Infantry | 15th December 1899 |
| **SAMANA** | 36th Sikhs | 36th (Sikh) Regt. of Bengal Infantry | 15th December 1899 |
| **TIRAH** | The Queen's (Royal West Surrey Regt.) | 1st Bn. The Queen's (Royal West Surrey Regt.) | 15th December 1899 |
| | The Devonshire Regt. | 1st Bn. The Devonshire Regt. | 15th December 1899 |
| | The Yorkshire Regt. | 2nd Bn. The Princess of Wales's Own (Yorkshire Regt.) | 15th December 1899 |
| | The Royal Scots Fusiliers | 2nd Bn. The Royal Scots Fusiliers | 15th December 1899 |
| | The King's Own Scottish Borderers | 2nd Bn. The King's Own Scottish Borderers | 15th December 1899 |
| | The Dorsetshire Regt. | 1st Bn. The Dorsetshire Regt. | 15th December 1899 |
| | The Sherwood Foresters | 2nd Bn. The Sherwood Foresters (Derbyshire Regt.) | 15th December 1899 |
| | The Northamptonshire Regt. | 1st Bn. The Northamptonshire Regt. | 15th December 1899 |
| | The Gordon Highlanders | 1st Bn. The Gordon Highlanders | 15th December 1899 |

|  |  | Indian Army |  |
|---|---|---|---|
| **TIRAH (Cont.)** | | INDIAN ARMY | |
| | 18th K.G.O. Lancers | 18th Regt. of Bengal Lancers | 15th December 1899 |
| | 21st Kohat Mountain Battery (F.F.) | No. 1 (Kohat) Mountain Battery, Punjab Frontier Force | 15th December 1899 |
| | 22nd Derajat Mountain Battery (F.F.) | No. 2 (Derajat) Mountain Battery, Punjab Frontier Force | 15th December 1899 |
| | 25th Mountain Battery | No. 5 Bombay Mountain Battery | 15th December 1899 |
| | 1st K.G.O. Sappers & Miners | Corps of Bengal Sappers & Miners | 15th December 1899 |
| | 2nd Q.V.O. Sappers & Miners | Queen's Own Corps of Madras Sappers & Miners | 15th December 1899 |
| | 3rd Sappers & Miners | Corps of Bombay Sappers & Miners | 15th December 1899 |
| | 15th Ludhiana Sikhs | 15th Regt. of Bengal Infantry (The Ludhiana Sikhs) | 15th December 1899 |
| | 30th Punjabis | 30th (Punjab) Regt. of Bengal Infantry | 15th December 1899 |
| | 36th Sikhs | 36th (Sikh) Regt. of Bengal Infantry | 15th December 1899 |
| | 53rd Sikhs (F.F.) | 3rd Regt. of Sikh Infantry, Punjab Frontier Force | 15th December 1899 |
| | 56th Punjabi Rifles | 2nd Regt. of Infantry, Punjab Frontier Force | 15th December 1899 |
| | 81st Pioneers | 21st Regt. of Madras Infantry (Pioneers) | 15th December 1899 |
| | 128th Pioneers | 28th (Pioneer) Regt. of Bombay Infantry | 15th December 1899 |
| | 1st K.G.O. Gurkha Rifles | 1st Gurkha (Rifle) Regt. | 15th December 1899 |
| | 2nd K.E.O. Gurkha Rifles | 2nd (Prince of Wales's Own) Gurkha (Rifle) Regt. (The Sirmoor Rifles) | 15th December 1899 |
| | 3rd Q.A.O. Gurkha Rifles | 3rd Gurkha (Rifle) Regt. | 15th December 1899 |
| | 4th Gurkha Rifles | 4th Gurkha (Rifle) Regt. | 15th December 1899 |
| **PUNJAB FRONTIER** | 3rd Skinners Horse | 3rd Regt. of Bengal Cavalry | 15th December 1899 |
| | 6th K.E.O. Cavalry | 6th (Prince of Wales's) Regt. of Bengal Cavalry | 15th December 1899 |
| | 9th Hodson's Horse | 9th Regt. of Bengal Lancers | 15th December 1899 |
| | 11th K.E.O. Lancers | 11th (The Prince of Wales' Own) Regt. of Bengal Lancers | 15th December 1899 |
| | 13th D.o.C. Lancers | 13th (Duke of Connaught's) Regt. of Bengal Lancers | 15th December 1899 |
| | 18th K.G.O. Lancers | 18th Regt. of Bengal Lancers | 15th December 1899 |
| | 38th K.G.O. Central India Horse | 1st Regt. Central India Horse | 15th December 1899 |
| | 39th K.G.O. Central India Horse | 2nd Regt. Central India Horse | 15th December 1899 |

| | | | |
|---|---|---|---|
| **PUNJAB FRONTIER (Cont.)** | Q.V.O. Corps of Guides (F.F.) | Queen's Own Corps of Guides, Punjab Frontier Force | 15th December 1899 |
| | 21st Kohat Mountain Battery (F.F.) | No. 1 (Kohat) Mountain Battery, Punjab Frontier Force | 15th December 1899 |
| | 22nd Derajat Mountain Battery (F.F.) | No. 2 (Derajat) Mountain Battery, Punjab Frontier Force | 15th December 1899 |
| | 25th Mountain Battery | No. 5 Bombay Mountain Battery | 15th December 1899 |
| | 28th Mountain Battery | No. 8 (Bengal) Mountain Battery | 15th December 1899 |
| | 1st K.G.O. Sappers & Miners | Corps of Bengal Sappers & Miners | 15th December 1899 |
| | 2nd Q.V.O. Sappers & Miners | Queen's Own Corps of Madras Sappers & Miners | 15th December 1899 |
| | 3rd Sappers & Miners | Corps of Bombay Sappers & Miners | 15th December 1899 |
| | 12th Pioneers | 12th (Kelat-i-Ghilzie) Regt. of Bengal Infantry | 15th December 1899 |
| | 15th Ludhiana Sikhs | 15th Regt. of Bengal Infantry (The Ludhiana Sikhs) | 15th December 1899 |
| | 20th D.C.O. Infantry | 20th (Duke of Cambridge's Own Punjab) Regt. of Bengal Infantry | 15th December 1899 |
| | 22nd Punjabis | 22nd (Punjab) Regt. of Bengal Infantry | 15th December 1899 |
| | 24th Punjabis | 24th (Punjab) Regt. of Bengal Infantry | 15th December 1899 |
| | 30th Punjabis | 30th (Punjab) Regt. of Bengal Infantry | 15th December 1899 |
| | 31st Punjabis | 31st (Punjab) Regt. of Bengal Infantry | 15th December 1899 |
| | 34th Sikh Pioneers | 34th (Punjab) Regt. of Bengal Infantry (Pioneers) | 15th December 1899 |
| | 35th Sikhs | 35th (Sikh) Regt. of Bengal Infantry | 15th December 1899 |
| | 36th Sikhs | 36th (Sikh) Regt. of Bengal Infantry | 15th December 1899 |
| | 37th Dogras | 37th (Dogra) Regt. of Bengal Infantry | 15th December 1899 |
| | 38th Dogras | 38th (Dogra) Regt. of Bengal Infantry | 15th December 1899 |
| | 39th Garhwal Rifles | 39th (The Garhwal Rifles) Regt. of Bengal Infantry | 15th December 1899 |
| | 45th Rattray's Sikhs | 45th (Rattray's Sikh) Regt. of Bengal Infantry | 15th December 1899 |
| | 53rd Sikhs (F.F.) | 3rd Regt. Sikh Infantry, Punjab Frontier Force | 15th December 1899 |
| | 56th Punjabi Rifles (F.F.) | 2nd Regt. of Infantry, Punjab Frontier Force | 15th December 1899 |
| | 81st Pioneers | 21st Regt. of Madras Infantry (Pioneers) | 15th December 1899 |
| | 128th Pioneers | 28th (Pioneer) Regt. of Bombay Infantry | 15th December 1899 |
| | 1st K.G.O. Gurkha Rifles | 1st Gurkha (Rifle) Regt. | 15th December 1899 |
| | 2nd K.E.O. Gurkha Rifles | 2nd (Prince of Wales's Own) Gurkha (Rifle) Regt. (The Sirmoor Rifles) | 15th December 1899 |
| | 3rd Q.A.O. Gurkha Rifles | 3rd Gurkha (Rifle) Regt. | 15th December 1899 |

| | | | |
|---|---|---|---|
| **PUNJAB FRONTIER (Cont.)** | 4th Gurkha Rifles | 4th Gurkha (Rifle) Regt. | 15th December 1899 |
| | 5th Gurkha Rifles (F.F.) | 5th Gurkha (Rifle) Regt. | 15th December 1899 |
| | 9th Gurkha Rifles | 9th Gurkha (Rifle) Regt. of Bengal Infantry | 15th December 1899 |
| **PEKIN 1900** | The Royal Welsh Fusiliers | The Royal Welsh Fusiliers | AO 271/1902 |
| | | INDIAN ARMY | |
| | 1st D.Y.O. Lancers | 1st (The Duke of York's Own) Regt. of Bengal Lancers | 23rd April 1903 |
| | 7th D.C.O. Rajputs | 7th (The Duke of Connaught's Own) Regt. of Bengal Infantry | 23rd April 1903 |
| | 24th Punjabis | 24th (Punjab) Regt.of Bengal Infantry | 23rd April 1903 |
| | 51st Sikhs (F.F.) | 1st Regt. Sikh Infantry, Punjab Frontier Force | 23rd April 1903 |
| **CHINA 1900** | 16th Cavalry | 16th Regt. of Bengal Lancers | 23rd April 1903 |
| | 33rd Q.V.O. Light Cavalry | 3rd (Queen's Own) Regt. of Bombay Light Cavalry | 23rd April 1903 |
| | 1st K.G.O. Sappers & Miners | Corps of Bengal Sappers & Miners | 23rd April 1903 |
| | 2nd Q .V.O. Sappers & Miners | Queen's Own Corps of Madras Sappers & Miners | 23rd April 1903 |
| | 3rd Sappers & Miners | Corps of Bombay Sappers & Miners | 23rd April 1903 |
| | 2nd Q.V.O. Rajput Light Infantry | 2nd (Queen's Own) Rajput Regt. of Bengal (Light) Infantry | 23rd April 1903 |
| | 6th Jat Light Infantry | 6th (Jat) Regt. of Bengal (Light) Infantry | 23rd April 1903 |
| | 14th K.G.O. Ferozepore Sikhs | 14th Regt. of Bengal Infantry (The Ferozepore Sikhs) | 23rd April 1903 |
| | 20th D.C.O. Infantry | 20th (The Duke of Cambridge's Own Punjab) Regt. of Bengal Infantry | 23rd April 1903 |
| | 34th Sikh Pioneers | 34th (Punjab) Regt. of Bengal Infantry (Pioneers) | 23rd April 1903 |
| | 57th Wilde's Rifles (F.F.) | 4th Regt. of Infantry, Punjab Frontier Force | 23rd April 1903 |
| | 61st K.G.O. Pioneers | 1st Regt. of Madras Infantry (Pioneers) | 23rd April 1903 |
| | 63rd Palamcottah Light Infantry | 3rd (or Palamcottah) Regt. of Madras (Light) Infantry | 23rd April 1903 |
| | 88th Carnatic Infantry | 28th Regt. of Madras Infantry | 23rd April 1903 |
| | 91st Punjabis (Light Infantry) | 31st Regt. (6th Burma Bn) of Madras (Light) Infantry | 23rd April 1903 |
| | 98th Infantry | 5th Infantry, Hyderabad Contingent | 23rd April 1903 |
| | 122nd Rajputana Infantry | 22nd Regt. of Bombay Infantry | 23rd April 1903 |
| | 126th Baluchistan Infantry | 26th (Baluchistan) Regt. of Bombay Infantry | 23rd April 1903 |

| | | | |
|---|---|---|---|
| **CHINA 1900** | 130th K.G.O. Baluchis | 30th Regt. of Bombay Infantry (3rd Baluch Battalion) | 23rd April 1903 |
| **(Cont.)** | 4th Gurkha Rifles | 4th Gurkha (Rifle) Regt. | 23rd April 1903 |

# AFRICA

H•

| | | |
|---|---|---|
| **TANGIER** | Defence | 1662-1680 |
| **MANDORA** | French Revolutionary Wars 1793-1802 | 13th March 1801 |
| **MARABOUT** | ,, ,, | 21st August 1801 |
| **EGYPT** (With Sphinx) | ,, ,, | 1801 |
| **CAPE OF GOOD HOPE** | Expedition against the Dutch | 7th to 9th January 1806 |
| **SOUTH AFRICA 1835** | 6th Kaffir War | 1835 |
| **SOUTH AFRICA 1846-1847** | 7th Kaffir War | 1846-1847 |
| **SOUTH AFRICA 1851-1853** | 8th Kaffir War | 1851-1853 |
| **ABYSSINIA** | Abyssinian War | 1867-1868 |
| **ASHANTEE** | Ashantee War | 1873-1874 |
| **SOUTH AFRICA 1878-1879** | Zulu & Basuto War | 1878-1879 |
| **TEL-EL-KEBIR** | Revolt of Arabi Pasha | 13th September 1882 |
| **EGYPT 1882** | 1st Sudan War | 1882 |
| **EGYPT 1884** | ,, | 1884 |
| **ABU KLEA** | Egyptian Campaign | 17th January 1885 |
| **KIRBEKAN** | ,, ,, | 10th February 1885 |
| **NILE** | ,, ,, | 1884-1885 |
| **SUAKIN** | ,, ,, | 22nd March 1885 |
| **TOFREK** | ,, ,, | 23rd March 1885 |
| **WEST AFRICA** | Minor Campaigns in West Africa | 1887, 1892-1894 |
| **SIERRA LEONE** | ,, ,, | 1898-1899 |
| **ASHANTI** | ,, ,, | 1900 |
| **BRITISH EAST AFRICA** | Minor Campaigns in East Africa | 1896-1901 |
| **HAFIR** | Reconquest of the Sudan | 19th September 1896 |
| **ATBARA** | ,, ,, | 8th April 1898 |
| **KHARTOUM** | ,, ,, | 2nd September 1898 |
| **MODDER RIVER** | South African War 1899-1902 | 28th November 1899 |
| **DEFENCE OF KIMBERLEY** | ,, ,, | October 1899 to February 1900 |
| **RELIEF OF KIMBERLEY** | ,, ,, | 15th February 1900 |

| | | |
|---|---|---|
| PAARDEBURG | South African War 1899-1902 | 18th to 27th February 1900 |
| DEFENCE OF LADYSMITH | " " | November 1899 to February 1900 |
| RELIEF OF LADYSMITH | " " | 28th February 1900 |
| SOUTH AFRICA 1899-1902 | " " | 1899-1902 |
| * MEDITERRANEAN | " " | 1901-1902 |
| * ST HELENA | " " | 1901-1902 |

NOTE 'The honours after 1881 i.e. from EGYPT 1882 were awarded to amalgamated Regiments. From this point the titles shown were those, with minor changes, which were borne by Regiments in 1914. For the British Army there is no column giving the previous title. The Indian Army however altered their titles in 1903 on reorganisation, in order that the titles of 1882 could be shown, the honours granted for TEL EL KEBIR, EGYPT 1882, SUAKIN AND TOFREK have been moved from their strict sequence and placed before the 1887 honours.

* To be precise these two honours should appear under EUROPE, they are placed here in order that the SOUTH AFRICAN honours should be kept together.

| | ABBREVIATED TITLE | FORMER TITLE | DATE OF AWARD |
|---|---|---|---|
| **ANGIER 1662-1680** | 1st Royal Dragoons | Tangier Troop of Horse | Army Order 180/1909 |
| | The Queen's (Royal West Surrey Regt.) | *Tangier Regt. of Foot | Army Order 180/1909 |
| | * Colonels of the Regt. from 1662-1680. | | |
| | 1662-1663 The Earl of Peterborough | | |
| | 1663-1664 The Earl of Teviot | | |
| | 1664-1668 Lt-Gen. H. Norwood | | |
| | 1668-1675 The Earl of Middleton | | |
| | 1675-1680 The Earl of Inchiquin | | |
| **TANGIER 1680** | Grenadier Guards | The King's Royal Regt. of Guards | Army Order 180/1909 |
| | Coldstream Guards | Coldstream Regt. of Foot Guards | Army Order 180/1909 |
| | The Royal Scots | The Earl of Dumbarton's Regt. of Foot | Army Order 180/1909 |
| **MANDORA** | 2nd Bn. The Cameronians | 90th Regt. of Foot (Perthshire Volunteers) | 7th March 1817 |
| | 2nd Bn. The Gordon Highlanders | 92nd Regt. of Foot | 15th February 1813 |
| **MARABOUT** | 2nd Bn. The Dorsetshire Regt. | 54th (West Norfolk) Regt. of Foot | 18th December 1841 |
| **EGYPT 1801** | 11th Hussars | 11th Regt. of Light Dragoons | 6th July 1802 |
| (With Sphinx) | 12th Lancers | 12th (Prince of Wales's) Regt. of (Light) Dragoons | 6th July 1802 |
| | Coldstream Guards | Coldstream Regt. of Foot Guards | 6th July 1802 |
| | Scots Guards | 3rd Regt. of Foot Guards | 6th July 1802 |
| | The Royal Scots | 1st (Royal) Regt. of Foot | 6th July 1802 |
| | The Queen's (Royal West Surrey Regt.) | 2nd (Queen's Royal) Regt. of Foot | 6th July 1802 |
| | The King's (Liverpool Regt.) | 8th (The King's) Regt. of Foot | 6th July 1802 |
| | The Lincolnshire Regt. | 10th (North Lincolnshire) Regt. of Foot | 6th July 1802 |
| | The Somerset L.I. | 13th (1st Somersetshire) Regt. of Foot | 6th July 1802 |
| | The Royal Irish Regt. | 18th (Royal Irish) Regt. of Foot | 6th July 1802 |
| | The Lancashire Fusiliers | 20th (East Devonshire) Regt. of Foot | 6th July 1802 |
| | The Royal Welsh Fusiliers | 23rd Regt. of Foot (Royal Welsh Fusiliers) | 6th July 1802 |
| | The South Wales Borderers | 24th (2nd Warwickshire) Regt. of Foot | 6th July 1802 |

| | | | |
|---|---|---|---|
| **EGYPT 1801 (Cont.)** | The King's Own Scottish Borderers | 25th (Sussex) Regt. of Foot | 6th July 1802 |
| | 1st Bn. The Cameronians | 26th (Cameronian) Regt. of Foot | 6th July 1802 |
| | 2nd Bn. The Cameronians | 90th Regt. of Foot (Perthshire Volunteers) | 6th July 1802 |
| | 1st Bn. The Royal Inniskilling Fusiliers | 27th (Inniskilling) Regt. of Foot | 6th July 1802 |
| | 1st Bn. The Gloucestershire Regt. | 28th (North Gloucestershire) Regt. of Foot | 6th July 1802 |
| | 2nd Bn. The Gloucestershire Regt. | 61st (South Gloucestershire) Regt. of Foot | 6th July 1802 |
| | 1st Bn. The East Lancashire Regt. | 30th (Cambridgeshire) Regt. of Foot | 6th July 1802 |
| | 2nd Bn. The South Staffordshire Regt. | 80th Regt. of Foot (Staffordshire Volunteers) | 6th July 1802 |
| | 2nd Bn. The Dorsetshire Regt. | 54th (West Norfolk) Regt. of Foot | 6th July 1802 |
| | 1st Bn. P.W.V. (South Lancashire Regt.) | 40th (2nd Somersetshire) Regt. of Foot | 6th July 1802 |
| | 1st Bn. The Black Watch | 42nd (Royal Highland) Regt. of Foot | 6th July 1802 |
| | 1st Bn. The Essex Regt. | 44th (East Essex) Regt. of Foot | 6th July 1802 |
| | 2nd Bn. The Northamptonshire Regt. | 58th (Rutlandshire) Regt. of Foot | 6th July 1802 |
| | 1st Bn. The Queen's Own (Royal West Kent Regt.) | 50th (West Kent) Regt. of Foot | 6th July 1802 |
| | 2nd Bn. The Manchester Regt. | *97th (Queen's Own) Regt. of Foot | 6th July 1802 |
| | 2nd Bn. The Gordon Highlanders | 92nd Regt. of Foot | 6th July 1802 |
| | The Queen's Own Cameron Highlanders | 79th Regt. of Foot (Cameronian Volunteers) | 6th July 1802 |
| | 2nd Bn. The Royal Irish Rifles | 86th Regt. of Foot | 6th July 1802 |
| | 2nd Bn. The Royal Irish Fusiliers | 89th Regt. of Foot | 6th July 1802 |
| | 1st Bn. The Connaught Rangers | 88th Regt. of Foot (Connaught Rangers) | 6th July 1802 |
| | | INDIAN ARMY | |
| | 2nd Q.V.O. Sappers & Miners | **Madras Pioneers | July 1802 |
| | 102nd K.E.O. Grenadiers | 2nd Bn. 1st Regt. Bombay Native Infantry | Bombay GO 14th April 1804 |
| | 113th Infantry | 1st Bn. 7th Regt. Bombay Native Infantry | Bombay GO 14th April 1804 |

* In 1801 was 97th (Queen's German) Regt. of Foot Renumbered 96th in 1816 and disbanded in 1818 as 96th (Queen's Own) Regt. of Foot. A new 96th Regiment was raised in 1824, and the honours of the disbanded Regiment regranted in 1874.

** Addition of Sphinx to EGYPT granted in 1879.

| Battle Honour | Present Title | Title at Time of Action | Date Awarded |
|---|---|---|---|
| **CAPE OF GOOD HOPE 1806 (Date added 25th July 1882)** | The South Wales Borderers | 24th (2nd Warwickshire) Regt. of Foot | 21st June 1824 |
| | 2nd Bn. The East Lancashire Regt. | 59th (2nd Nottinghamshire) Regt. of Foot | 3rd March 1836 |
| | 1st Bn. The Highland L.I. | 71st (Highland) Regt. of Foot | 8th June 1835 |
| | 1st Bn. Seaforth Highlanders | 72nd (Highland) Regt. of Foot | 3rd March 1836 |
| | 1st Bn. The Royal Irish Rifles | 83rd Regt. of Foot | 3rd March 1836 |
| | 2nd Bn. The Argyll & Sutherland Highlanders | 93rd Regt. of Foot | 1st December 1835 |
| **SOUTH AFRICA 1835** | 1st Bn. The Royal Inniskilling Fusiliers | 27th (Inniskilling) Regt. of Foot | 25th July 1882 |
| | 1st Bn. Seaforth Highlanders | 72nd (Duke of Albany's Own Highlanders) Regt. of Foot | 25th July 1882 |
| | 1st Bn. The Gordon Highlanders | 75th Regt. of Foot | 25th July 1882 |
| **SOUTH AFRICA 1846-1847** | 7th Dragoon Guards | 7th (The Princess Royal's) Regt. of Dragoon Guards | 25th July 1882 |
| | The Royal Warwickshire Regt. | 6th (Royal 1st Warwickshire) Regt. of Foot | 25th July 1882 |
| | 2nd Bn. The Cameronians | 90th Regt. of Foot (Perthshire Volunteers) Light Infantry | 25th July 1882 |
| | 1st Bn. The Royal Inniskilling Fusiliers | 27th (Inniskilling) Regt. of Foot | 25th July 1882 |
| | 2nd Bn. The Black Watch | 73rd Regt. of Foot | 25th July 1882 |
| | 1st Bn. The Sherwood Foresters | 45th (Nottinghamshire) Regt. of Foot | 25th July 1882 |
| | 1st Bn. The Argyll & Sutherland Highlanders | 91st (Argyllshire) Regt. of Foot | 25th July 1882 |
| | The Rifle Brigade | The Rifle Brigade | 25th July 1882 |
| **SOUTH AFRICA 1851-52-53** | 12th Lancers | 12th (The Prince of Wales's) Royal Regt. of Lancers | 25th July 1882 |
| | The Queen's (Royal West Surrey) Regt. | 2nd (The Queen's Royal) Regt. of Foot | 25th July 1882 |
| | The Royal Warwickshire Regt. | 6th (Royal 1st Warwickshire) Regt. of Foot | 25th July 1882 |
| | The Suffolk Regt. | 12th (East Suffolk) Regt. of Foot | 25th July 1882 |
| | 2nd Bn. The Black Watch | 73rd Regt. of Foot | 25th July 1882 |
| | 1st Bn. Oxf & Bucks Lt. Infty. | 43rd (Monmouthshire) Regt. of Foot (Light Infantry) | 25th July 1882 |
| | The King's Royal Rifle Corps | 60th (The King's Royal Rifle Corps) | 25th July 1882 |
| | 2nd Bn. The Highland L.I. | 74th (Highland) Regt. of Foot | 25th July 1882 |

| Campaign | Present title | Title at time of award | Date of award |
|---|---|---|---|
| **SOUTH AFRICA 1851-52-53 (Cont.)** | 1st Bn. The Argyll & Sutherland Highlanders | 91st (Argyllshire) Regt. of Foot | 25th July 1882 |
| | The Rifle Brigade | The Rifle Brigade | 25th July 1882 |
| **ABYSSINIA** | 3rd Dragoon Guards | 3rd (Prince of Wales's) Dragoon Guards | 21st September 1868 |
| | The King's (Royal Lancaster Regt.) | 4th (The King's Own Royal) Regt. of Foot | 21st September 1868 |
| | 1st Bn. The Cameronians | 26th (The Cameronian) Regt. of Foot | 21st September 1868 |
| | 1st Bn. The Duke of Wellington's Regt. | 33rd (The Duke of Wellington's) Regt. of Foot | 21st September 1868 |
| | 1st Bn. The Sherwood Foresters | 45th (Nottinghamshire) Regt. of Foot Sherwood Foresters | 21st September 1868 |
| | | INDIAN ARMY | |
| | 10th D.C.O. Lancers | 10th Regt. of Bengal Light Cavalry (Lancers) | 9th August 1869 |
| | 12th Cavalry | 12th Regt. of Bengal Cavalry | 9th August 1869 |
| | 33rd Q.V.O. Light Cavalry | 3rd Regt. of Bombay Light Cavalry | 9th August 1869 |
| | 25th Mountain Battery | No. 1 Company, Bombay Native Artillery | 9th August 1869 |
| | 2nd Q.V.O. Sappers & Miners | Corps of Madras Sappers & Miners | 9th August 1869 |
| | 3rd Sappers & Miners | Corps of Bombay Sappers & Miners | 9th August 1869 |
| | 21st Punjabis | 21st (Punjab) Regt. Bengal Native Infantry | 9th August 1869 |
| | 23rd Sikh Pioneers | 23rd (Punjab) Regt. Bengal Native Infantry (Pioneers) | 9th August 1869 |
| | 102nd K.E.O. Grenadiers | 2nd or Grenadier Regt., Bombay Native Infantry | 9th August 1869 |
| | 103rd Mahratta Light Infantry | 3rd Regt. Bombay Native Infantry | 9th August 1869 |
| | 110th Mahratta Light Infantry | 10th Regt. Bombay Native Infantry | 9th August 1869 |
| | 121st Pioneers | 21st Regt. Bombay Native Infantry (The Marine Battalion) | 9th August 1869 |
| | 125th Napier's Rifles | 25th Regt. Bombay Native (Light) Infantry | 9th August 1869 |
| | 127th Q.M.O. Baluch Light Infantry | 27th Regt. Bombay Native Infantry or 1st Baluch Battalion | 9th August 1869 |
| **ASHANTEE 1873-1874** | The Royal Welsh Fusiliers | 23rd Regt. of Foot (Royal Welch Fusiliers) | 18th October 1876 |
| | 1st Bn. The Black Watch | 42nd (Royal Highland) Regt. of Foot (The Black Watch) | 18th October 1876 |
| | The Rifle Brigade | The Rifle Brigade (The Prince Consort's Own) | 18th October 1876 |
| | The West India Regt. | 1st & 2nd Bns The West India Regt. | 18th October 1876 |

| Battle Honour | Regiment | Regiment at time | Date |
|---|---|---|---|
| SOUTH AFRICA 1877-78-79 | The South Wales Borderers | 24th (2nd Warwickshire) Regt. of Foot | 25th July 1882 |
| | 2nd Bn. The Cameronians | 90th Regt. of Foot (Perthshire Volunteers) (Light Infantry) | 25th July 1882 |
| | 1st Bn. The Connaught Rangers | 88th Regt. of Foot (Connaught Rangers) | 25th July 1882 |
| | 2nd Bn. The Connaught Rangers | 94th Regt. of Foot | 25th July 1882 |
| SOUTH AFRICA 1878-1879 | The Somerset L.I. | 13th (1st Somersetshire) or Prince Albert's Regt. of Light Infantry | 25th July 1882 |
| | 2nd Bn. The South Staffordshire Regt. | 80th Regt. of Foot (Staffordshire Volunteers) | 25th July 1882 |
| SOUTH AFRICA 1879 | 1st King's Dragoon Guards | 1st (The King's) Regt. of Dragoon Guards | 25th July 1882 |
| | 17th Lancers | 17th (Duke of Cambridge's Own) Regt. of Lancers | 25th July 1882 |
| | The Buffs (East Kent Regt.) | 3rd (East Kent) Regt. of Foot (The Buffs) | 25th July 1882 |
| | The King's Own (Royal Lancaster Regt.) | 4th (The King's Own Royal) Regt. of Foot | 25th July 1882 |
| | The Royal Scots Fusiliers | 21st Regt. of Foot (Royal Scots Fusiliers) | 25th July 1882 |
| | 2nd Bn. The Northamptonshire Regt. | 58th (Rutlandshire) Regt. of Foot | 25th July 1882 |
| | 1st Bn. The Middlesex Regt. | 57th (West Middlesex) Regt. of Foot | 25th July 1882 |
| | The King's Royal Rifle Corps | 60th (The King's Royal Rifle Corps) | 25th July 1882 |
| | 2nd Bn. The Wiltshire Regt. | 99th (The Duke of Edinburgh's) Regt. of Foot | 25th July 1882 |
| | 1st Bn. The Argyll & Sutherland Highlanders | 91st (Princess Louise's Argyllshire Highlanders) Regt. of Foot | 25th July 1882 |
| * TEL EL KEBIR | | 1st Life Guards | GO 32/1883 |
| | | 2nd Life Guards | GO 32/1883 |
| | | Royal Horse Guards | GO 32/1883 |
| | | 4th Dragoon Guards | GO 32/1883 |
| | | 7th Dragoon Guards | GO 32/1883 |
| | | 19th Hussars | GO 32/1883 |
| | | Grenadier Guards | GO 32/1883 |
| | | Coldstream Guards | GO 32/1883 |
| | | Scots Guards | GO 32/1883 |
| | | The Royal Irish Regt. | GO 32/1883 |

| Battle Honour | Regiment | Authority |
|---|---|---|
| **TEL EL KEBIR (Cont.)** | The Duke of Cornwall's L.I. | GO 32/1883 |
| | The Black Watch | GO 32/1883 |
| | The King's Royal Rifle Corps | GO 32/1883 |
| | The York & Lancaster Regt. | GO 32/1883 |
| | The Highland Light Infantry | GO 32/1883 |
| | Seaforth Highlanders | GO 32/1883 |
| | The Gordon Highlanders | GO 32/1883 |
| | The Queen's Own Cameron Highlanders | GO 32/1883 |
| | The Royal Irish Fusiliers | GO 32/1883 |
| **EGYPT 1882** | 1st Life Guards | GO 32/1883 |
| | 2nd Life Guards | GO 32/1883 |
| | Royal Horse Guards | GO 32/1883 |
| | 4th Dragoon Guards | GO 32/1883 |
| | 7th Dragoon Guards | GO 32/1883 |
| | Grenadier Guards | GO 32/1883 |
| | Coldstream Guards | GO 32/1883 |
| | Scots Guards | GO 32/1883 |
| | The Royal Irish Regt. | GO 32/1883 |
| | The Duke of Cornwall's L.I. | GO 32/1883 |
| | The Royal Sussex Regt. | GO 32/1883 |
| | The South Staffordshire Regt. | GO 32/1883 |
| | The Sherwood Foresters | GO 32/1883 |
| | The Royal Berkshire Regt. | GO 32/1883 |
| | The Queen's Own (Royal West Kent Regt.) | GO 32/1883 |
| | The King's Shropshire L.I. | GO 32/1883 |
| | The Manchester Regt. | GO 32/1883 |
| | The Highland L.I. | GO 32/1883 |
| | Seaforth Highlanders | GO 32/1883 |
| | The Queen's Own Cameron Highlanders | GO 32/1883 |
| | 8th (City of London) Bn. The London Regt. Post Office Rifles | GO 32/1883 |

| | | |
|---|---|---|
| **EGYPT 1882, 1884** (Date '1884' added G.O. 10/1885) | 19th Hussars | GO 32/1883 |
| | The Black Watch | GO 32/1883 |
| | The King's Royal Rifle Corps | GO 32/1883 |
| | The York & Lancaster Regt. | GO 32/1883 |
| | The Gordon Highlanders | GO 32/1883 |
| | The Royal Irish Fusiliers | GO 32/1883 |
| **EGYPT 1884** | 10th Hussars | |
| **ABU KLEA** | 19th Hussars | GO 18/1886 |
| | 1st Bn. The Royal Sussex Regt. | GO 18/1886 |
| **KIRBEKAN** | 1st Bn. The South Staffordshire Regt. | GO 18/1886 |
| | 1st Bn. The Black Watch | GO 18/1886 |
| **NILE 1884-1885** | 19th Hussars | GO 10/1886 |
| | 1st Bn. The Royal Irish Regt. | GO 10/1886 |
| | 2nd Bn. The Duke of Cornwall's L.I. | GO 10/1886 |
| | 1st Bn. The Royal Sussex Regt. | GO 10/1886 |
| | 1st Bn. The South Staffordshire Regt. | GO 10/1886 |
| | 1st Bn. The Black Watch | GO 10/1886 |
| | 2nd Bn. The Essex Regt. | GO 10/1886 |
| | 1st Bn. The Queen's Own (R.W.K.) | GO 10/1886 |
| | 1st Bn. The Gordon Highlanders | GO 10/1886 |
| | 1st Bn. The Queen's Own Cameron Highlanders | GO 10/1886 |
| **SUAKIN 1885** | 5th (Royal Irish) Lancers | GO 10/1886 |
| | 20th Hussars | GO 10/1886 |
| | Grenadier Guards | GO 10/1886 |
| | Coldstream Guards | GO 10/1886 |
| | Scots Guards | GO 10/1886 |
| | 1st Bn. The East Surrey Regt. | GO 10/1886 |

| | | | |
|---|---|---|---|
| **SUAKIN 1885 (Cont.)** | | 1st Bn. The Royal Berkshire Regt. | GO 10/1886 |
| | | 1st Bn. The King's Shropshire L.I. | GO 10/1886 |
| **TOFREK** | | 1st Bn. The Royal Berkshire Regt. | GO 10/1886 |
| **TEL EL KEBIR** | | INDIAN ARMY | |
| | 2nd Lancers | 2nd Regt. of Bengal Cavalry | GGO 341/1883 |
| | 6th K.E.O. Cavalry | 6th Regt. of Bengal Cavalry | GGO 341/1883 |
| | 13th DoC Lancers | 13th Regt. of Bengal Lancers | GGO 341/1883 |
| | 2nd Q.V.O. Sappers & Miners | Queen's Own Corps of Sappers & Miners | GGO 341/1883 |
| | 7th D.C.O. Rajputs | 7th Regt. Bengal Native Infantry | GGO 341/1883 |
| | 20th D.C.O. Infantry (Brownlow's Punjabis) | 20th (Punjab) Regt. Bengal Native Infantry | GGO 341/1883 |
| | 129th D.C.O. Baluchis | 29th Regt. Bombay Native Infantry or 2nd Baluch Battalion | GGO 341/1883 |
| **EGYPT 1882** | | INDIAN ARMY | |
| | 2nd Lancers | 2nd Regt. of Bengal Cavalry | GGO 341/1883 |
| | 6th K.E.O. Cavalry | 6th Regt. of Bengal Cavalry | GGO 341/1883 |
| | 13th DoC Lancers | 13th Regt. of Bengal Lancers | GGO 341/1883 |
| | 2nd Q.V.O. Sappers & Miners | Queen's Own Corps of Sappers & Miners | GGO 341/1883 |
| | 7th D.C.O. Rajputs | 7th Regt. Bengal Native Infantry | GGO 341/1883 |
| | 20th D.C.O. Infantry (Brownlow's Punjabis) | 20th (Punjab) Regt. Bengal Native Infantry | GGO 341/1883 |
| | 129th D.C.O. Baluchis | 29th Regt. Bombay Native Infantry or 2nd Baluch Battalion | GGO 341/1883 |
| **SUAKIN 1885** | | INDIAN ARMY | |
| | 9th Hodson's Horse | 9th Regt. of Bengal Cavalry | GGO 478/1886 |
| | 2nd Q.V.O. Sappers & Miners | Queen's Own Corps of Sappers & Miners | GGO 478/1886 |
| | 15th Ludhiana Sikhs | 15th Regt. of Bengal Infantry (The Ludhiana Sikhs) | GGO 478/1886 |
| | 17th Infantry | 17th (The Loyal Purbiah) Regt. of Bengal Infantry | GGO 478/1886 |
| | 128th Pioneers | 28th Regt. of Bombay Infantry | GGO 478/1886 |

| | | | |
|---|---|---|---|
| **WEST AFRICA 1887** | The West India Regt. | | 21st December 1896 |
| **WEST AFRICA 1892-93-94** | The West India Regt. | | 21st December 1896 |
| **SIERRA LEONE 1898** | The West India Regt.<br>The West African Regt. | | Army Order 21/1903<br>Army Order 296/1908 |
| **ASHANTI 1900** | The West African Regt.<br>The Nigeria Regt. West African Frontier Force<br>The Gold Coast Reg. West African Frontier Force<br>1st (Central Africa) Bn. The King's African Rifles | | Army Order 296/1908 |
| **BRITISH EAST AFRICA 1896** | 124th D.C.O. Baluchistan Infantry | 24th (Duchess of Connaught's Own Baluchistan) Regt. of Bombay Infantry | G.O. 65/1901 |
| **BRITISH EAST AFRICA 1897-1899** | 127th Q.MO. Baluch Light Infantry | 27th (1st Baluch Battalion) Bombay Light Infantry | G.O. 65/1901 |
| **BRITISH EAST AFRICA 1898** | 104th Wellesley's Rifles | 4th Regt. 1st Bn. Rifle Regt., Bombay Infantry | G.O. 65/1901 |
| **BRITISH EAST AFRICA 1901** | 116th Mahrattas | 16th Regt. Bombay Infantry | 1st August 1905 |
| | | INDIAN ARMY | |
| **TOFREK** | 2nd Q.V.O. Sappers & Miners | Queen's Own Corps of Sappers & Miners | GGO 478/1886 |
| | 15th Ludhiana Sikhs | 15th Regt. of Bengal Infantry (The Ludhiana Sikhs) | GGO 478/1886 |
| | 17th Infantry | 17th (The Loyal Purbiah) Regt. of Bengal Infantry | GGO 478/1886 |
| | 128th Pioneers | 28th Regt. of Bombay Infantry | GGO 478/1886 |

| | | |
|---|---|---|
| **HAFIR** | The North Staffordshire Regt. | 24th April 1899 |
| **ATBARA** | The Royal Warwickshire Regt. | 24th April 1899 |
| | The Lincolnshire Regt. | 24th April 1899 |
| | Seaforth Highlanders | 24th April 1899 |
| | The Queen's Own Cameron Highlanders | 24th April 1899 |
| **KHARTOUM** | 21st Lancers | 24th April 1899 |
| | Grenadier Guards | 24th April 1899 |
| | The Northumberland Fusiliers | 24th April 1899 |
| | The Royal Warwickshire Regt. | 24th April 1899 |
| | The Lincolnshire Regt. | 24th April 1899 |
| | The Lancashire Fusiliers | 24th April 1899 |
| | Seaforth Highlanders | 24th April 1899 |
| | The Queen's Own Cameron Highlanders | 24th April 1899 |
| | The Rifle Brigade | 24th April 1899 |

## BATTLE HONOURS FOR THE SOUTH AFRICAN WAR

NOTE: As there were few changes in the titles of regiments after the South African War, for the remainder of the book, for reasons of space the regiments will be shown in two columns, in order of precedence. The bulk of the honours were authorised in Army Order 3 of 1905.

**MODDER RIVER**

9th Lancers
Grenadier Guards
Coldstream Guards
Scots Guards
The Northumberland Fusiliers
The Northamptonshire Regt.
The King's Own Yorkshire L.I.
The Highland L.I.
The Argyll & Sutherland Highlanders

**DEFENCE OF KIMBERLEY**

The Loyal North Lancashire Regt.

**RELIEF OF KIMBERLEY**

1st Life Guards
2nd Life Guards
16th Lancers
The Buffs (East Kent Regt.)

**RELIEF OF KIMBERLEY (Cont.)**

Royal Horse Guards
6th Dragoon Guards
Royal Scots Greys
9th Lancers
10th Hussars
12th Lancers
+The Princess of Wales's Own (Yorkshire Regt.)
The Gloucestershire Regt.
The Duke of Wellington's (West Riding Regt.)
The Welsh Regt.
++The Oxfordshire Light Infantry
The Essex Regt.

**PAARDEBURG**

1st Life Guards
2nd Life Guards
Royal Horse Guards
6th Dragoon Guards
Royal Scots Greys
9th Lancers
10th Hussars
12th Lancers
16th Lancers
The Buffs (East Kent Regt.)
The Norfolk Regt.
The Lincolnshire Regt.
The Prince of Wales's Own (Yorkshire Regt.)
The King's Own Scottish Borderers
The Gloucestershire Regt.
The Duke of Cornwall's L.I.
The Duke of Wellington's (West Riding Regt.)
The Hampshire Regt.
The Welsh Regt.
The Black Watch
The Oxfordshire Light Infantry
The Essex Regt.
The King's Shropshire L.I.
Seaforth Highlanders
The Gordon Highlanders
The Argyll & Sutherland Highlanders

**DEFENCE OF LADYSMITH**

5th Dragoon Guards
5th Lancers
18th Hussars
19th Hussars
The King's (Liverpool Regt.)
The Devonshire Regt.
The Leicestershire Regt.
The Gloucestershire Regt.
The King's Royal Rifle Corps
The Manchester Regt.
The Gordon Highlanders
The Rifle Brigade

\+ Title changed to Alexandra, Princess of Wales's Own (Yorkshire Regt.) 17th June 1902.

++ Title changed to The Oxfordshire & Buckinghamshire Light Infantry 3rd October 1908.

**RELIEF OF LADYSMITH**

1st Royal Dragoons
13th Hussars
14th Hussars
The Queen's (Royal West Surrey Regt.)
The King's Own (Royal Lancaster Regt.)
The Royal Fusiliers
The Devonshire Regt.
The Somerset Light Infantry
The West Yorkshire Regt.
The Lancashire Fusiliers
The Royal Scots Fusiliers
The Royal Welsh Fusiliers
The Cameronians
The Royal Inniskilling Fusiliers
The East Surrey Regt.
The Border Regt.
The Dorsetshire Regt.
P.W.V. (South Lancashire Regt.)
The Middlesex Regt.
The King's Royal Rifle Corps
The York & Lancaster Regt.
The Durham Light Infantry
The Royal Irish Fusiliers
The Connaught Rangers
The Royal Dublin Fusiliers
The Rifle Brigade

**SOUTH AFRICA 1899-1900**

1st Life Guards
2nd Life Guards
Royal Horse Guards

**SOUTH AFRICA 1899-1902**

5th Dragoon Guards
6th Dragoon Guards
1st Royal Dragoons
Royal Scots Greys
5th Royal Irish Lancers
6th (Inniskilling) Dragoons
9th Lancers
10th Hussars
12th Lancers
13th Hussars
18th Hussars
19th Hussars
Grenadier Guards
Coldstream Guards
Scots Guards
The Royal Scots
The Queen's (Royal West Surrey Regt.)
The King's Own (Royal Lancaster Regt.)
The Northumberland Fusiliers
The Royal Warwickshire Regt.
The Royal Fusiliers
The King's (Liverpool Regt.)
The Devonshire Regt.
The Suffolk Regt.
The Somerset Light Infantry
The West Yorkshire Regt.
The Leicestershire Regt.
The Yorkshire Regt.

**SOUTH AFRICA 1899-1902 (Cont.)**

The Lancashire Fusiliers
The Royal Scots Fusiliers
The Royal Welsh Fusiliers
The Cameronians
The Royal Inniskilling Fusiliers
The Gloucestershire Regt.
The East Surrey Regt.
The Duke of Cornwall's Light Infantry
The Border Regt.
The Dorsetshire Regt.
The Prince of Wales's Volunteers (S.Lancashire Regt.)
The Welsh Regt.
The Black Watch
The Essex Regt.
The Sherwood Foresters
The Loyal North Lancashire Regt.
The Northamptonshire Regt.
The Royal Berkshire Regt.
The King's Own (Yorkshire Light Infantry)
The King's (Shropshire Light Infantry)
The King's Royal Rifle Corps
The Manchester Regt.
The York & Lancaster Regt.
The Durham Light Infantry
The Highland Light Infantry
Seaforth Highlanders
The Gordon Highlanders
The Royal Irish Rifles
The Royal Irish Fusiliers
The Connaught Rangers
The Argyll & Sutherland Highlanders
The Royal Munster Fusiliers
The Royal Dublin Fusiliers
The Rifle Brigade
8th (City of London) Bn. The London Regt. (Post Office Rifles)

**SOUTH AFRICA 1900**

4th (City of London) Bn. The London Regt. (Royal Fusiliers)

**SOUTH AFRICA 1900-1901**

Berkshire Yeomanry
Buckinghamshire Yeomanry (Royal Bucks Hussars)
Cheshire Yeomanry (Earl of Chester's)
Denbighshire Yeomanry (Hussars)
Derbyshire Yeomanry
Royal 1st Devon Yeomanry
Royal North Devon Yeomanry (Hussars)
Dorsetshire Yeomanry (Queen's Own)
Fife & Forfar Yeomanry
Gloucestershire Yeomanry (Royal Gloucestershire Hussars)
Hampshire Yeomanry (Carabiniers)
Hertfordshire Yeomanry
Royal East Kent Yeomanry (Duke of Connaught's Own) (Mounted Rifles)
West Kent Yeomanry (Queen's Own)
Lanarkshire Yeomanry (Queen's Own Royal Glasgow & Lower Ward of Lanarkshire)
1st County of London Yeomanry (Middlesex, Duke of Cambridge's Hussars)
Lothians & Border Horse
Oxfordshire Yeomanry (Queen's Own Oxfordshire Hussars)
North Somerset Yeomanry

**SOUTH AFRICA 1900-1901 (Cont.)**

West Somerset Yeomanry
Staffordshire Yeomanry (Queen's Own Royal Regt.)
Suffolk Yeomanry (Duke of Kent's Own Loyal Suffolk Hussars)
Warwickshire Yeomanry
Westmorland & Cumberland Yeomanry
Royal Wiltshire Yeomanry (Prince of Wales's Own Royal Regt.)
6th (Rifle) Bn. The King's (Liverpool Regt.)
9th Bn. The King's (Liverpool Regt.)
4th Bn. The Devonshire Regt.
5th (Prince of Wales's) Bn. The Devonshire Regt.
6th Bn. The Devonshire Regt.
4th Bn. The Somerset Light Infantry
5th Bn. The Somerset Light Infantry
4th Bn. The East Yorkshire Regt.
5th Bn. The Royal Scots Fusiliers
7th (Merioneth & Montgomery) Bn. The Royal Welsh Fusiliers
Brecknockshire Bn. The South Wales Borderers
7th Bn. The Worcestershire Regt.
4th Bn. The Duke of Cornwall's Light Infantry
5th Bn. The Duke of Cornwall's Light Infantry
8th (Isle of Wight Rifles) Bn. The Hampshire Regt.
4th Bn. The Dorsetshire Regt.
5th Bn. The P.W.V. (South Lancashire Regt.)
4th Bn. The Oxf & Bucks Light Infantry
5th (Buchan & Formatin) Bn. The Gordon Highlanders
28th (County of London) Bn. The London Regt. (Artists Rifles)
1st Bn. The Cambridgeshire Regt.
Inns of Court Officer's Training Corps.

**SOUTH AFRICA 1900-1902**

7th Dragoon Guards
8th Hussars
14th Hussars
16th Lancers
17th Lancers
The Buffs (East Kent Regt.)
The Norfolk Regt.
The Lincolnshire Regt.
The East Yorkshire Regt.
The Bedfordshire Regt.
The Royal Irish Regt.
The Cheshire Regt.
The South Wales Borderers
The King's Own Scottish Borderers
The Worcestershire Regt.
The East Lancashire Regt.
The Duke of Wellington's Regt.
The Royal Sussex Regt.
The Hampshire Regt.
The South Staffordshire Regt.
The Oxf & Bucks Light Infantry
The Queen's Own (Royal West Kent Regt.)
The Middlesex Regt.
The Wiltshire Regt.
The North Staffordshire Regt.
The Queen's Own Cameron Highlanders
The Leinster Regt.
The Honourable Artillery Company
Ayrshire Yeomanry (Earl of Carrick's Own)
Lanarkshire Yeomanry
Lancashire Hussars
Duke of Lancaster's Own Yeomanry
Leicestershire Yeomanry (Prince Albert's Own)
City of London Yeomanry (Roughriders)

**SOUTH AFRICA 1900-1902 (Cont.)**

3rd County of London Yeomanry (Sharpshooters)
1st Lovat's Scouts
2nd Lovat's Scouts
Northumberland Hussars
Nottinghamshire Yeomanry (Sherwood Rangers)
Nottinghamshire Yeomanry (South Nottinghamshire Hussars)
Scottish Horse
Shropshire Yeomanry
The Queen's Own Worcestershire Hussars
Yorkshire Dragoons (Queen's Own)
Yorkshire Hussars (Alexandra, Princess of Wales's Own)
4th Bn. The Royal Scots (Queen's Edinburgh Rifles)
5th Bn. The Royal Scots (Queen's Edinburgh Rifles)
7th Bn. The Royal Scots
4th Bn. The Queen's (Royal West Surrey Regt.)
5th Bn. The Queen's (Royal West Surrey Regt.)
4th Bn. The Buffs (East Kent Regt.)
5th (Weald of Kent) Bn. The Buffs (East Kent Regt.)
4th Bn. The King's Own (Royal Lancaster Regt.)
5th Bn. The King's Own (Royal Lancaster Regt.)
4th Bn. The Northumberland Fusiliers
5th Bn. The Northumberland Fusiliers
6th Bn. The Northumberland Fusiliers
5th & 6th Bns. The Royal Warwickshire Regt.
7th Bn. The Royal Warwickshire Regt.
1st (City of London) Bn. The London Regt. (Royal Fusiliers)
2nd (City of London) Bn. The London Regt. (Royal Fusiliers)
3rd (City of London) Bn. The London Regt. (Royal Fusiliers)
5th Bn. The King's (Liverpool Regt.)
7th Bn. The King's (Liverpool Regt.)
8th (Irish) Bn. The King's (Liverpool Regt.)
4th Bn. The Norfolk Regt.
5th Bn. The Norfolk Regt.
4th Bn. The Lincolnshire Regt.
5th Bn. The Lincolnshire Regt.
4th Bn. The Suffolk Regt.
5th Bn. The Suffolk Regt.
5th Bn. The West Yorkshire Regt.
6th Bn. The West Yorkshire Regt.
7th & 8th Bns. The West Yorkshire Regt. (Leeds Rifles)
5th Bn. The Bedfordshire Regt.
4th Bn. The Leicestershire Regt.
5th Bn. The Leicestershire Regt.
4th Bn. The Yorkshire Regt.
5th Bn. The Yorkshire Regt.
5th Bn. The Lancashire Fusiliers
6th Bn. The Lancashire Fusiliers
7th Bn. The Lancashire Fusiliers
8th Bn. The Lancashire Fusiliers
4th Bn. The Royal Scots Fusiliers
5th (Earl of Chester's) Bn. The Cheshire Regt.
6th Bn. The Cheshire Regt.
4th (Denbighshire) Bn. The Royal Welsh Fusiliers
5th (Flintshire) Bn. The Royal Welsh Fusiliers
6th (Carnarvon & Anglesey) Bn. The Royal Welsh Fusiliers
4th (The Border) Bn. The King's Own Scottish Borderers
5th (Dumfries & Galloway) Bn. The King's Own Scottish Borderers
5th Bn. The Cameronians
6th Bn. The Cameronians
7th Bn. The Cameronians

**SOUTH AFRICA 1900-1902 (Cont.)**

8th Bn. The Cameronians
4th (City of Bristol) Bn. The Gloucestershire Regt.
5th Bn. The Gloucestershire Regt.
8th Bn. The Worcestershire Regt.
4th Bn. The East Lancashire Regt.
5th Bn. The East Lancashire Regt.
5th Bn. The East Surrey Regt.
6th Bn. The East Surrey Regt.
4th Bn. The Duke of Wellington's Regt.
5th Bn. The Duke of Wellington's Regt.
6th Bn. The Duke of Wellington's Regt.
7th Bn. The Duke of Wellington's Regt.
4th (Cumberland & Westmorland) Bn. The Border Regt.
4th Bn. The Royal Sussex Regt.
5th (Cinque Ports) Bn. The Royal Sussex Regt.
4th Bn. The Hampshire Regt.
5th Bn. The Hampshire Regt.
6th Bn. (Duke of Connaught's) Bn. The Hampshire Regt.
7th Bn. The Hampshire Regt.
5th Bn. The South Staffordshire Regt.
6th Bn. The South Staffordshire Regt.
4th Bn. P.W.V. (South Lancashire Regt.)
4th Bn. The Welsh Regt.
5th Bn. The Welsh Regt.
6th (Glamorgan) Bn. The Welsh Regt.
4th (City of Dundee) Bn. The Black Watch
5th (Angus & Dundee) Bn. The Black Watch
6th (Perthshire) Bn. The Black Watch
7th (Fife) Bn. The Black Watch
Buckinghamshire Bn. Oxf & Bucks Lt. Infty
4th Bn. The Essex Regt.
5th Bn. The Essex Regt.
6th Bn. The Essex Regt.
7th Bn. The Essex Regt.
5th Bn. The Sherwood Foresters
6th Bn. The Sherwood Foresters
7th (Robin Hood) Bn. The Sherwood Foresters
8th Bn. The Sherwood Foresters
4th Bn. The Loyal North Lancashire Regt.
5th Bn. The Loyal North Lancashire Regt.
4th Bn. The Northamptonshire Regt.
4th Bn. The Royal Berkshire Regt.
4th Bn. The Queen's Own (Royal West Kent Regt.)
5th Bn. The Queen's Own (Royal West Kent Regt.)
4th Bn. The King's Own (Yorkshire Light Infantry)
5th Bn. The King's Own (Yorkshire Light Infantry)
4th Bn. The King's (Shropshire Light Infantry)
7th Bn. The Middlesex Regt.
8th Bn. The Middlesex Regt.
9th Bn. The Middlesex Regt.
4th Bn. The Wiltshire Regt.
5th Bn. The Manchester Regt.
6th Bn. The Manchester Regt.
7th Bn. The Manchester Regt.
8th (Ardwick) Bn. The Manchester Regt.
9th Bn. The Manchester Regt.
5th Bn. The North Staffordshire Regt.
6th Bn. The North Staffordshire Regt.
4th (Hallamshire) Bn. The York & Lancaster Regt.
5th Bn. The York & Lancaster Regt.
5th Bn. The Durham Light Infantry
6th Bn. The Durham Light Infantry
7th Bn. The Durham Light Infantry
8th Bn. The Durham Light Infantry
9th Bn. The Durham Light Infantry
5th (City of Glasgow) Bn. The Highland Light Infantry
6th (City of Glasgow) Bn. The Highland Light Infantry
7th (Blythswood) Bn. The Highland Light Infantry
8th (Lanark) Bn. The Highland Light Infantry
9th (Glasgow Highland) Bn. The Highland Light Infantry

**SOUTH AFRICA 1900-1902 (Cont.)**

4th (Ross Highland) Bn. Seaforth Highlanders
5th (Sutherland & Caithness) Bn. Seaforth Highlanders
6th (Morayshire) Bn. Seaforth Highlanders
4th Bn. The Gordon Highlanders
6th (Banff & Donside) Bn. The Gordon Highlanders 13
7th (Deeside) Bn. The Gordon Highlanders
4th Bn. The Queen's Own Cameron Highlanders
5th (Renfrew) Bn. The Argyll & Sutherland Highlanders
6th (Renfrew) Bn. The Argyll & Sutherland Highlanders
7th Bn. The Argyll & Sutherland Highlanders
8th (Argyllshire) Bn. The Argyll & Sutherland Highlanders
9th (Dumbartonshire) Bn. The Argyll & Sutherland Highlanders
1st Bn. The Monmouthshire Regt.
2nd Bn. The Monmouthshire Regt.
3rd Bn. The Monmouthshire Regt.
5th (City of London) Bn. The London Regt. (London Rifle Brigade)
6th (City of London) Bn. The London Regt. (Rifles)
7th (City of London) Bn. The London Regt.
9th (County of London) Bn. The London Regt. (Queen Victoria's Rifles)
11th (County of London) Bn. The London Regt. (Finsbury Rifles)
12th (County of London) Bn. The London Regt. (The Rangers)
13th (County of London) Bn. The London Regt. (Kensington)
14th (County of London) Bn. The London Regt. (London Scottish)
15th (County of London) Bn. The London Regt. (Prince of Wales's Own, Civil Service Rifles)
16th (County of London) Bn. The London Regt. (Queen's Westminster Rifles)
17th (County of London) Bn. The London Regt. (Poplar & Stepney Rifles)
18th (County of London) Bn. The London Regt. (London Irish Rifles)
19th (County of London) Bn. The London Regt. (St.Pancras)
20th (County of London) Bn. The London Regt. (Blackheath & Woolwich)
21st (County of London) Bn. The London Regt. (1st Surrey Rifles)
22nd (County of London) Bn. The London Regt. (Queen's)
23rd (County of London) Bn. The London Regt.
24th (County of London) Bn. The London Regt. (Queen's)
The Highland Cyclist Battalion

**SOUTH AFRICA 1901**

Montgomeryshire Yeomanry
Pembrokeshire Yeomanry
8th Bn. The Royal Scots

**SOUTH AFRICA 1901-1902**

1st King's Dragoon Guards
2nd Dragoon Guards
3rd Dragoon Guards
7th Hussars
20th Hussars
6th Bn. The Royal Scots
9th (Highlanders) Bn. The Royal Scots
10th (Cyclist) Bn. The Royal Scots
4th Bn. The Cheshire Regt.
5th (Cumberland) Bn. The Border Regt.
10th Bn. The Manchester Regt.

| | |
|---|---|
| **SOUTH AFRICA 1902** | 3rd Hussars<br>2nd County of London Yeomanry (Westminster Dragoons)<br>10th (Scottish) Bn. The King's (Liverpool Regt.) |
| **ST. HELENA 1901** | 4th Bn. The Gloucestershire Regt. |
| **ST. HELENA 1901-1902** | 3rd Bn. The Wiltshire Regt. (Royal Wiltshire Militia) |
| **MEDITERRANEAN 1900-1901** | 3rd Bn. The Loyal North Lancashire Regt. (3rd Royal Lancashire Militia)<br>5th Bn. The Northumberland Fusiliers<br>3rd Bn. The Queen's Own (Royal West Kent Regt.) (West Kent Militia)<br>3rd Bn. Seaforth Highlanders (Highland (Rifles) Militia) |
| **MEDITERRANEAN 1901** | 5th Bn. The Royal Munster Fusiliers (Royal Limerick County Militia) |
| **MEDITERRANEAN 1901-1902** | 3rd Bn. The West Yorkshire Regt. (2nd West Yorkshire Militia)<br>3rd Bn. The King's Own (Yorkshire Light Infantry) (1st West Yorkshire Militia) |

# AMERICA
# WEST INDIES
# ANTIPODES

## AMERICA
## (NORTH, CENTRAL & SOUTH)

| | | | |
|---|---|---|---|
| LOUISBURG | Seven Years War (French & Indian Wars) | | 8th June to 27th July 1758 |
| QUEBEC | " | | 27th June to 18th September 1759 |
| NORTH AMERICA 1763/64 | Pontiac's Conspiracy | | 1763-1764 |
| DETROIT | War of 1812 | | 16th August 1812 |
| QUEENSTOWN | " | | 13th October 1812 |
| MIAMI | " | | 5th May 1813 |
| NIAGARA | " | | 19th December 1813 |
| BLADENSBURG | " | | 24th August 1814 |
| SURINAM | Expedition against Dutch | | 30th April 1804 |
| MONTE VIDEO | Expedition against Spanish | | 3rd February 1807 |

## WEST INDIES

| | | | |
|---|---|---|---|
| GUADALOUPE 1759 | Seven Years War | | 22nd January to 1st May 1759 |
| MARTINIQUE 1762 | " | | 7th January to 12th February 1762 |
| MORO | " | | 1st July to 14th August 1762 |
| HAVANNAH 1762 | " | Capitulated | 14th August 1762 |
| ST LUCIA 1778 | American War of Independence | | 12th to 28th December 1778 |
| NAVAL CROWN | Battle of the Saints | | 12th April 1782 |
| MARTINIQUE 1794 | French Revolutionary Wars 1793-1802 | | 5th February to 23rd March 1794 |
| ST LUCIA 1796 | " | | 26th April to 15th May 1796 |
| ST LUCIA 1803 | Napoleonic Wars | | 21st to 22nd June 1803 |
| DOMINICA | " | | 22nd February 1805 |
| MARTINIQUE 1809 | " | | 30th January to 4th February 1809 |
| GUADALOUPE 1810 | " | | January to February 1810 |

## ANTIPODES

| | | |
|---|---|---|
| NEW ZEALAND | 1st Maori War | 1846-1847 |
| | 2nd Maori War | 1860-1861 |
| | 3rd Maori War | 1863-1866 |

| | ABBREVIATED TITLE | FORMER TITLE | DATE OF AWARD |
|---|---|---|---|
| **LOUISBURG** | The Royal Scots | 2nd Bn. 1st (or Royal) Regt. of Foot<br>(Col: Lt-Gen. James Sinclair) | 13th March 1882 |
| | The East Yorkshire Regt. | 15th Regt. of Foot<br>(Col: Maj-Gen. Jeffery Amherst) | 13th March 1882 |
| | The Leicestershire Regt. | 17th Regt. of Foot<br>(Col: Brig. John Forbes) | 13th March 1882 |
| | The Cheshire Regt. | 22nd Regt. of Foot<br>(Col: Brig. Edward Whitmore) | 13th March 1882 |
| | 1st Bn. The Gloucestershire Regt. | 28th Regt. of Foot<br>(Col: Lt-Gen. Philip Bragg) | 13th March 1882 |
| | 1st Bn. The Royal Sussex Regt. | 35th Regt. of Foot<br>(Col: Lt-Gen. Charles Otway) | 13th March 1882 |
| | 1st Bn. P.W.V. (South Lancashire Regt.) | 40th Regt. of Foot<br>(Col: Maj-Gen. Peregrine Thomas Hopson) | 13th March 1882 |
| | 1st Bn. The Sherwood Foresters | 45th Regt. of Foot<br>(Col: Lt-Gen. Hugh Warburton) | 13th March 1882 |
| | 1st Bn. The Loyal North Lancashire Regt. | 47th Regt. of Foot<br>(Col: Lt-Gen. Peregrine Lascelles) | 13th March 1882 |
| | 1st Bn. The Northamptonshire Regt. | *48th Regt. of Foot<br>(Col: Col. Daniel Webb) | 13th March 1882 |
| | The King's Royal Rifle Corps | **2nd & 3rd Bns. 60th (or Royal American) Regt. of Foot<br>(Col-in-Chief: Maj-Gen. James Abercrombie) | 13th March 1882 |
| | 1st Bn. The Wiltshire Regt. | 62nd Regt. of Foot<br>(Col: Maj-Gen. William Strode) | Army Order 97/1910 |

* 2nd Bn. 58th Foot were also present

** Colonels Commandant: 2nd Bn. Joseph Duseaux; 3rd Bn. Charles Lawrence.

| | | | |
|---|---|---|---|
| **QUEBEC 1759** | The East Yorkshire Regt. | 15th Regt. of Foot<br>(Col: Maj-Gen. Jeffery Amherst) | 13th March 1882 |
| | 1st Bn. The Gloucestershire Regt. | 28th Regt. of Foot<br>(Col: Lt-Gen. Philip Bragg) | 13th March 1882 |

| Honour | Present Unit | Original Unit | | Date |
|---|---|---|---|---|
| QUEBEC 1759 (Cont.) | 1st Bn. The Royal Sussex Regt. | 35th Regt. of Foot (Col: Lt-Gen. Charles Otway) | | 13th March 1882 |
| | 1st Bn. Oxf & Bucks Lt. Infty. | 43rd Regt. of Foot (Col: Lt-Gen. James Kennedy) | | 13th March 1882 |
| | 1st Bn. The Loyal North Lancashire Regt. | 47th Regt. of Foot (Col: Lt-Gen. Peregrine Lascelles) | | 13th March 1882 |
| | 1st Bn. The Northamptonshire Regt. | 48th Regt. of Foot (Col: Col. Daniel Webb) | | 13th March 1882 |
| | The King's Royal Rifle Corps | 2nd & 3rd Bns. 60th (or Royal American) Regt. of Foot (Col-in-Chief: Jeffery Amherst) | | 13th March 1882 |
| NORTH AMERICA | 1st Bn. The Black Watch | 42nd (Royal Highland) Regt. of Foot | | Army Order 2/1914 |
| | The King's Royal Rifle Corps | 60th (or Royal American) Regt. of Foot | | Army Order 2/1914 |
| DETROIT | 1st Bn. The Welsh Regt. | 41st Regt. of Foot | | 2nd April 1816 |
| MIAMI | 1st Bn. The Welsh Regt. | 41st Regt. of Foot | | 2nd April 1816 |
| QUEENSTOWN | 1st Bn. The Welsh Regt. | 41st Regt. of Foot | | 2nd April 1816 |
| | 1st Bn. The Royal Berkshire Regt. | 49th (Hertfordshire) Regt. of Foot | | 27th January 1816 |
| NIAGARA | 19th Hussars | *19th Regt. of (Light) Dragoons | | 5th May 1815 |
| | The Royal Scots | 1st Bn. 1st (or Royal Scots) Regt. of Foot | | 5th May 1815 |
| | The Royal Warwickshire Regt. | 1st Bn. 6th (1st Warwickshire) Regt. of Foot | | 28th September 1816 |
| | The King's (Liverpool Regt.) | 1st Bn. 8th (or the King's) Regt. of Foot | | 5th May 1815 |
| | 2nd Bn. P.W.V. (South Lancashire Regt.) | 1st Bn. 82nd Regt. of Foot (Prince of Wales's Volunteers) | | 27th June 1816 |
| | 1st Bn. The Welsh Regt. | 1st Bn. 41st Regt. of Foot | To Flank Companies | 5th May 1815 |
| | | | Distinction to Regt. | 20th September 1824 |
| | 2nd Bn. The Royal Irish Fusiliers | 2nd Bn. 89th Regt. of Foot | | 5th May 1815 |
| | | 2nd Bn. disbanded 1816 | Award to Regt. | 29th August 1831 |
| | 1st Bn. The Leinster Regt. | **100th (HRH the Prince Regent's County of Dublin) Regt. of Foot | | 5th May 1815 |

* Disbanded 1821. Reformed in 1860 from HEIC Bengal European Light Cavalry; Granted original regiments honours in 1874.

** Disbanded 1818. Regranted to Leinster Regt. 22.3.1875.

| | | | |
|---|---|---|---|
| **BLADENSBURG** | The King's Own (Royal Lancaster Regt.) | 4th (The King's Own) Regt. of Foot | 31st May 1827 |
| | The Royal Scots Fusiliers | 21st (Royal North British Fuziliers) Regt. of Foot | 7th January 1854 |
| | 1st Bn. The Essex Regt. | 44th (East Essex) Regt. of Foot | 31st May 1827 |
| | 2nd Bn. The King's Shropshire L.I. | 85th (Bucks Volunteers) (Light Infantry) Regt. | 18th August 1826 |
| **SURINAM** | The Bedfordshire Regt. | 16th (Buckinghamshire) Regt. of Foot | Army Order 108/1898 |
| | 1st Bn. The North Staffordshire Regt. | 64th (2nd Staffordshire) Regt. of Foot | 31st January 1818 |
| **MONTE VIDEO** | 1st Bn. The South Staffordshire Regt. | 38th (1st Staffordshire) Regt. of Foot | 19th March 1817 |
| | 1st Bn. P.W.V. (South Lancashire Regt.) | 40th (2nd Somersetshire) Regt. of Foot | 27th April 1824 |
| | 1st Bn. The Royal Irish Fusiliers | 87th (Prince of Wales's Own Irish) Regt. of Foot | 12th January 1824 |
| | The Rifle Brigade | 95th Regt. of Foot (or Rifle Corps) | 15th March 1821 |
| **GUADALOUPE 1759** | The Buffs (East Kent Regt.) | 3rd Regt. of Foot or The Buffs (Col: Maj-Gen. George Howard) | Army Order 295/1909 |
| | The King's Own (Royal Lancaster Regt.) | 4th (King's Own) Regt. of Foot (Col: Maj-Gen. Alexander Duroure) | Army Order 295/1909 |
| | 1st Bn. The Gloucestershire Regt. | 28th Regt. of Foot (Col: Lt-Gen. Philip Bragg) | Army Order 295/1909 |
| | 1st Bn. The South Staffordshire Regt. | 38th Regt. of Foot (Col: Maj-Gen. Sir James Ross) | Army Order 295/1909 |
| | 1st Bn. The Black Watch | 42nd (Royal Highland) Regt. of Foot (Col: Lt-Gen. Lord John Murray) | Army Order 295/1909 |
| | 1st Bn. The Manchester Regt. | 63rd Regt. of Foot (Col: Maj-Gen. David Watson) | Army Order 295/1909 |
| | 1st Bn. The North Staffordshire Regt. | 64th Regt. of Foot (Col: Col. Hon. George Townshend) | Army Order 295/1909 |
| | 1st Bn. The York & Lancaster Regt. | 65th Regt. of Foot (Col: Col. Robert Armiger) | Army Order 295/1909 |

| | | | |
|---|---|---|---|
| **MARTINIQUE 1762** | The East Yorkshire Regt. | 15th Regt. of Foot<br>(Col: Maj-Gen. Jeffery Amherst) | Army Order 295/1909 |
| | The Leicestershire Regt. | 17th Regt. of Foot<br>(Col: Maj-Gen. Hon. Robert Monckton) | Army Order 295/1909 |
| | The Cheshire Regt. | 22nd Regt. of Foot<br>(Col: Maj-Gen. Hon. Thomas Gage) | Army Order 295/1909 |
| | 1st Bn. The Royal Inniskilling Fusiliers | 27th (Inniskilling) Regt. of Foot<br>(Col: Lt-Gen. Hugh Warburton) | Army Order 295/1909 |
| | 1st Bn. The Gloucestershire Regt. | 28th Regt. of Foot<br>(Col: Maj-Gen. Viscount Townshend) | Army Order 295/1909 |
| | 1st Bn. The Royal Sussex Regt. | 35th Regt. of Foot<br>(Col: Gen. Charles Otway) | Army Order 295/1909 |
| | 1st Bn. The South Staffordshire Regt. | 38th Regt. of Foot<br>(Col: Maj-Gen. Hon. Sharington Talbot) | Army Order 295/1909 |
| | 1st Bn. P.W.V. (South Lancashire Regt.) | 40th Regt. of Foot<br>(Col: Maj-Gen. Robert Armiger) | Army Order 295/1909 |
| | 2nd Bn. The Welsh Regt. | 69th Regt. of Foot<br>(Col: Maj-Gen. Hon. Charles Colville) | Army Order 295/1909 |
| | 1st Bn. The Black Watch | 42nd (Royal Highland) Regt. of Foot<br>(Col: Lt-Gen. Lord John Murray) | Army Order 295/1909 |
| | 1st Bn. Oxf & Bucks Lt. Infty. | 43rd Regt. of Foot<br>(Col: Lt-Gen. Bennet Noel) | Army Order 295/1909 |
| | 1st Bn. The Northamptonshire Regt. | 48th Regt. of Foot<br>(Col: Maj-Gen. Daniel Webb) | Army Order 295/1909 |
| | The King's Royal Rifle Corps | 60th (Royal American) Regt. of Foot<br>(Col-in-Chief: Maj-Gen. Sir Jeffery Amherst) | Army Order 295/1909 |
| **MORO** | 2nd Bn. The Essex Regt. | 56th Regt. of Foot<br>(Col: Maj-Gen. Hon. William Keppel) | * 27th December 1827 |
| **HAVANNAH** | The Royal Scots | 1st (or Royal) Regt. of Foot<br>(Col: Gen. Hon. James St.Clair) | Army Order 295/1909 |
| | The Norfolk Regt. | 9th Regt. of Foot<br>(Col: Lt-Gen. William Whitmore) | Army Order 295/1909 |



* Permitted to resume.

| | | | |
|---|---|---|---|
| **HAVANNAH (Cont.)** | The East Yorkshire Regt. | 15th Regt. of Foot<br>(Col: Maj-Gen. Sir Jeffery Amherst) | Army Order 295/1909 |
| | The Leicestershire Regt. | 17th Regt. of Foot<br>(Col: Maj-Gen. Hon. Robert Monckton) | Army Order 295/1909 |
| | The Cheshire Regt. | 22nd Regt. of Foot<br>(Col: Maj-Gen. Hon. Thomas Gage) | Army Order 295/1909 |
| | 1st Bn. The Royal Inniskilling Fusiliers | 27th (Inniskilling) Regt. of Foot<br>(Col: Lt-Gen. Hugh Warburton) | Army Order 295/1909 |
| | 1st Bn. The Gloucestershire Regt. | 28th Regt. of Foot<br>(Col: Maj-Gen. Viscount Townshend) | Army Order 295/1909 |
| | 1st Bn. The Border Regt. | 34th Regt. of Foot<br>(Col: Maj-Gen. Lord Frederick Cavendish) | Army Order 295/1909 |
| | 1st Bn. The Royal Sussex Regt. | 35th Regt. of Foot<br>(Col: Gen. Charles Otway) | Army Order 295/1909 |
| | 1st Bn. P.W.V. (South Lancashire Regt.) | 40th Regt. of Foot<br>(Col: Maj-Gen. Robert Armiger) | Army Order 295/1909 |
| | 1st Bn. The Black Watch | 42nd (Royal Highland) Regt. of Foot<br>(Col. Lt-Gen. Lord John Murray) | Army Order 295/1909 |
| | 1st Bn. Oxf & Bucks Lt. Infty. | 43rd Regt. of Foot<br>(Col: Lt-Gen. Hon. Bennet Noel) | Army Order 295/1909 |
| | 2nd Bn. The Essex Regt. | 56th Regt. of Foot<br>(Col: Maj-Gen. Hon. William Keppel) | Army Order 295/1909 |
| | 1st Bn. The Northamptonshire Regt. | 48th Regt. of Foot<br>(Col: Maj-Gen. Daniel Webb) | Army Order 295/1909 |
| | The King's Royal Rifle Corps | 60th (Royal American) Regt. of Foot<br>(Col-in-Chief: Maj-Gen. Sir Jeffery Amherst) | Army Order 295/1909 |
| **ST LUCIA 1778** | The King's Own (Royal Lancaster Regt.) | 4th (The King's Own) Regt. of Foot<br>(Col: Gen. Studholme Hodgson) | Army Order 295/1909 |
| | The Northumberland Fusiliers | 5th Regt. of Foot<br>(Col: Lt-Gen. Earl Percy) | Army Order 295/1909 |

| | | | |
|---|---|---|---|
| **ST LUCIA 1778 (Cont.)** | The East Yorkshire Regt. | 15th Regt. of Foot<br>(Col: Maj-Gen. William Fawcett) | Army Order 295/1909 |
| | 1st Bn. The Royal Inniskilling Fusiliers | 27th (Inniskilling) Regt. of Foot<br>(Col: Maj-Gen. Eyre Massey) | Army Order 295/1909 |
| | 1st Bn. The Gloucestershire Regt. | 28th Regt. of Foot<br>(Col: Maj-Gen. Charles Grey) | Army Order 295/1909 |
| | 2nd Bn. The Duke of Cornwall's L.I. | 46th Regt. of Foot<br>(Col: Maj-Gen. John Vaughan) | Army Order 295/1909 |
| | 2nd Bn. The Border Regt. | 55th Regt. of Foot<br>(Col: Maj-Gen. James Grant) | Army Order 295/1909 |
| | 1st Bn. The Royal Sussex Regt. | 35th Regt. of Foot<br>(Col: Lt-Gen. Harry Fletcher) | Army Order 295/1909 |
| | 1st Bn. P.W.V. (South Lancashire Regt.) | 40th Regt. of Foot<br>(Col: Lt-Gen. Sir Robert Hamilton) | Army Order 295/1909 |
| | 1st Bn. The Royal Berkshire Regt. | 49th Regt. of Foot<br>(Col: Lt-Gen. Hon. Alexander Maitland) | Army Order 295/1909 |
| **NAVAL CROWN (Superscribed 12th April 1782)** | 2nd Bn. The Welsh Regt. | 69th Regt. of Foot<br>(Col: Lt-Gen. Hon. Philip Sherard) | Army Order 312/1909 |
| **MARTINIQUE 1794** | The Royal Warwickshire Regt. | 6th (Royal 1st Warwickshire) Regt. of Foot<br>(Col: Maj-Gen. Ralph Abercromby) | Army Order 295/1909 |
| | The Norfolk Regt. | 9th (East Norfolk) Regt. of Foot<br>(Col: Maj-Gen. Albermarle Bertie) | Army Order 295/1909 |
| | The East Yorkshire Regt. | 15th (Yorkshire, East Riding) Regt. of Foot<br>(Col: Maj-Gen. Henry Watson Powell) | Army Order 295/1909 |
| | The Royal Scots Fusiliers | 21st Regt. of Foot (or Royal North British Fusiliers)<br>(Col: Maj-Gen. James Hamilton) | Army Order 295/1909 |
| | 2nd Bn. The East Surrey Regt. | 70th (Surrey) Regt. of Foot<br>(Col: Maj-Gen. The Earl of Suffolk) | Army Order 295/1909 |
| | 1st Bn. The Dorsetshire Regt. | 39th (East Middlesex) Regt. of Foot<br>(Col: Maj-Gen. Nisbett Balfour) | Army Order 295/1909 |

| | | | |
|---|---|---|---|
| MARTINIQUE 1794 (Cont.) | 1st Bn. Oxf & Bucks Lt. Infty. | 43rd (Monmouthshire) Regt. of Foot (Col: Maj-Gen. Edward Smith) | Army Order 295/1909 |
| | 2nd Bn. The Northamptonshire Regt. | 58th (Rutlandshire) Regt. of Foot (Col: Lt-Gen. George Scott) | Army Order 295/1909 |
| | 1st Bn. The North Staffordshire Regt. | 64th (2nd Staffordshire) Regt. of Foot (Col: Maj-Gen. James Leland) | Army Order 295/1909 |
| | 1st Bn. The York & Lancaster Regt. | 65th (2nd Yorkshire, North Riding) Regt. of Foot (Col: Maj-Gen. James Gunning) | Army Order 295/1909 |
| ST LUCIA 1796 (Date 1796 added, Army Order 295/1909) | 1st Bn. The Royal Inniskilling Fusiliers | 27th (Inniskilling) Regt. of Foot (Col: Gen. Eyre Massey) | 28th March 1836 |
| | 1st Bn. The King's Shropshire L.I. | 53rd (Shropshire) Regt. of Foot (Col: Maj-Gen. Gerard Lake) | 10th March 1825 |
| ST LUCIA 1803 (Date 1803 added, Army Order 295/1909) | The Royal Scots | 1st (or Royal) Regt. of Foot | 25th July 1821 |
| | 1st Bn. The North Staffordshire Regt. | 64th (2nd Staffordshire) Regt. of Foot | 31st January 1818 |
| DOMINICA | 2nd Bn. The Duke of Cornwall's L.I. | 46th (South Devonshire) Regt. of Foot | 9th February 1808 |
| | The West India Regt. | 1st Bn. The West India Regt. | 9th February 1808 |
| MARTINIQUE 1809 Date 1809 added, Army Order 295/1909 | The Royal Fusiliers | 7th Regt. of Foot (or Royal Fusiliers) | 5th September 1816 |
| | The King's (Liverpool Regt.) | 8th (The King's) Regt of Foot | 5th September 1816 |
| | The Somerset L.I. | 13th (1st Somersetshire) Regt. of Foot | 19th November 1816 |
| | The East Yorkshire Regt. | 15th (Yorkshire, East Riding) Regt. of Foot | 31st May 1817 |
| | The Royal Welsh Fusiliers | 23rd Regt. of Foot (or Royal Welsh Fuzileers) | 18th November 1816 |
| | The King's Own Scottish Borderers | 25th (The King's Own Borderers) Regt. of Foot | 9th December 1819 |
| | 2nd Bn. The Cameronians | 90th Regt. of Foot (or Perthshire Volunteers) | 7th March 1817 |
| | The King's Royal Rifle Corps | 3rd Bn. 60th (Royal American) Regt. of Foot | 28th August 1817 |
| | 1st Bn. The Manchester Regt. | 63rd (West Suffolk) Regt. of Foot | 1st October 1819 |
| | The West India Regt. | 1st Bn. The West India Regt. | 17th October 1817 |

| | | | |
|---|---|---|---|
| **GUADALOUPE 1810**<br>Date 1810 added,<br>Army Order 295/1909 | The East Yorkshire Regt. | 15th (Yorkshire, East Riding) Regt. of Foot | 31st May 1817 |
| | 2nd Bn. The Cameronians | 90th Regt. of Foot (or Perthshire Volunteers) | 7th March 1817 |
| | 2nd Bn. The East Surrey Regt. | 70th (Surrey) Regt. of Foot | 22nd October 1867 |
| | 1st Bn. The Manchester Regt. | 63rd (West Suffolk) Regt. of Foot | 1st October 1819 |
| | The West India Regt. | 1st Bn. The West India Regt. | 17th October 1817 |

| | | | |
|---|---|---|---|
| NEW ZEALAND (For services 1846-1847) | 2nd Bn. The Northamptonshire Regt. | 58th (Rutlandshire) Regt. of Foot | 17th May 1870 |
| | 2nd Bn. The Manchester Regt. | 96th Regt. of Foot | 17th May 1870 |
| | 2nd Bn. The Wiltshire Regt. | 99th (Lanarkshire) Regt. of Foot | 17th May 1870 |
| NEW ZEALAND (For services 1860-1861) | The Suffolk Regt. | 12th (East Suffolk) Regt. of Foot | 17th May 1870 |
| | The West Yorkshire Regt. | 14th (Buckinghamshire) Regt. of Foot | 17th May 1870 |
| | 1st Bn. P.W.V. (South Lancashire Regt.) | 40th (2nd Somersetshire) Regt. of Foot | 17th May 1870 |
| | 1st Bn. The Middlesex Regt. | 57th (West Middlesex) Regt. of Foot | 17th May 1870 |
| | 1st Bn. The York & Lancaster Regt. | 65th (2nd Yorkshire, North Riding) Regt. of Foot | 17th May 1870 |
| NEW ZEALAND (For services 1863-1866) | The Suffolk Regt. | 12th (East Suffolk) Regt. of Foot | 17th May 1870 |
| | The West Yorkshire Regt. | 14th (Buckinghamshire) Regt. of Foot | 17th May 1870 |
| | The Royal Irish Regt. | 18th (Royal Irish) Regt. of Foot | 17th May 1870 |
| | 2nd Bn. The East Surrey Regt. | 70th (Surrey) Regt. of Foot | 17th May 1870 |
| | 1st Bn. Oxf & Bucks Lt. Infty. | 43rd (Monmouthshire Light Infantry) Regt. of Foot | 17th May 1870 |
| | 1st Bn. The Queen's Own (Royal West Kent Regt.) | 50th (Queen's Own) Regt. of Foot | 17th May 1870 |
| | 1st Bn. The Durham L.I. | 68th (Durham Light Infantry) Regt. of Foot | 17th May 1870 |

# INDEX

APPENDIX

## BATTLE HONOURS BORNE BY MUTINEER REGIMENTS OF THE BENGAL ARMY

| | |
|---|---|
| AFGHANISTAN | 2nd, 3rd. Regts. Light Cavalry<br>4th Regt. Irregular Cavalry<br>16th, 35th, 37th, 48th. Regts. Native Infantry |
| ALLIWAL | 1st, 3rd, 5th. Regts. Light Cavalry<br>4th Regt. Irregular Cavalry<br>24th, 30th, 36th, 48th. Regts. Native Infantry |
| ALLYGHUR | 7th, 23rd, 35th. Regts. Native Infantry |
| ARRACAN | 2nd Regt. Irregular Cavalry<br>26th, 40th, 49th, 62nd. Regts. Native Infantry |
| ASSAM | 46th, 57th, Regts. Native Infantry |
| AVA | 40th. Regt. Native Infantry |
| BHURTPORE | 3rd, 4th, 6th, 8th, 9th, 10th. Regts. Light Cavalry<br>1st Regt. Irregular Cavalry<br>6th, 11th, 15th, 18th, 23rd, 35th, 36th, 37th, 41st, 58th, 60th, 63rd. Regts. Native Infantry |
| BUXAR | 2nd, 3rd, 5th, 8th, 9th, 10th. Regts. Native Infantry |
| CABOOL 1842 | 1st, 5th, 10th. Regts. Light Cavalry<br>3rd Regt. Irregular Cavalry<br>2nd, 6th, 16th, 26th, 30th, 35th, 38th, 53rd, 60th, 64th. Regts. Native Infantry |
| CANDAHAR 1842 | 1st Regt. Irregular Cavalry<br>2nd, 16th, 38th. Regts. Native Infantry |
| CARNATIC | 4th, 5th, 12th, 22nd Regts. Native Infantry |
| CHILLIANWALLAH | 1st, 5th, 6th, 8th. Regts. Light Cavalry<br>3rd, 9th. Regts. Irregular Cavalry<br>15th, 20th, 25th, 30th, 36th, 45th, 46th, 56th, 69th, Regts. Native Infantry |
| DEIG | 2nd, 3rd, Regts. Light Cavalry<br>5th, 7th, 9th, 30th, 44th. Regts. Native Infantry |
| DELHI | 2nd, 3rd, Regts. Light Cavalry<br>1st, 5th, 22nd, 23rd, 28th, 29th, 30th, 35th. Native Infantry |
| FEROZESHUHUR | 4th, 5th, 8th. Regts. Light Cavalry<br>3rd, 4th, 8th, 9th. Regts. Irregular Cavalry<br>2nd, 12th, 14th, 16th, 24th, 26th, 44th, 45th, 48th, 54th, 73rd. Regts. Native Infantry |
| GHUZNEE | 2nd, 3rd. Regts. Light Cavalry<br>4th Regt. Irregular Cavalry<br>2nd, 16th, 35th, 38th, 48th. Regts. Native Infantry |
| GOOJERAT | 1st, 5th, 6th, 8th. Regts. Light Cavalry<br>3rd, 9th, 11th, 12th, 13th, 14th. Regts. Irregular Cavalry<br>8th, 13th, 15th, 20th, 25th, 30th, 36th, 45th, 46th, 51st, 52nd, 56th, 69th, 72nd. Regts. Native Infantry |
| GUZERAT | 2nd, 3rd, 5th, 7th, 11th, 13th. Regts. Native Infantry |
| HYDRABAD | 9th Regt. Light Cavalry |
| JAVA | 25th, 40th, Regts. Native Infantry |
| JELLALABAD | 5th Regt. Light Cavalry<br>35th Regt. Native Infantry |
| KELAT | 4th Regt. Irregular Cavalry |
| KORAH | 1st, 10th. Regts. Native Infantry |
| LASWARRIE | 1st, 2nd, 3rd, 4th, 6th. Regts. Light Cavalry<br>1st, 12th, 24th, 30th. Regts. Native Infantry |
| MAHARAJPOOR | 1st, 4th, 5th, 8th, 10th. Regts. Light Cavalry<br>4th Regt. Irregular Cavalry<br>2nd, 14th, 16th, 39th, 56th. Regts. Native Infantry |

| | |
|---|---|
| MEEANEE 1843 | 9th. Regt. Light Cavalry |
| MOODKEE | 4th, 5th. Regts. Light Cavalry<br>4th, 8th, 9th. Regt. Irregular Cavalry<br>2nd, 16th, 24th, 26th, 45th, 48th, 73rd. Regts. Native Infantry |
| MOOLTAN | 2nd, Regt. Light Cavalry<br>7th, 11th, 14th. Regts. Irregular Cavalry<br>8th, 49th, 51st, 52nd, 72nd. Regts. Native Infantry |
| MYSORE | 4th, 6th, 13th, 16th. Regts. Native Infantry |
| PEGU | 10th, 40th, 67th, 68th. Regts. Native Infantry |
| PLASSEY | 1st. Regt. Native Infantry |
| PUNNIAR | 2nd, 5th, 8th. Regts. Light Cavalry<br>8th Regt. Irregular Cavalry<br>39th, 50th, 51st, 58th. Regts. Native Infantry |
| PUNJAUB | 1st, 2nd, 5th, 6th, 7th. 8th. Regts. Light Cavalry<br>2nd, 3rd, 7th, 9th, 11th, 12th, 13th, 14th, 15th, 16th, 17th Regts. Irregular Cavalry<br>1st, 3rd, 4th, 8th, 13th, 15th, 18th, 20th, 22nd, 25th, 29th, 30th, 36th, 37th, 45th, 46th, 49th, 50th, 51st, 52nd, 53rd, 56th, 69th, 71st, 72nd, 73rd. Regts. Native Infantry |
| SEETABULDEE | 6th Regt. Light Cavalry |
| SERINGAPATAM | 14th, 16th, 36th, 37th, 38th, 39th, Regts. Native Infantry |
| SUBRAON | 3rd, 4th, 5th. Regts. Light Cavalry<br>2nd, 8th, 9th Regt. Irregular Cavalry<br>7th, 16th, 26th, 41st, 68th. Regts. Native Infantry |

NOTE : Awards of MAHARAJPORE & PUNNIAR to 5th and 8th Light Cavalry and 35th Native Infantry. Detachments of these regiments were awarded the honour.

2nd Light Cavalry mutinied in 1850, the 11th renumbered 2nd inherited their honours.

## MUTINEER REGIMENTS OF THE BENGAL ARMY

### CAVALRY

| | |
|---|---|
| 1st Regt. Light Cavalry | Mutinied at Mhow |
| 2nd Regt. Light Cavalry | Mutinied at Cawnpore |
| 3rd Regt. Light Cavalry | Mutinied at Meerut |
| 4th Regt. Light Cavalry | Disarmed at Umballa |
| 5th Regt. Light Cavalry | Disarmed at Peshawar |
| 6th Regt. Light Cavalry | Mutinied at Jullundur |
| 7th Regt. Light Cavalry | Mutinied at Lucknow |
| 8th Regt. Light Cavalry | Disarmed at Mian Mir |
| 9th Regt. Light Cavalry | Mutinied at Sialkote |
| 10th Regt. Light Cavalry | Mutinied at Ferozepore |
| 3rd Regt. Irregular Cavalry | Mutinied at Saugor |
| 4th Regt. Irregular Cavalry | Mutinied at Hansi |
| 5th Regt. Irregular Cavalry | Mutinied at Rohni |
| 9th Regt. Irregular Cavalry | Mutinied at Hoshiarpore & Bunnu |
| 10th Regt. Irregular Cavalry | Disbanded at Nowshera |
| 11th Regt. Irregular Cavalry | Disarmed at Berhampore |
| 12th Regt. Irregular Cavalry | Mutinied at Sewgowlie |
| 13th Regt. Irregular Cavalry | Mutinied at Benares |
| 14th Regt. Irregular Cavalry | Mutinied at Jhansi & Nowgong |
| 15th Regt. Irregular Cavalry | Mutinied at Sultanpore |
| 16th Regt. Irregular Cavalry | Disarmed at Rawal Pindi |
| 17th Regt. Irregular Cavalry | Disarmed |
| 18th Regt. Irregular Cavalry | Disarmed at Peshawar |

NOTE: The following Regiments of Irregular Cavalry survived, and although some partially mutinied they were reconstituted and by 1914 had become

1st Regiment became 1st Duke of York's Own Lancers (Skinners Horse)
2nd Regiment became 2nd Lancers (Gardner's Horse)
4th Regiment became 3rd Skinner's Horse
6th Regiment became 4th Cavalry
7th Regiment became 5th Cavalry
8th Regiment became 6th King Edward's Own Cavalry
17th Regiment became 7th Hariana Lancers
18th Regiment became 8th Cavalry.

### INFANTRY

| | |
|---|---|
| 1st Regt. Native Infantry | Mutinied at Cawnpore |
| 2nd Regt. | Disarmed at Barrackpore |
| 3rd Regt. | Mutinied at Phillour |
| 4th Regt. | Disarmed at Nurpur & Hoshiarpore |
| 5th Regt. | Disbanded at Umballa |
| 6th Regt. | Mutinied at Allahabad |
| 7th Regt. | Mutinied at Dinapore |
| 8th Regt. | Mutinied at Dinapore |
| 9th Regt. | Mutinied at Aligarh |
| 10th Regt. | Mutinied at Fatehgarh |
| 11th Regt. | Mutinied at Meerut |
| 12th Regt. | Mutinied at Nowgong & Jhansi |
| 13th Regt. | Mutinied at Lucknow |
| 14th Regt. | Mutinied at Jhelum |
| 15th Regt. | Mutinied at Nasirabad |
| 16th Regt. | Disarmed at Mian Mir |
| 17th Regt. | Mutinied at Azamgarh |
| 18th Regt. | Mutinied at Bareilly |
| 19th Regt. | Disbanded at Barrackpore |
| 20th Regt. | Mutinied at Meerut |
| 22nd Regt. | Mutinied at Fyzabad |
| 23rd Regt. | Mutinied at Mhow |
| 24th Regt. | Disarmed at Peshawar |
| 25th Regt. | Disarmed |

| | | | |
|---|---|---|---|
| 26th Regt. | Mutinied at Mian Mir | 57th Regt. | Disbanded at Ferozepore |
| 27th Regt. | Disarmed at Peshawar | 58th Regt. | Disarmed at Rawal Pindi |
| 28th Regt. | Mutinied at Shahjehanpore | 60th Regt. | Mutinied at Umballa |
| 29th Regt. | Mutinied at Moradabad | 61st Regt. | Mutinied at Jullundur |
| 30th Regt. | Mutinied at Nasirabad | 62nd Regt. | Disarmed at Multan |
| 34th Regt. | Mutinied at Barrackpore | 63rd Regt. | Disarmed at Berhampore |
| 35th Regt. | Disarmed at Amritsar | 64th Regt. | Disarmed at Peshawar |
| 36th Regt. | Mutinied at Jullundur | 67th Regt. | Mutinied at Agra |
| 37th Regt. | Mutinied at Benares | 68th Regt. | Mutinied at Bareilly |
| 38th Regt. | Mutinied at Delhi | 69th Regt. | Disarmed at Multan |
| 39th Regt. | Disarmed at Dera Ismail Khan | 71st Regt. | Mutinied at Lucknow |
| 40th Regt. | Mutinied at Dinapore | 72nd Regt. | Mutinied at Neemuch |
| 41st Regt. | Mutinied at Sitapore | 73rd Regt. | Disarmed at Jalpaigori & Dacca |
| 44th Regt. | Disarmed at Agra | 74th Regt. | Mutinied at Delhi |
| 45th Regt. | Disbanded at Ferozepore | | |
| 46th Regt. | Mutinied at Sialkote | | |
| 48th Regt. | Mutinied at Lucknow | | |
| 49th Regt. | Disarmed at Mian Mir | | |
| 50th Regt. | Mutinied at Nagode | | |
| 51st Regt. | Mutinied at Peshawar | | |
| 52nd Regt. | Mutinied at Jubbulpore | | |
| 53rd Regt. | Mutinied at Cawnpore | | |
| 54th Regt. | Mutinied at Delhi | | |
| 55th Regt. | Mutinied at Nowshera | | |
| 56th Regt. | Mutinied at Cawnpore | | |

NOTE: The following regiments survived and although some partially mutinied or were disarmed they were reconstituted and by 1914 had become
21st Regt. Disarmed at Peshawar became 1st Brahmans
31st Regt. became 2nd Queen Victoria's Own Rajput Light Infantry
32nd Regt. A portion mutinied became 3rd Brahmans
33rd Regt. Disarmed Jullundur became 4th Prince Albert Victor's Rajputs
42nd Regt. Mutinied at Saugor reconstituted to become 5th Light Infantry
43rd Regt. Disarmed reconstituted as 6th Jat Light Infantry
47th Regt. Disarmed at Mirzapore became 7th Duke of Connaught's Own Rajputs
59th Regt. Disarmed at Amritsar reconstituted as 8th Rajputs
63rd Regt. Disarmed Berhampore. Reconstituted as 9th Bengal Infantry, and later 9th Gurkha Rifles
65th Regt. Disarmed became 10th Jats
66th Regt. Original 66th disbanded for mutiny in 1850 reconstituted as 66th Gurkha Regt. 1850. Subsequently 1st Gurkhas
70th Regt. Disarmed became 11th Rajputs